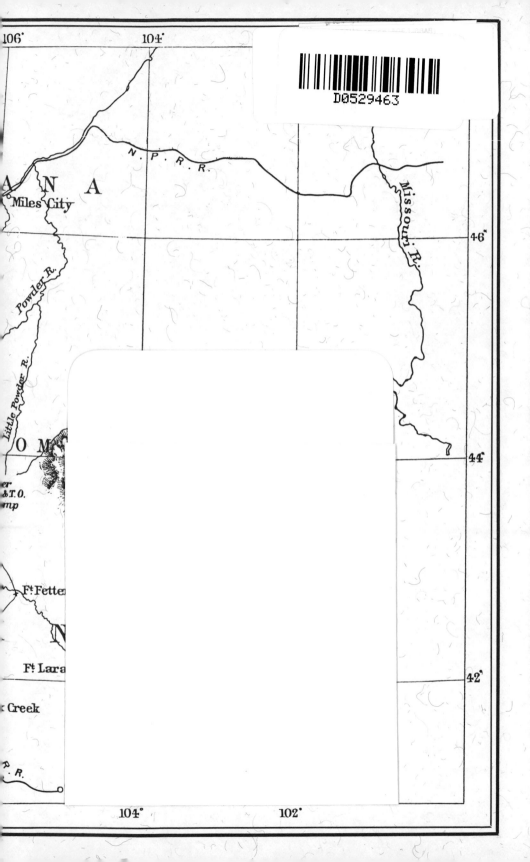

106°   104°

N. P. R. R.

A N A   A

Miles City

Missouri R.

46°

Powder R.

Little Powder R.

O M

44°

er
& T.O.
mp

Ft Fetter

N

Ft Lara

42°

Creek

R. R.

104°   102°

MORETON FREWEN'S
WESTERN ADVENTURES

WESTERN ADVENTURES

by

L. Milton Woods

American Heritage Center
University of Wyoming
in cooperation with
Roberts Rinehart, Inc. Publishers

Copyright © 1986 by L. Milton Woods
Published by Roberts Rinehart, Inc. Publishers
Post Office Box 3161
Boulder, Colorado 80303
for the American Heritage Center, University of Wyoming
International Standard Book Number 0-911797-26-2
Library of Congress Catalog Card Number 86-062432
Printed in the United States of America
Designed by Linda Seals

Contents

Preface

·*1*·

Wyoming Beginnings   1

·*2*·

Moreton Frewen of England   19

·*3*·

The Frewen Brothers on the Powder River   31

·*4*·

Diversions of one Sort or Other   44

·*5*·

The Powder River Cattle Company, Limited   63

·*6*·

A (Very Brief) Peaceful Interlude   79

·7·

To Superior and Beyond   95

·8·

Envoy Extraordinary   106

·9·

Sniping from the Sidelines   120

·10·

Of Lawsuits and Other Alarums   138

·11·

Director at Last   147

·12·

The Liquidator Liquidates   167

·13·

War and Winter   174

·14·

Eastern Interlude   182

·15·

Eheu Fugaces   191

Preface

I have been asked why a person interested in the history of the western United States would be writing about an aristocratic English gentleman, who lives on in the works of others under the disparaging nickname "Mortal Ruin."

Certainly, there is no lack of writing on Moreton Frewen, some of which emerged from his own prolific pen. And there are places where his sojourn in Wyoming are treated. Yet, none that I have read capture the way in which this man — this unfortunate man — was entranced by the strange "savage" land he found along the eastern slope of the Big Horn mountains in northern Wyoming, or the way he sought to make a statement of himself in that alien country.

Only twenty-five years old when he left England for Wyoming, after losing a good portion of his inheritance in the pursuit of fast horses and lovely ladies (including Lillie Langtry), Frewen plunged into the open range cattle business with the same enthusiasm he had brought to the chase at home. Purchasing herds two or three at a time and throwing up a headquarters, complete with a telephone, that was respectable by English country standards, but which the cowboys in remote Wyoming called a castle, he at once earned the attention and sometimes the admiration or enmity of those he met.

The new land seemed to offer endless suggestions for making (and losing) fortunes, and Moreton exploited a good number of them. It was a credit to his salesmanship, but also to his analysis and intelligence, that he was joined in these ventures by some of the great names of both Great Britain and the United States, including several peers, Pierre Lorillard, and his father-in-law, Leonard Jerome.

That he did not succeed is well known, but the reasons behind his failure, including his own numerous shortcomings, should not obscure the fundmental understanding that he had of those critical days of the range cattle industry or the vision he had for meeting the crises that it faced. That his ideas were not adopted in time to avert the catastrophe that engulfed his own company and many like it was partly his fault and partly the fault of those who had lost confidence in a spirit that seemed perpetually confident that over the next hill might stand the pot of gold he so badly needed to meet his pecuniary needs.

The Wyoming episode of Moreton's life occupied only a portion of the autobiography he was working on when he died, and there were other adventures that he undoubtedly thought were more exciting. But while he was in the West, that region consumed his enormous energies; he was ultimately to make more than one hundred ocean crossings in furtherance of his work there. That so little physical evidence remains for that period is more a phenomenon of the range cattle industry than solely the case of Moreton Frewen. Built as it was on the principle of using government lands for so long as they remained otherwise unoccupied, that industry has left few footprints to testify to its once great extent. Yet, extensive it was, and while it was those like Moreton Frewen walked and rode very tall, indeed. He was, after all, a gentleman, and, as he said, "Being a gentleman is much against one here, as in the colonies generally."

So it is, that yet another account of a portion of Moreton Frewen's life has been written — this time covering those hectic years when he was trying to become the greatest cattle baron on the western range. I hope the reader may come to feel that his strivings were actuated by an attractive spirit, although his execution was fatally flawed.

· 1 ·

Wyoming Beginning

The corpse was a horrid sight; the man had been shot in the trail above the KC ranch, then dragged by the feet about fifty yards into a gulch. The inquest was held on the site: "It would have shocked the steady British jury to see us eight of us—our horses browsing around—not a roof within twenty miles, 'sitting on' that gruesome thing," wrote Moreton Frewen, the ad hoc foreman of the inquest. The jury returned a verdict of "wilful murder" against some person unknown, although Moreton supposed the man was killed by Indians. He remarked that the death was "rather characteristic of this savage country."[1] This happened in 1884, and Frewen had already been six years in this "savage" country.

When Frewen came to Wyoming in 1878, the territory had already been organized for nine years—a long time on that fast-moving frontier. It was a territory like no other before it. In 1867, the hinterland that swept endlessly north and south from the line of the railroad was, for all intents and purposes, unsettled. To be sure, gold had been discovered at South Pass in the 1860s, causing a rush of miners to that region, but the major long-term contribution of the mining country was to force the creation of a county to govern the western part of the territory (then part of Dakota). It was also the home of Mrs. Esther Morris, who would successfully urge the introduction of the woman suffrage bill at the first session of the territorial legislature in 1869. By 1878 the mining country was on the decline and would never again play a pivotal role in territorial politics.

After a slow start following its incorporation in 1862, the Pacific railroad reached Crow Creek in what is now southeastern Wyoming in the fall of 1867 and stopped there until spring. A town, a military camp, and a large supply organization had thoughtfully been provided for the large assemblage of people there to experience their first

Wyoming winter. As the child of the railroad, the new town had been surveyed by corporate surveyors, and its name—Cheyenne—was given by General Grenville M. Dodge, who himself personified the cooperative venture that was the Union Pacific: he was the newly-elected congressman from Iowa, the chief engineer of the Union Pacific Railroad, and an officer in the army during the Civil War. His close ties to the military were evident that day in the summer of 1867 when he came to choose the townsite: he was accompanied by Generals Christopher C. Auger and John A. Rawlins (who would later give his name to a Wyoming town), two companies of cavalry, and two of infantry. It was a proper entourage.

The new territory had also launched the range cattle industry. At first, the impetus for bringing a large number of beef cattle to the area was the need to supply the construction crews, and John Wesly Iliff, who would later be one of the greatest cattle kings, set up his cow camp on Crow Creek a few miles from Cheyenne to carry out his contract with Jack Casement. In 1868, Iliff moved to Cheyenne, where he remained for a time. But it was the open range that transformed these relatively modest beginnings into the great industry that territorial governor Francis E. Warren thought was more profitable than any other honest business.

Wyoming was created from all of the western part of Dakota Territory (except for a tiny piece along the western border that was forgotten by the draftsmen and finally given to Montana in 1873), together with a chunk of the ever-unpopular Utah territory (other parts of that unhappy territory had previously been hacked off and given to Nevada and Colorado). It was the Dakota area that created the necessity for territorial division, for the workers building the Union Pacific Railroad had a disturbing proclivity for voting Democratic, and their numbers threatened the Republican control of the Dakota power center far to the east, at Yankton. Accordingly, Dakota was happy to be rid of pesky Wyoming, and the new settlers in that region were equally glad to be freed from the distant connection to the east.

The organic act for Wyoming Territory was passed in the dying months of Andrew Johnson's administration, but the conflict between the Radical Republicans and the president made it impossible for any territorial officials to be confirmed until after the Grant administration took office the following year. Then, in the summer of 1869, Wyoming Territory was organized with its own legislature and appointed officials, and the business of providing government for the few settlers there was taken over from the Dakota Territory.

In the fall of 1867, Cheyenne had a population of 3,000, but it would fall to just over 2,300 two years later, and to 1,450 when the census of 1870 was taken. In the entire territory there were — not counting the Indians — only 8,000 people in 1869 (just over 9,000 a year later). It was overwhelmingly male, and nearly 73 percent of the people had jobs (compared with only 33 percent for the country as a whole). There was thus a strong economic base for future growth. A mere 3 percent of the population in 1870 were born in Wyoming and 39 percent were foreign-born, with Ireland leading the list. Altogether, the British Isles accounted for more than half the foreign-born population (two-thirds if we include the Canadian provinces).

The first legislature had acknowledged its legal roots by adopting the common law of England, but the English visitor — of whom there would soon be many — would have been amazed at the novel tinkering of these lawmakers with British practice. In that famous first session, the franchise was extended to women (but the vote was also given to every male over the age of twenty-one who had been in the territory ninety days and was either a citizen of the country or had declared his intention to become one). This was not the first example of woman suffrage in the United States (widows had limited suffrage in New Jersey early in the century), but the idea was novel enough in the United States to cause "much amusement" when it was suggested by Mrs. Horace Greeley for adoption in New York.[2]

In the mother country, the time for woman suffrage had not yet come; indeed, not all men could vote. Agricultural laborers and a good many industrial workers were still outside the franchise, even after the Second Reform Bill of 1867, and when John Stuart Mill introduced female suffrage during the debate on that bill, it was easily defeated.[3] Certainly, Moreton Frewen would have thought little of the idea of extending the vote to women; he was not overly fond of extension to the wrong sort of men. "There is no doubt that the lower you carry a franchise," he said, "the less it is worth to anyone." He repeated a conversation between two Kentish "rustics": " 'Bill,' said his pal, 'this day will get us the vote.' Says Bill, 'Blow the vote, I don't want the vote, I want the franchise, that's what they have been promising us!' " "Most of them think the franchise is some sort of farm, rent free!" said Frewen.

But an unenlightened attitude on woman suffrage was common among the gentlemen of those days. Frewen's nephew, Winston Churchill, declared in 1897 that he would "unswervingly" oppose the "ridiculous" movement, although he later would espouse the cause.[4]

The second Wyoming legislature tried to undo female suffrage by repealing it, but the governor vetoed the repealer; the territory then settled down to accommodate itself to what it had done, if not always to enjoy it. The Wyoming press recognized that the suffrage novelty was good advertising for them and for the territory and often printed commentaries on the subject, including a letter written to her hometown newspaper by a displaced Texas lady residing in Cheyenne. While she felt that many ladies "disapproved" of voting, conditions were in fact quite civilized: separate ballot boxes at *separate* places were provided for the ladies, so that they need have nothing to do with men nor even to see them! She noted that the gentlemen accompanied their wives when voting, and then the ladies returned "immediately home." Thus, she seemed to be saying, voting need not damage one's reputation at all. Jury service, she said, was quite a different matter and had died a "natural death." As for office holding, it was just as bad; one lady got herself elected justice of the peace, served until she was satisfied, and then "subsided." So much for liberation in the 1870s.[5]

Dakota had organized four counties in the area given to Wyoming (Laramie, Carter, Albany, and Carbon); the first Wyoming legislature renamed Carter (to Sweetwater) and created a fifth—Uinta—along the western border to complete the map. These old counties were long strips running north and south, but their northern reaches were mere geographical conveniences to include the entire rectangle that was Wyoming and not to be of concern to the officials in the county seats along the railroad.

And with good reason. A series of treaties with the Indians had freed the route of the railroad from Indian control, but at the price of continued Indian presence in the north. The entire Powder River region north of the North Platte River and east of the Big Horn mountains was an unceded Sioux hunting ground (although the Sioux were supposed to reside more or less permanently on their large reservation in Dakota Territory). In the central part of Wyoming Territory, the Shoshoni reservation blocked access to the Big Horn Basin. And the entire northwestern sector was occupied by the vast Yellowstone region, soon to become the nation's first national park.

Before these treaties were signed there had been islands of white influence in the area. There had been a military post on the Powder River since the summer of 1865, when Camp Connor was established to protect travel on the Montana road, the famous old Bozeman Trail. This post evolved into Fort Reno, which was built in 1866. In the same year another fort, Fort Philip Kearny, was located on the Piney, and still another, Fort C. F. Smith, was built to the north across the Montana line.

These posts almost immediately came under pressure from the Indians, who bitterly resented the intrusion on their hunting grounds. The Fetterman massacre and the Wagon Box Fight are only two of the resulting engagements, the former, with its loss of eighty officers and men, being the record disaster in Indian fighting up to that point. When the Fort Laramie Treaty of 1868 was signed with the Sioux, the United States government agreed to abandon the Bozeman Trail posts; they were burned by the Indians within sight of the departing troops.

The continuing Indian presence was a sore point to the Wyoming settlers, and they immediately commenced agitation to eliminate it. A party of goldseekers penetrated the Big Horn Basin in 1870, but they did not find the yellow metal, and further efforts in that direction were delayed for a time. But the basin was Crow country; the Sioux presented a more serious problem. Not only did they have the entire Powder River basin as a hunting ground, they persisted in staying there, refusing to return to the reservations. Occasionally, they would also sally forth and shoot up the Crow Agency in southern Montana. For his part, Red Cloud complained that a portion of the Oregon Trail still ran north of the North Platte River, in violation of the treaty. Despite the risk, miners were swarming into the Black Hills region, where gold had been discovered, putting the government clearly on the spot. In 1875 an attempt was made to buy the Black Hills from the Sioux, but no agreement could be reached even with the reservation Indians, to say nothing of the hostiles somewhere out in the Powder River region.

Then the government threw down the gauntlet. In November 1875, the Sioux were ordered to return to their reservation from the

Powder River region by January 31, 1876. The timing of this ultimatum was such that a reply could not have been received before the deadline, and apparently none was expected. The military "solution" to the problem was to begin.

General Phil Sheridan, commanding the Military Division of the Missouri, devised a three-pronged offensive. In the spring of 1876, the so-called "Montana Column" under Colonel John Gibbon moved down the Yellowstone, while a "Dakota Column" under General Alfred Terry moved west, and a third force under General George Crook moved north from Fort Fetterman (down on the Platte River). According to the plan, the Sioux would find themselves surrounded by this formidable military array, and a final settlement would be reached with them. Every schoolchild now knows how badly the plan failed. The Indians mustered in numbers far exceeding the total military force sent against them, but even then the result might have been different had the three columns been able to bring their combined strength into play. Instead, Colonel George A. Custer, one of Terry's officers, raced to join action with the Indians, not even waiting for the rest of Terry's force to come up. Foolishly dividing his own Seventh Cavalry into three smaller units (one supposes to prevent the escape of the enormous force camped in the valley of the Little Bighorn), Custer placed his portion of that regiment athwart the route the Sioux would take as they broke up camp. Custer earned his place in history when the Indian horde quite literally ran over his position on the low bluffs along the river, killing every white man in the command.

Terry came up shortly after the battle and buried the dead, but the Indians were now long gone, having undoubtedly realized that their brief victory was to be their last, as indeed it was. Some years would pass before the stragglers returned from Canada (Frewen actually met Sitting Bull at the Custer battlefield in 1886), but the days of carefree hunting in the Power River country were over.

Even before the Custer battle, the Wyoming legislature had acted to place its stamp on the north country. In December 1875, two new counties were created in the northeastern part of the territory, the eastern one from the north end of Laramie and Albany counties, and the western one from the north end of Carbon County and a portion of Sweetwater County. The eastern county was named Crook, after the general. The other occupied the Powder River country and included the Big Horn mountains and all of the Big Horn Basin east of the river; it was named Pease, in honor of Dr. Eugene L. Pease, a representative of Uinta County and president of the Council in the first territorial legislature. Four years later, the name was changed to Johnson County, to honor Edward Payson Johnson, a Cheyenne attorney who was elected to the 1879 legislature but died before it convened.

Settlers did not rush into the new counties; indeed, the two counties were to gain national attention quite because of their lack of population, in connection with the "sagebrushing" of Judge Peck. Judge William Ware Peck arrived from New York in 1877 to be territorial judge in Uinta and Sweetwater counties, where he soon gained an unfavorable reputation for dispensing "eastern" style justice and in the process costing the taxpayers more than three times what his predecessor had spent during a term of court. In December, the legislature, unable to get rid of a presidential appointee, hit upon the novel idea of assigning Peck where he could do no harm: a judicial district was organized for Crook and Pease counties, and Peck was given the job. To avoid angering the other judges who would have to take over Peck's work in the western part of the territory, $1,800 was appropriated to compensate for the added workload there. Governor John M. Thayer signed the bill because, he said rather lamely, the legislature was going to override his veto if he did not, and besides a veto would have delayed the organization of Crook County. News of this "sagebrushing" of Peck soon reached Washington (Crook and Pease counties were thought to be chiefly occupied by that ubiquitous plant rather than by people), where it was not found amusing. Acting in much the same indirect fashion as the legislature had, the president, who could not get rid of the lawmakers, took the only action available to him: he removed Governor Thayer, who had signed the offending measure. (The "sagebrushing" bill provided for immediate organization of Crook County; this gives a clue to the scarcity of settlers in the county, since the original county legislation provided for organization when five hundred voters petitioned.)

Peck went to Washington to try to secure the annulment of the measure assigning him to the northeast; he was able to get a bill passed by the Senate, but it died in the House under the watchful eye of Delegate William W. Corlett of Wyoming.[6] And neither of the two northern counties were organized after all. There was agitation for organization from time to time, but the parent counties were reluctant to lose the tax revenues. The *Cheyenne Daily Leader* snidely commented that there might be "half a dozen" inhabitants in the two counties, and suggested that they might be organized by detailing soldiers to fill the offices, and by giving Sitting Bull the post of sheriff.[7] Both counties had to wait until the next decade before they were established as functioning units (Johnson, the former Pease, in 1881 and Crook in 1885).

While Moreton Frewen called himself the first settler in the Powder River country, he was clearly defining the term "settler" in a limited way. A similar claim is made for Oliver Perry Hanna, who is said to have arrived in the Powder River country on August 11, 1878 (he did not stay the winter, returning to break ground for his ranch above Big Horn in April 1879). Hanna laid out the town of Big Horn and named it; later he guided for guests who came to hunt at the Frewen ranch.[8]

While not civilian settlements, Forts Reno and Philip Kearney had been permanent establishments in the country in the sixties, and there were post sutlers serving both posts until they were abandoned in 1868. In 1876, after the Custer battle, the Army established a new fort on the Powder River about three miles upstream from old Fort Reno, and the following year it was designated Fort McKinney. Unfortunately, the site lacked sufficient drinking water, forage, and construction materials; accordingly, it was abandoned in favor of a site on Clear Creek (or Clear Fork, as the army referred to it), where there was pine (only cottonwood grew on the Powder River). The post trader at the Powder River location was E. U. Snider; he moved with the post to Clear Creek, and the following year Frewen was permitted to open a store and eating house at the old location (he was prohibited from opening a bar).[9]

We do not know when Augustus Trabing (of Medicine Bow) established his store at the Crazy Woman crossing of the Bozeman Trail; it was certainly there in the fall of 1878, under the management of A. M. Bowman. The following year Trabing moved the store, first to a site four miles south of the present location of Buffalo, and then, when the Fort McKinney military reservation was reduced, to the future site of Buffalo itself.

Buffalo arose as a tent town on Clear Creek, along the eastern boundary of the (now reduced) Fort McKinney reservation, centered on the predecessor of the old Occidental Hotel. The proprietor,

Charley Buell, provided lodging for miners and a place of safekeeping for the gold dust that the fortunate ones possessed.[10] Mail service was provided on a tri-weekly basis under a government contract, which was apparently so indifferently performed that one patron remarked that "tri-weekly" meant the contractor delivered the mail one week and then "tried" to deliver it the next.[11] Early in 1879 it was reported that there were already twenty settlers on Goose Creek (near the town of Big Horn), and by the middle of that year, emigrants were leaving daily for that region; in a single day, thirteen wagons passed through Cheyenne on the way north.[12] The town of Big Horn got its own post office in June.[13]

While these settlements were growing up, the major (nongovernmental) economic interest was being conducted out on the range, away from town. The range cattle business had started almost by accident. For years, it was generally believed that the Wyoming country was in truth a part of that Great American Desert described by Major Stephen Long in 1820, and generally inhospitable. But as early as 1860, a strange phenomenon was observed. When the expedition headed by Captain William F. Raynolds went into winter quarters on Deer Creek in that year, the captain said, ". . . but few animals in the train were in condition to have continued the march without a generous grain diet. . . . In the spring all were in as fine condition . . . as could be desired." On further investigation it was noted that the dry grasses on the plains were extremely nutritious, and beef cattle could subsist comfortably on them. This interesting and valuable knowledge was circulated in a book prepared by the surgeon of the Union Pacific Railroad, and the rush was soon on.[14]

There now developed a huge but peculiar industry, characterized by its lack of land ownership; the mighty herds merely foraged freely on the public domain. Since the situation was surely anomalous, the government had pondered over alternatives, and in 1879 and 1880 hearings were held throughout the West to learn the stockmen's attitude toward a suggestion of lease or purchase of the grazing lands. At a meeting of the Wyoming Stock Growers Association, all but three members were opposed to proposed sale of the land at five cents per acre, and they were unanimous in opposition to lease of the land at one-half cent per acre with right to purchase at five cents at any time during the twenty-year lease term. The association went on record as opposing acquisition of public lands in large parcels and favoring the existing system; if the government did decide to sell the land, then the price should not exceed five cents per acre, sales should only be made to actual occupants, and deferred payment should be permitted.[15] The reason for this attitude was simple: so great were the land requirements for these huge grazing outfits that even a nickel an acre would have been a considerable financial burden.

Huge herds of Texas and Oregon cattle were brought to graze on the open range; in the spring of 1879 it was estimated that 200,000 might come in that year alone. But even then it was apparent that the resource was not unlimited, for the Cheyenne papers were bragging that Wyoming cattle were fat, while Nebraska herds were in poor shape, the consequence of overstocking on the ranges in that state. Contagious diseases were feared on the open range because there was no way to isolate sick animals. And it was difficult to improve the herds, as the cows ranged freely with bulls of indifferent quality. Some operators imported blooded stock (the Stanleys of Rock Creek brought in thirty-one Shorthorn bulls in 1878), but controlled breeding required fencing, which was only rarely used in the early days of the industry.

Aside from considerations of their cost, fences were also a danger to the cattle during bad storms. Cattle drifted across the prairie in search of shelter, but when they came to a fence, they would pile up along it and freeze to death.

Yet, if there were to be no fences, some means had to be devised to differentiate one's cattle from those of others. Branding served to identify the mature animals, but this would not suffice to identify calves. (The humorist Bill Nye said he was working on a way to have the cow pass on her brand to the calf, but there were no practical solutions to the problem.) So it was that the roundup was conceived. Every spring, all of the big outfits would ride the range together, rounding up the cattle and branding the calves running with their mothers. Occasionally a calf was found without a mother — she had either died or abandoned her calf — and there was thus no brand that could be used for it. The solution ultimately adopted for this orphan, or "maverick," situation was to require the calf to be branded with the "M" brand and sold, the proceeds going to support the regulation of the industry.

Natural disasters were an ever-present danger. The winters varied considerably, and if a hard one followed a bad summer, losses would be heavy. Then there was fire. Prairie fires were remarked upon by passengers on the railroad (the steam engines may have set some of them), and in the fall of 1879 a bad fire burned the entire area between Tongue River and Clear Creek in the Powder River country. For ten days the fire raged, beyond the power of human hands to control it. Afterward the bloated carcasses of wild animals testified to its ferocity and speed. The fire not only killed the animals, but it also destroyed the forage for the coming winter.[16]

Such a widespread industry created administrative problems for government. The theory in Wyoming was that taxes were to be assessed on the animals according to the residence of the owner. But the counties to the west of Laramie County (with its large number of ranch owners) chose to assess animals that were permanently grazing in their county regardless of the county of residence of the owner. Naturally the owners sought to avoid double taxation and chose to short the Laramie County returns.[17]

It is not particularly remarkable that a regulatory system would develop for such an industry, but it is remarkable that the system that arose was almost entirely a *private* system, the creature of the Wyoming Stock Growers Association. There had been an earlier stockmen's organization in Albany County since 1871, and in 1873 the Laramie County Stock Growers Association was organized; in 1879, its name was changed to Wyoming Stock Growers Association. By this time its ranks had swelled to nearly two hundred, and these members were leading men of the territory. In the 1882 legislature, half the members of the Council were stockmen, and at least a third of those were members of the association; in the House, five of the eight Laramie County representatives were members of the association.

For a number of years the association's sway in the territory was unchecked. Already in 1875 the legislature had provided that the counties could appoint (and pay for) stock detectives; these county employees were to be appointed only on the recommendation of the county cattlemen's organization. The 1882 legislature directed the governor to appoint the territorial veterinarian on the recommendation of the association, and at the following session the Maverick Bill gave the association control over the supervision of roundups, including the branding and sale of mavericks, with the proceeds going into the association treasury to help pay for cattle inspectors.

The association meeting in the spring of 1879 set five roundups to cover the area under association control. Since the Powder River country was then largely vacant, only one roundup was set on the north side of the North Platte, and it only proceeded as far north as Rawhide Buttes. All of the roundups commenced on May 20 and were expected to take five to seven weeks to complete. Where one roundup met another there was coordination to ensure that the country was fully covered.

Roundups were grand affairs, even in the early days; one writer thought they were reminiscent of the annual assemblages of the fur traders, a time of "wild and boisterous excitement."[18] During 1881, one of the roundups camped close to Cheyenne, and a large number of the cowboys came to town. They would ride full tilt toward the door of the saloon and then vault over their horses' heads. After they had "satisfied the inner man," they would jump into the saddle without aid of stirrup. Not a line would have to be rewritten for a modern western movie![19]

The *Cheyenne Daily Sun* sent a reporter along on Roundup No. 5 in 1880, and he was duly impressed. At least 150 men were involved in the operation, which was expected to gather 65,000 to 70,000 head of cattle. The number of horses involved was very large, as they were worked hard; on one roundup involving only 35 men and 30 wagons, there were 1,260 horses.[20] There was also ample opportunity to see the contest of men against bucking broncos, and to show off the skills of the range. In one display of speed and coordination, three ropers succeeded in branding 166 calves in 80 minutes for Judge J. M. Carey's CY outfit.[21]

Roundup was also hard, risky work. Soon after the roundups began, the casualties began trickling back into town, mostly broken bones from encounters with spirited horses.[22] One steer became so enraged at being roped that he turned and gored the pursuing horse. The wounded animal threw his rider, who in the confusion had got his hand tangled in the rope, jerking off his thumb and forefinger. The steer then turned upon the injured and unseated cowboy, who was luckily rescued by others.[23]

To some people, the association at times seemed larger than the territory, and in a sense it really was. When stock inspector Frank Canton was elected sheriff in Johnson County and ran into difficulty having his election certified by the county clerk, it was to Sturgis, secretary of the association, that he complained, not to the Wyoming officialdom![24] By 1879, association stock inspectors were located at

Kansas City, Council Bluffs, and Clinton, Iowa, to detect any attempted sale of branded animals by unauthorized individuals. The roundups in eastern Wyoming were coordinated with the Nebraska roundups and covered some of that state, and in 1881, the executive committee was enlarged to include representation for Cheyenne and Sioux counties, Nebraska, which then became a branch of the Wyoming organization as their stock association had disbanded.[25]

While stockmen might be expected to respect the decisions of the association as being in their own best interests, those outside the membership were often less inclined to such an uncritical view. One of the duties of the inspectors was to monitor beef being purchased by butchers, and if unbranded animals were found, they would secure the arrest of the butcher. One such case brought forth an exchange of letters in the newspaper, the butcher complaining that stockmen often bought unbranded calves from each other and were not arrested, and the secretary of the association responding that such sales only involved sucking calves, whose ownership was not in doubt.[26]

Even the Indians were occasionally cowed by the great association. When Frank Canton was assigned as a stock inspector to the Powder River area, he learned that two Arapahoes from the Wind River reservation had butchered beef animals, and he at once set out for the reservation to arrest the guilty braves. After a tense scene, he was able to bring them back for trial (although not before the squaw of one insisted that she accompany Canton back to Buffalo). Canton could write triumphantly to the secretary of the association that he had returned with his men.

The association also kept a vigilant eye on potential troublemakers among cowhands. When it came to the attention of the secretary that Fred Hesse had hired one Bill Smith to work on Frewen's Powder River spread, Sturgis wrote sternly to Hesse, telling him that Smith was "liable to work much injury to the stock interests," because he had three or four brothers who were "notoriously bad characters." This was not merely friendly information. The Executive Committee of the association had directed Sturgis to tell Hesse to "cease to give further employment to the man." Sturgis noted that he had had to give the same sort of advice to three or four other outfits in the Powder River region.[27]

The request was taken seriously. After a long interview with Smith and some considerable checking on the outside, Moreton

Frewen asked Hebert E. Teschemacher, of the Executive Committee, to reconsider the decision. While he freely admitted that Smith's brothers were involved in the "gang," Moreton believed that Bill had done his utmost to dissuade them from their enterprise. Moreover, there was a far more significant witness supporting Smith: Frank Canton, who stood ready to go to Cheyenne and appear before "your worships." But there was another reason. The chief villain in the area was Mat Murphy, who employed twenty-six men, including every useful man on the blacklist. He had sent over to ask Smith to join him, and it is particularly for this reason that Moreton asked that Smith be "whitewashed."[28] Apparently it was done, because Smith remained in the employment of the Powder River company.

It was another characteristic of this closed society of "gentlemen" that the accounting was necessarily conducted according to the same rules, and it became customary for large herds to change hands based upon a "book count" rather than upon actual tally. The book count was maintained with standard estimates for increases and losses. This system only broke down after disastrous winters caused foreign shareholders to question the integrity of their managers in the field.

So large an industry would be expected to leave a considerable number of footprints. Yet, today when one examines the public records for this period in the county seats, for many of these mighty outfits there is little evidence that they ever existed. The big cattlemen owned little, if any, land until much later. They altered the landscape so little that the evidence of their passing can be observed only here and there. Even the magnificent "Frewen Castle" has long been gone, and when Moreton's daughter came to look for it, she could locate the site where it had been only with considerable difficulty (some of the insulators on the telephone line survived longer, as forlorn testimony to a marvelous lifestyle).

No description of the range cattle industry and its foreign antecedents would be complete without mention of the Cheyenne Club. The club, incorporated in 1880, has been much remarked upon because it stands as an unusual example of luxury and privilege in a land that was largely primitive and among people who at least gave lip service to egalitarian principles. First organized in the summer of 1880 as the Cactus Club, its original members included both Moreton and Richard Frewen, as well as their neighbor, Horace Plunkett. There was a brief discussion whether a separate dining room should be built to admit ladies, but this idea was handily voted down.[29] Then there was a search for a more appropriate name, with Cheyenne Club winning out of a field of eighteen.

Richard Frewen was one of the first directors of the club. Limited by its bylaws to a membership of two hundred, the club was the meeting place of the wealthy, where they could for a time avoid the rigors of the range. The bylaws made drunkenness and profanity grounds for expulsion, as was "any act so dishonorable in social life as to unfit the guilty person for the society of gentlemen."[30] Nor were these rules lightly disregarded; one member was expelled for shooting a hole in an oil painting of a cow and bull (he said it was a travesty on pure-bred stock).[31]

When the Frewens' friend Charles M. Oelrichs struck the club bartender, and brother Harry Oelrichs uttered some appropriate profanity, a special meeting of the board was called to consider the offenses. Harry apologized for the language, and Charley said he was "full" at the time; the board censured the former and suspended the latter for thirty days. However, Charley then wrote what the board characterized as a "dictatorial" and "disrespectful" letter, which quickly earned him expulsion! Harry was also in trouble for tearing down the notice of the first action by the board; he was suspended for a year but permitted to stay in his room until he recovered from some current illness.[32]

Moreton did not approve of these decisions. "There has been a most troublesome row here," he said, "and the Club behaved like brutes and Charley and Harry left."[33] Some years later, the secretary of the club censured Moreton's own assistant ranch manager, Frank Kemp, for calling Judge Joseph M. Carey "a G-d d-n s-n of a b-h," to quote the official minutes. In what may have been the same argument, the club's president, Phil Dater, had called Carey a liar. The penalty for Kemp was a five-month suspension, and Dater was given two weeks; we do not know if the difference in language or the difference in rank distinguished the two cases.[34]

There were also darker spirits in the area. The vacuum that the former Indian hunting ground represented was soon filled by those who needed to shun the close companionship of society, where lawmen were in residence. The Trabing store on Crazy Woman was a popular target for the operations of these so-called "road agents," and in the fall of 1878 the *Leader* reported that the store had been hit for the third time in three weeks, the last time while eight or nine of Trabing's employees were present, together with a noncom from the army and a teamster named Eels. Notwithstanding the firepower represented by such a large group (arms were "convenient to them"), the seven or eight desperados carried away enough to require twelve pack animals and also made off with one U.S. Army horse (presumably the unlucky sergeant's mount). The *Leader* thought the whole affair strange.[35] A few months later, a peddler was relieved of $250 three miles north of the store.[36]

Each foray by the road agents called forth another cry for protection from the settlers, but the army lamely replied that there were too few soldiers available, and the county governments safely located along the line of the railroad debated whether the Trabing store might be in Albany County or in Carbon County (it was in Carbon, but there had as yet been no survey in the north). The disgusted editor of the Laramie *Sentinel* suggested that armed citizens should be sent to the region to "capture or shoot" all the outlaws they might find, apparently on the assumption that these miscreants would be easy for such "citizens" to identify.[37]

The notorious "Doc" Middleton, later known as the premier horse thief of Nebraska, was about during this period. His real name was James Riley and his life of crime started with a shooting in Sidney, Nebraska, in 1877, after which he organized a gang that supported itself by stealing horses and cattle.[38] The *Leader* estimated that he stole at least three thousand horses (the *Sun* estimated two thousand — the matter was not an exact science), which he reportedly had little difficulty reselling. About thirty-five years old, he was tall and wore a moustache and full beard; a broken upper front tooth had been replaced with gold, giving him a striking smile. A buxom girl named Richards lost her heart to him, and they eloped. Thereafter, the county where her family lived was spared the visitations of his gang.[39] Noted as a crack rifle shot, he carried two needle guns as well as four revolvers (two on his person, and two on his saddle). His horse, a brown mare, was "fleet as the wind."[40] Finally, in 1879, he was wounded by a Wyoming Stock Growers Association inspector and captured. Brought to Cheyenne, he was tried and convicted, drawing five years in the federal penitentiary at Lincoln.[41]

The presence of large herds unattended on the range was doubtless a temptation to weaker souls, and some stealing took place. As

we have noted, the largely uninhabited northeast was a handy location for the shelter of one whose past might be too hot on his trail.
A particular piece of geography contributed to that objective. About
thirty miles west of Kaycee there is a narrow defile, "just wide enough
to allow passage of a wagon . . ."; it was only one hard day's ride
from Casper and the overland trail, and here outlaws on occasion
took their rest. This was the famed Hole in the Wall (the name did
not appear in print until the nineties). That there were outlaws, and
that some of them spent time at the Hole in the Wall is certain, but
so much folklore has been built around the facts that one cannot be
sure how many there were, nor for how long they were in residence
there. The James brothers were seen there as early as 1877, and
Moreton Frewen was amused in the fall of 1881 to read that one of
the James brothers (Moreton records the name as "Joe") was sup-
posedly in northern Wyoming, ready to seize the ranch and store of
the Frewen brothers. He put the story down as "newspaper humbug."[42]
Not all who sought sanctuary there were rustlers, of course, as other
miscreants recognized the value of a safe place, including Butch
Cassidy and Big Nose George, before his untimely end in Rawlins
(where a part of his skin was fashioned into a pair of moccasins that
can still be seen there).[43] Perhaps it was a "savage" country.

Notes to Chapter 1

1. Moreton Frewen to Clara Frewen, June 19, 21, 1884, Frewen Papers, American Heritage Center, University of Wyoming (hereafter cited as Frewen Papers).

2. *The New York Times,* July 18, 1867.

3. George M. Trevelyan, *British History in the Nineteenth Century and After (1782–1919)*
(London, 1937), 347; and Robert Blake, *Disraeli* (New York, 1967), 472–73.

4. Randolph S. Churchill, *Winston S. Churchill,* vol. 1 (Boston, 1966), 325.

5. *Cheyenne Daily Sun,* March 20, 1879.

6. John D. W. Guice, *The Rocky Mountain Bench* (New Haven, Connecticut, 1972),
81–87.

7. *Cheyenne Daily Leader,* November 19, 1878.

8. *Historical Sheridan and Sheridan County* (Sheridan, Wyoming, 1959), 13; and Lorah
B. Chaffin, *Sons of the West* (Caldwell, Idaho, 1941), 177.

9. Robert A. Murray, *Military Posts in the Powder River Country of Wyoming,
1865–1894* (Lincoln, Nebraska, 1968), 111, 117, and 124; and Robert A. Murray, *Military Posts of Wyoming* (Fort Collins, Colorado, 1974), 80.

10. Howard B. Lott, "The Old Occidental," *Annals of Wyoming* 27(1) (April 1955):
25.

11. *Cheyenne Daily Leader,* March 12, 1879.

12. *Cheyenne Daily Leader,* March 27, June 7, 8, 1879.

13. *Cheyenne Daily Leader,* June 12, 1879.

14. Dr. H. Latham, *The Pasture Lands of North America: Winter Grazing* (Omaha, Nebraska, 1871), 33.

15. Taft A. Larson, *History of Wyoming* (Lincoln, Nebraska, 1965), 176; and *Cheyenne Daily Leader,* November 20, 1879.

16. *Cheyenne Daily Sun,* September 23, 1879.

17. *Cheyenne Daily Sun,* June 5, 11, 1879.

18. *Cheyenne Daily Sun,* December 18, 1880.

19. *Cheyenne Daily Sun,* June 16, 1881.

20. *Cheyenne Daily Sun,* December 18, 1880.

21. *Cheyenne Daily Sun,* April 12, 1879.

22. *Cheyenne Daily Sun,* May 26, 1881.

23. *Cheyenne Daily Sun,* August 24, 1881.

24. Frank M. Canton, *Frontier Trails* (New York, 1930), 49-73; and Frank M. Canton to Thomas Sturgis, *passim,* Wyoming Stock Growers Association Papers, American Heritage Center, University of Wyoming (hereafter cited as WSGA Papers).

25. Maurice Frink, *Cow Country Cavalcade* (Denver, 1954), 39-56.

26. *Cheyenne Daily Leader,* December 12, 13, 16, 1880.

27. Thomas Sturgis to Fred Hesse, April 23, 1884, WSGA Papers.

28. Frewen to H. E. Teschemacher, June 3, 1884, Frewen Papers.

29. Minutes of the Cheyenne Club, June 5, 22, 1880, American Heritage Center, University of Wyoming (hereafter cited as Minutes of the Cheyenne Club).

30. L. G. "Pat" Flannery, ed., *John Hunton's Diary,* vol. 6 (Glendale, California, 1970), 86.

31. David Dary, *Cowboy Culture* (New York, 1981), 267.

32. Minutes of the Cheyenne Club, September 16, 21, 1882.

33. Frewen to Clara Frewen, September 29, 1882, Frewen Papers.

34. Minutes of the Cheyenne Club, October 6, November 8, 1884.

35. *Cheyenne Daily Leader,* October 13, 1878.

36. *Cheyenne Daily Leader,* March 14, 1879.

37. *Laramie Daily Sentinel,* December 2, 1878.

38. Doug Engebretson, *Empty Saddles, Forgotten Names* (Aberdeen, South Dakota, 1982), 131; and C. R. (Mose) Cooksey, "Robbers' Roost Station," *Annals of Wyoming* 38(1) (April 1966): 93-94.

39. *Cheyenne Daily Sun,* July 9, 1879.

40. *Cheyenne Daily Leader,* April 8, 1879.

41. *Cheyenne Daily Sun,* September 30, 1879.

42. Frewen to Clara Frewen, October 25, 1881, Frewen Papers.

43. Charles Kelly, *The Outlaw Trail* (New York, 1959), 107-111.

· 2 ·

Moreton Frewen of England

A great deal has been written about Moreton Frewen — a good bit of it from his own pen, for Moreton was not shy or withdrawn. Indeed, he quoted for his wife the following description of him given by a "good" friend: "Your present manner of life promises to confirm what always was a true fault in your nature. You are self confident to the borderland of conceit, and when last home on at least one occasion your utter disregard of another's opinion was a very near approach to actual rudeness." Then, in case Clara might have missed the point, he explained, "Which plainly expressed means that in the opinion of those less friendly I *am* conceited and *am* rude."[1] While one can admire such candor, it did not help him in later years to form lasting relationships, either personally or in business. Nevertheless, he had uncanny success in making new friends and securing new support, even though one would suppose that the brashness of a young man of twenty-seven might be more easily forgiven than would be the case some years later. He was variously known by two nicknames, "Mortal Ruin" and "Silver Tongue." The first was testimony to his disastrous record of failed businesses, and the second explains the success he enjoyed in recruiting the widespread participation of others in these enterprises.

In addition to his own writings, among them the autobiography he was working on at the time of his death and a diary covering about two years, which he modestly allowed had "started me in the footsteps of Pepys and Greville," we have several books, including one full-length biography from the prolific Leslie family (descendants of his sister-in-law Leonie Jerome Leslie); all of which throw light on various aspects of Moreton's life.

There are a few (mostly unfavorable) comments from his nephew, Winston Churchill. When Winston was preparing to publish his first book, he sought help from the "literary" member of the family, Uncle Moreton, who had published a slender work on bimetallism. Moreton thereupon proceeded to edit the Churchillian prose! In a letter to his mother, Winston indignantly wrote, "With great courage Moreton has in places altered what I wrote and made it appear nice and plain and simple so that an idiot in an almshouse could make no mistake." He added, "as far as Moreton is concerned, I now understand why his life has been a failure in the city and elsewhere."[2]

Of old Sussex stock, Frewen was born May 8, 1853, the fourth surviving son of a wealthy Sussex squire. Although Moreton was sometimes incorrectly referred to as Lord Frewen, his family was not noble. It nevertheless was a "good" family (an ancestor had been knighted in 1684), and Moreton was proud of a pair of green velvet slippers on display at his birthplace, Brickwall, that once had been cadged from Queen Elizabeth I (he told Clara the family would sooner the Queen had given them a small grant of crown lands).[3] Moreton was a son of his father's second marriage. The eldest son of the first marriage predeceased his father, and the second son had been disinherited during the father's lifetime. When he died, the squire left the bulk of his estate to Edward, the eldest son of the second marriage, but the old man's concern for family ties caused him to burden the estate with a £50,000 payment to the disinherited son, John. As a consequence, Edward was soon in financial difficulty. Moreton wrote to Clara Jerome in the fall of 1880 that Ted was in a "great state of dismay" about his rents. "Farms by the half dozen, both in Sussex and in Leicestershire are falling in — no tenants are to be had." Later in the year he commented that the estate of Cold Overton was still unlet; it would eventually have to be sold, and Ted would have to mortgage his family birthplace, Brickwall, in Northiam, Sussex.

The younger sons, Richard, Moreton, and Stephen, each received cash settlements of £16,000 from their father. Richard received property in Innishannon, County Cork, Ireland, but it was burdened by payments of £800 per year (for twenty-five years) to brother Edward. Moreton had an interest in Galway property, but his tenants did not pay rent. Moreton's lack of large inheritance was only an early example of a string of financial disappointments he would suffer during his life.

For a time he moderated his life in the hopes that his efforts would influence his uncle, Charles Hay Frewen of Cold Overton, in Leicestershire, to name Moreton in his will. Later, he described the situation to Leonard Jerome: "I was rather tacitly encouraged to live carelessly and take no thought for the morrow by a rich childless uncle, who led me not by words merely, but in writing, to form extravagant expectations as to what he would do for me." But these efforts were in vain, and according to Moreton, the uncle sensed that the lad was only acting: "He probably knew, for I was a bad actor, that I had less than no affection for him; in any case, he died two years since, leaving me nothing but a legacy of dislike for his memory."[4] Another version of this story is given by Frewen's biographer, quoting Hugh Lowther (later the earl of Lonsdale). Lowther said that Uncle Charles had paid Moreton's gambling debts, on condition that he never play cards again; when the pledge was broken, the uncle swore not to leave Moreton the Cold Overton estate or to pay his debts again.[5]

In any case, Uncle Charles died September 1, 1878, during the Derby races, and it was on the second day of the races that he was buried. Moreton had entered Rusk, a mare he owned, in the races; he had bet £800 on her, but she "never showed in front." Thinking there might yet be good news from the estate of Uncle Charles, he asked his lawyer how much had been left him, and the answer came back: nothing. "I was down in the depths, the only time in my life," he wrote, although we do not know which loss pained him the most. Whatever the reason for his disinheritance, the lost legacy did not soon pass from Moreton's mind, for a year later he was still moved to refer to "that vulgar beast C. Martin," explaining, "I hate all the Martins. . . . It was the Martins who got all my beastly old uncle's hoarded wealth."[6] Actually, brother Stephen inherited an estate in Yorkshire from Uncle Charles, so the Martins did not get it all.

Of course, Moreton still had received £16,000 from his father, a not inconsiderable sum in those days (roughly $77,000), but this sum was to prove unequal to the needs he would discover. An avid follower of the ponies, Moreton went to the Doncaster races in the fall of 1878 and, in his own words, had been "betting heavily," so that up to the last day he had won a "small fortune." He then determined to risk all his winnings on a single race and thereby secure his financial future. "So after a long consultation with Fred Archer, who was to ride, I put all of my winnings on Hampton for the Cup." Archer was to ride Lord Ellesmere's Hampton, and he was stoutly opposed by Mr. Gretton's horse Pageant. Alas, it was Pageant's day, and, said

Moreton, "Instead of winning nearly eight 'thou,' I left Doncaster little the richer, save in memory." Many years later, Moreton remarked that it was Lord Ellesmere's horse that dispatched him to America.[7]

This was in 1878, just before he left England, and we are getting ahead of the story, for Moreton had other ways of straining his finances. A handsome man and a striking horseman, he found he could attract the attention of the first lady of Professional Beauties, Lillie Langtry.

Christened on the island of Jersey as Emilie Charlotte Le Breton, this remarkable woman had by now settled in London with her husband, Richard. We have a description of Lillie from the man who was to become Moreton's brother-in-law, Lord Randolph Churchill. He thought her "a most beautiful creature, quite unknown, very poor, and they say has but one black dress."[8] Moreton recalled meeting Lillie at a dinner given by Lady Manners. "I arrived grievously late," he said, "the diners had coupled up. I was introduced amid the confusion of my apologies to my companion, 'Mrs. Langtry.'"[9] Lillie was wearing the black gown that had become her trademark, and Frewen said, "All London had been talking of this phenomenon for a week, but I had never seen her before." We are told that Lillie tried to open the conversation by asking, "What are your spiritual beliefs?" Although one doubts the story, Moreton is supposed to have been "dumb-struck."[10] He was to see much of her after that. (Also vying for her favors was John Leslie, who one day would marry Leonie Jerome and thereby become Moreton's brother-in-law.)

Seven years later, when Moreton was happily married to Clara, he still was enchanted by the memory of Lillie: "She was in those days, quiet — though without being the least stupid, rather dreamy and so unconscious and unworldly." To his diary he confided his fury when she was seen in the company of Freddie Gebhard, "that black, greasy brute" (who also happened to be rich). "There is an inevitable shrinking from the contact, however slight, of a lower order of nature . . . ," and so on.[11]

It seems certain Moreton was one of Lillie's several lovers but found himself overmatched by "an inconveniently frequent visitor," whom he identified as Crown Prince Rudolph of Austria, the Hapsburg heir, although others would have named a royal closer to home, the Prince of Wales (whom Moreton and many others irreverently called "Tum," one can be sure only behind the Prince's back.[12] One unfortunate was drunk enough to use the nickname to the Prince's face and had to depart without breakfast in punishment for the indiscretion).[13]

As a farewell present to Lillie, Moreton gave her his horse Redskin. Later, he had to explain this act of charity to Clara. "Quite true," he admitted, "Mrs. Langtry has dear 'Redskin'. I was very fond of him and so wouldn't sell when I left England. She is fonder of him than of anything or anyone and he is in the best of hands." Not certain that this explanation had been adequate, he returned to the subject a few days later by emphasizing that Redskin had been with Lillie since February 1878, although he neglected to mention that he had not departed London until the fall of that year, leading one to suppose that the gift may not have been final the previous winter. Whatever the circumstances, Lillie made good use of the horse by riding him in Hyde Park in company with His Royal Highness.

It would surely have wounded Moreton's pride to read Lillie's account of her acquisition of Redskin. She said, "Then someone presented me with a thoroughbred hack named Redskin (a perfect gentleman in appearance and manner), and he, too, became a member of the family."[14] Although this passage is typical of the way Lillie deals with her male friends in her memoirs, it is curious that we learn something of Redskin's disposition ("a perfect gentleman"), but absolutely nothing of the "someone" who had given him to her!

So it was that, bereft of the lovely Lillie and of a good portion of his original inheritance, Moreton determined to seek his fortune elsewhere. His friend Hugh Lowther, who had already run interference for Moreton with Uncle Charles, now bought all Moreton's horses, apparently as a favor, since he shortly after resold them at a loss, which Moreton put at £400. Later on, Moreton learned of the loss and wrote to Lowther, offering him the horse Moonlight as a small offset to the balance. Waiting a mere week for a reply, he then gave the horse to his younger brother Stephen, only to hear from Lowther that he would accept the offer. This, of course, disappointed Stephen, and Moreton so informed Lowther. The gentleman thereupon insisted that the horse go back to Stephen.[15] Moreton was never troubled by these endless assaults on his friends' good nature. Five years later, when things were going poorly on the Wyoming ranch, he approached Lowther again, asking him to buy a portion of the operation.

Moreton had already visited America in the spring of 1878, as the guest of John Adair at the Adair Ranch in Texas. On this first of more than one hundred crossings of the Atlantic, he went first to New York, then to Chicago (via Philadelphia and Washington), where he met General Phil Sheridan, who told him of the wonders of the Yellowstone region. After a few weeks in Texas, he returned to England in July without visiting the Wyoming country that had been described to him.[16] It was fall of the same year when he made the decision to go to Wyoming to ranch, and it was mid-November when he got there, in the company of his brother Richard (who still had *his* £16,000), and four others who wanted to go hunting: Sir Charles Wolseley, and three of Moreton's Cambridge friends, James Boothby Burke Roche, son of Lord Fermoy, Jack Thornhill of Diddington, and Gilbert Leigh of Stoneleigh, heir to a barony. Leigh thus came for the first time to the region where he was to meet his death (of which more later).

Nothing was simple with Moreton, and his departure from England was no exception. He chartered a special train to race after the one he had missed — the fastest train in Ireland — which was to have taken him to the ship at Queenstown. If we are to believe him, a hundred people were collected at Cork station to cheer his progress. The line was under steam when he arrived, but a fast tender placed him on board.[17]

The group had originally set their sights on a hunt in the Yellowstone region, but they stopped in Chicago on their way west, where General Phil Sheridan dissuaded them from entering that area (the Indians were said to be aggressive). They therefore proceeded to Rawlins by rail and then set out in a northeasterly direction, encountering plenty of game. By December, the hunters from England were ready to return to the railhead and the journey home, and the Frewens were about to take on the serious business of selecting a ranch location.

Travelling with two companions enlisted by Moreton, a one-time prospector named Jack Hargreaves and a Texas cowboy named Tate, the two brothers struck out northeasterly toward the Powder River country. Even to someone familiar with the country such a trip in late December was fraught with considerable danger, but the Frewens were not without physical courage. Nevertheless, the expedition was soon in trouble. The snow in the passes was too deep for the horses, but a solution presented itself. A band of friendly Shoshonis on a buffalo hunt appeared, and the Englishmen obligingly assisted them in killing winter rations for "twenty lodges," according to Moreton. The herd, of "two or three thousand," had bunched up. Since Dick's horse had given out the day before in the deep snow, the situation was becoming desperate. Learning that the pass was a main buffalo trail, the four determined to try to use the buffalo as "snow plows." The magnificent beasts were stampeded through the pass, leaving a trail the tired horses could follow to the safety of the Powder River country. Moreton described the scene: "At one or two deep transverse drifts the leaders plunged in and went clean out of sight, but in a few yards they bobbed out again like porpoises playing through a wave."[18] It had been a close call but, as always, he took it in stride.

The two Frewen brothers make an interesting study. About the same size as Moreton (six feet three inches), Dick was a year older. He was the pessimist, while Moreton was the optimist. Moreton commented rather condescendingly that Dick "has never been submitted to society's looking glass — female influences — from his youth up, and so is still uncouth, and unspoiled, too." Presumably his own experiences entitled him to be considered an expert on the subject. Their feelings for each other took violent swings over the years. Moreton was seriously ill (he thought it was mountain fever) in the fall of 1880, and Dick was up at all hours to mix his quinine, a service that captured Moreton's heart and caused him to tell Clara that he was "so fond" of brother Dick. Less than a year later he was vowing to confront his brother, complaining how "insulting his letters have often been."

Later on, Dick, who *could* write astonishing letters, wrote to Leonard Jerome to complain that Moreton and Clara should not have married, since he must now support them.[19] All of these histrionics culminated in at least one physical encounter (". . . we had a fearful row," Moreton said, "and I shame to say I had to lay hand on him"); yet they always came back to their family ties in the end. Indeed, when Dick was drowned while yachting off Pembrokeshire, the life estate in the Innishannon property that passed to Moreton's family proved a godsend to poor Clara, as she tried to cope with her financial difficulties.

Moreton was also close to Edward and especially to his younger brother Stephen, both of whom eventually invested in his enterprises. While dabbling in nearly countless businesses, Dick and Moreton still had time to meddle in family affairs. Moreton complained that after a friend had arranged a transfer for Stephen to the much sought after "Blues," the boy had "thrown it up," as he expected to receive promotion faster in his own regiment.[20]

Dick and Moreton both took exceptional interest in the courting of Leonie Jerome, the younger sister of Clara and Jennie (Lady Randolph Churchill). It seems that Leonie had led their friend Charley Fitzwilliam to believe that she was seriously interested in him and then did not advance the matter, while poor Charley languished.

Late in 1881 Dick wrote what can only be called an intemperate letter to Clara, who had recently married Moreton. He started off by complaining that Moreton had not kept him informed about business matters, then moved at once into criticism of Clara for not writing, if she really cared for him. "But perhaps," he added, "you care for one in the same way that a good many people do, and that is in proportion to what they can get out of one." Having introduced the letter in this manner, he then wished her happiness in the coming year! "And lastly," he added, "if you care for me at all will you be kind enough to send me some straightforward answers about some of poor Charlie Fitzwilliams wretched business. I consider that Leo and your mother have behaved anything but well in the matter. Now do find out from Leo what she intends doing. Is she going to marry Freddy or not, and if so can't you prevail on her to write a nice womanly letter to Charlie asking him to set her free and telling him straight out that she finds she likes another better. It will be only right and it will be the best thing that can happen. Charlie who is too good a fellow to be ruined for any woman. Then will you find out if Leo has received Charlie's letters which he wrote 3 times a week during part of October and November, and if so did she answer them . . . ." There is more, but this will give the reader an adequate taste of the sort of outpouring that would often issue from Dick's pen. Two days later, he wrote again to Clara, asking her not to follow through on the previous letter, since Leonie had apparently done what was expected of her.[21]

Moreton weighed in with his own advice about Freddy Gebhard, another of Leonie's suitors, who also earned Moreton's wrath by pursuing Lillie Langtry with some success. "It's not that he's bad, snobbish or offensive," said he, "but he's of the class they make bank clerks in England."[22] Poor Leonie! She had no lack of advice, including some from Jennie, who thought Charlie a good sort but not much from the money standpoint.[23]

Moreton's courtship of Clara Jerome is an integral part of our story, not only because it was the underlying reason for much of the surviving correspondence, but because it affected so fundamentally the conduct of the business he was trying to conduct in America.

Born Clarita Jerome on April 15, 1851, she was nearly two years older than Moreton. Her father was Leonard Walter Jerome, a lawyer and small-town newspaper proprietor who came to New York in 1855, became for a time the principal proprietor of the *New York Times* (he apparently sold out before 1870), and earned several fortunes in Wall Street.[24] The family got a taste for continental living during the time when Leonard was American consul to Trieste, and as the eldest daughter of a millionaire Clara was received in the best social circles in Paris and later in London. Mrs. Jerome was seeking a titled suitor for her daughter but required that he also be Protestant. So, when the Duc de Lescera, a Spanish relative of the Empress Eugenie, became too interested in young Clara, the good mother ordered him from the house. Clara and Jennie contrived to admit the poor nobleman through the drawing room window, but Mrs. Jerome interrupted the tryst; happily, the nearsighted lady mistook the duke for a servant, and he escaped by taking a message to the cook.[25] Mrs. Jerome's search for a titled French connection for her daughter (a Huguenot, of course) was aborted when the foolish debacle of the Franco-Prussian War toppled the empire that formed the underpinnings of her Paris existence, and mother and daughters only escaped the Prussian conquest of the city by leaving on the last train to the Channel. After the war, Leonard made a hurried trip back to Paris to pack up some paintings, and his wife insisted on going, too; she was able to buy at auction the white porcelain dining service that had belonged to Napoleon III, featuring the golden "N" surmounted by the imperial crown.[26] It was small recompense for dashed hopes. Forced to take up quarters in London, the girls unhapply sought other diversions.

It was during this period that the second daughter (Jeanette, but always called Jennie) caught the eye of the second son of the duke of Marlborough, and they at once planned marriage, despite opposition from the duke and duchess (who thought Jennie unsuitable) and from Leonard (who was not impressed with English nobility). Eventually, the Churchills and Leonard relented, and Jennie married Lord Randolph, which permitted Clara to move in her sister's circle. But disaster soon struck again. A rift developed between Lord Randolph and the Prince of Wales as a result of the notorious Aylesford affair (Lord Randolph was even challenged to a duel by the Prince); the upshot of this unfortunate event was the ostracism of the Churchill family from the society of the prince.

Sadly, Clara returned to New York with her mother, and it was there that she first met Moreton Frewen, apparently in 1879. Although their first meeting did not strike the same sort of sparks as Jennie's first evening with Lord Randolph, Moreton was taken by the blonde beauty (he did not care for "dark" women, such as Jennie was). There then began a passionate correspondence that was to last a number of years. Writing long letters, sometimes more than one in a day, Moreton poured out his devotion for Clara, intermixed with profound and not so profound observations on things around him and his own view of the state of mankind.

Moreton admonished Clara to save his letters so that he could read them to her later, and she honored his request, except for those sent under a black seal, which we suppose were especially steamy (or at least he thought so). The courtship had to overcome some little difficulty about his past affairs, but this was apparently accommodated with some sort of mutual offset of indiscretions; Moreton did ask Clara to be kind to one of his old mistresses. It was all very civilized.

Through the summer of 1880, the outpouring of letters from the big ranch house on the Powder River was directed toward hastening the day when they could be married. Finally, Papa Jerome gave his consent, although not for such an early date as Moreton had desired. While pressing hard for an early marriage, Moreton was at the same time warning Clara that there would be "frequent intervals of separation." "I shall leave you with one of your sisters during my annual migrations west," he said, adding confidently, "a month will always do it."[27] Then he worried that Clara would be frightened at the wild West, and he proceeded to reassure her that she was of a "sporting" instinct. "You know the sporting instinct implies a great deal beyond *killing*. The love of new and wild experiences, the artist soul, the love of untutored nature and this sporting instinct your sex has in a great measure with ours; . . . So darling, don't anticipate disappointment for I'm certain I can make life oh, so happy for you here, for one bright brief summer."

The engagement was announced on both sides of the ocean, with the wedding to take place at Grace Church in New York on June 2, 1881. Then a major obstacle arose. The matter of a wedding settlement was gently broached. Jennie had had £2,000 a year (nearly $10,000) settled on her, and Moreton hoped for nothing less for the eldest daughter. But alas, Papa's finances were not what they once had been, and he demurred, even making the point that the engagement had been announced on the clear understanding that there would be no settlement. This was enough to get Moreton's attention. "Now there was no understanding of the sort," he thundered to Clara, "there was no such folly on your side or on mine. Quite the reverse, it was only after you felt confident that some provision would be forthcoming that you agreed to change your mind [and consent to marry]." Then to assure her that crass money considerations were not *completely* in control of him, he added, "You understand, you darling, that I am very far from complaining that I am to take you with nothing."[28] In the end, instead of nothing Leonard gave Clara a diamond necklace, but there was no cash.

In characteristic fashion, Moreton spent the day before his wedding at the Union Club with Leonard and Pierre Lorillard, whose horse Iroquois had been entered in the English Derby. When Iroquois won (the first American horse to do so), Leonard and Moreton spent the night helping Pierre celebrate.[29] It was not a traditional way to begin a marriage, but then almost nothing Moreton did was traditional.

Notes to Chapter 2

1. Frewen to Clara Jerome, August 3, 1880, Frewen Papers.
2. Churchill, *Winston S. Churchill*, vol. 1, 365.
3. Frewen to Clara Jerome, September 27, 1880, Frewen Papers.
4. Frewen to Clara Jerome, September 23, 1880, Frewen Papers.
5. Allen Andrews, *The Splendid Pauper* (New York, 1968), 53.
6. Frewen to Clara Frewen, December 17, 1881, Frewen Papers.
7. Morton Frewen, *Melton Mowbray* (London, 1924), 147–48.
8. The letter was apparently written early in 1878. Anita Leslie, *Lady Randolph Churchill* (New York, 1969), 76–77.
9. Frewen, *Melton Mowbray*, 101.
10. James Brough, *The Prince and the Lily* (New York, 1975), 157.
11. Frewen diary, June 16, 1884, Frewen Papers.

12. Frewen, *Melton Mowbray*, 101.

13. Philip Magnus, *King Edward the Seventh* (New York, 1964), 92.

14. Lillie Langtry, *The Days I Knew* (New York, 1925), 132–33.

15. Frewen diary, March 29, 1883, Frewen Papers.

16. Howard B. Lott, ed., "Diary of Major Wise, an Englishman, Recites Details of Hunting Trip in Powder River Country in 1880," *Annals of Wyoming* 12(2) (April 1940), 87.

17. Frewen, *Melton Mowbray*, 154.

18. Ibid., 166.

19. Frewen to Clara Frewen, October 29, 1881, Frewen Papers.

20. Frewen to Clara Jerome, May 1, 1880, Frewen Papers.

21. Richard Frewen to Clara Frewen, December 22, 24, 1881.

22. Frewen to Clara Jerome, April 1881, Frewen Papers.

23. Leslie, *Lady Randolph Churchill*, 84.

24. *New York Times*, July 4, 1880.

25. Anita Leslie, *The Remarkable Mr. Jerome* (New York, 1954), 124.

26. Ibid., 147.

27. Frewen to Clara Jerome, September 7, 1880, Frewen Papers.

28. Frewen to Clara Jerome, April 2, 1881, Frewen Papers.

29. Leslie, *The Remarkable Mr. Jerome*, 248.

· 3 ·

The Frewen Brothers
on the Powder River

I wonder who else has power to live as I have lived, to come abroad
in time, pioneer and open up a country nearly as large as Ireland,
and where was a desert to plant a thriving settlement — and this, too,
in the dead of winter and with Indians all about."[1] So Morton Frewen
once reflected on his venture in the Powder River country. Not
modest, but not far off the mark, either. His fondness for this wild
new land was apparently genuine and deep, for he returned often to
the theme. Once, he remarked wistfully, "The country is so lovely,
and for me, its first white settler, has such an indescribable interest
and charm that I should feel quite sad if I thought I was soon to drop
out of its life."[2]

The Frewen brothers began their ranching operations in partnership in the spring of 1879; the formal agreement was not drawn up
until 1880, to be effective at the beginning of 1881.[3] The operation was
styled the Big Horn Ranche, using the spelling then in vogue with
British investors.

We do not know where the brothers spent the early winter of
1878–79, but we know something of their whereabouts from a newspaper interview in April. They had just returned from three or four
months in the north, where they had been building what an excited
reporter called three fortified ranches, one on Powder River, one on
Crazy Woman, and one on Dry Fork. A newspaper account noted
with vast exaggeration that the two brothers were wealthy capitalists,
who had tried "the lions and elephants of Africa, the tigers and other
interesting brutes in the jungles of India, chased the bounding
kangaroo in the Australian brush."[4]

Yet, conditions were not good in the north; the Indians were restive, and the brothers decided they would delay actual transfer of cattle to their new range until things settled down a bit. Their opinion was that there would be an Indian uprising soon, and Moreton claimed that "hostile" bands of Sioux and Bannocks could be met at any time. He told of coming upon the graves of five white men who had been "jumped" by the Sioux at Dry Creek; they were buried at the headwaters of the Nowood by a contingent of the Fifth Cavalry, who came upon the bodies.

After these preliminaries in the north, the two embarked on a flurry of activity that must have astonished and amused the residents of Cheyenne. After Dick took a side trip to New York, they were both ready to commence serious cattle purchases. In mid-April, Dick left for New Mexico and there purchased 7,000 head, which were to be held on a southern range until they could safely be brought north. The two brothers had hoped to buy in Colorado but were unable to do so, causing Moreton to contemplate a trip to Oregon; Dick was to be dispatched to the Tongue River to build a fourth ranch for receiving the Oregon stock.

Then, on May 1, Moreton was able to close what the *Sun* called "one of the largest" cattle purchases of the season. For $70,000 cash they purchased 4,500 head from Tim Foley, and with it they acquired the brand they would later make famous, the "76." Foley's range was on the Sweetwater and the North Platte west of old Fort Casper; his ranch was on Sand Creek. A further 1,500 head were contracted from Foley for delivery from Montana in the fall. Dick and the foreman (Tate) were dispatched to pick up the cattle, and Moreton made ready to follow them.[5]

According to widely circulated gossip, the Foley herd was driven more than once around a hill for Frewen's inspection and purchase, a story that Moreton later hotly denied. Since so many of his mistakes are undisputed, there is no reason to suppose that he was also guilty of this example of naïveté, even though the story has been repeated a number of times.[6] Many years later, Moreton's friend Lord Lonsdale repeated the double purchase story as fact, but the earl must be forgiven for passing on fantasy, since in the same letter he also flatly denied that Moreton and Lillie Langtry were lovers. ("He was never very much interested in love of the ladies at all," said Lonsdale!)[7] In fact, it is quite out of character for Moreton to be hoodwinked in this simple fashion. Moreover, Foley had agreed to make up any shortfall in the 4,500 book count, so he would gain little by driving the same animals several times around the hill.[8]

Before their formal partnership agreement was drawn, Richard had already put a total of £13,000 sterling ($63,000) into the venture, and Moreton had put in £7,977 ($39,000); in spite of this disparity in capital, the partners were to share equally in profits and losses. Each was permitted to draw £200 (about $1,000) annually, in quarterly installments, against anticipated profits. The agreement contemplated that the capital might be reduced in the future, apparently in anticipation of abundant profits. Included in the numerous provisions in the agreement was the appointment of Stebbins, Post & Co. in Cheyenne as bankers for the partnership, a relationship that was to prove difficult on both sides in the years to come. Finally, the agreement provided that disputes should be resolved by arbitration under the procedures of the Common Law Procedure Act of 1854 of England. There were soon to be disputes aplenty to resolve, although none went to arbitration.

Soon they were sending supplies north to the new headquarters: arms, ammunition, tools, poultry, plows, brands, lumber, and glass sash.[9] Before the new operation was properly underway, the road agents infesting the Powder River country made a sally against the Frewen enterprise and got away with thirty to forty first class horses. Moreton thought the culprits were a group who had been apprehended by the authorities earlier and relieved of their mounts (which had been stolen).[10]

At first, things went quite well. In May 1880, Moreton noted that they had just sold £3,200 ($15,000) worth of beef and had reinvested the proceeds "and some more" in fresh cattle, everything paid. Nevertheless, there was undoubtedly friction between the brothers, even though Moreton claimed at one point that they were "getting on famously." Later, he remarked ominously that there was "constant risk of collision," and Moreton was already mulling over the possibility of buying Dick out, although the reader might be forgiven for wondering what he would use for capital.

There were the usual problems with employees. A foreman was leaving, Moreton supposed because of jealousy over the salary Fred Hesse was being paid by brother Ted on a nearby range. Some from Great Britain were hired, but such origins did not exempt them from Moreton's criticism. "I am quite angry with dear old Brock," he said to Clara. "He has sent out a most useless poor fellow, a parson's son. It is such folly the notion that because a man is in want at home he must come here. A man must have capital, strength and energy, and here is one poor fellow who is devoid of all three." The cowhands grew accustomed to the parade of guests at the ranch house, and it was perhaps inevitable that they would expect supervision to be slack during the heavy visiting season, especially when the foreman had to be in Rawlins for a law case. But Moreton had energy for more than one activity; he decided to ride over to see how the work was going, only to find that the crew had made for a "whiskey store" (presumably the Frewen establishment at Powder River crossing).

Moreton arranged for Ted to throw his cattle in with theirs under a different brand, with Ted taking responsibility for one-third of the expenses. By the fall of 1880, Moreton could write to Clara, ". . . things are looking unusually well," although he admitted that when they examined the household expenses they found that the massive two-story headquarters cost them £180 a month (about $900), a not inconsiderable sum. The main room of the house was forty feet square, "running up to the roof, and hung all round with Indian trophies and the spoils of the chase — elk and deer horns, buffalo robes and beaver skins — and lots of flowers and creepers."[11] There was also a mezzanine (Moreton called it a "musicians' gallery") where musicians could sit to play for guests dancing below. "Twenty of us can dine in the hall comfortably, and after we can move out and lounge on the piazza and watch the great purple shadows stealing down over the prairie from the mountains."[12] The walls were papered, and Moreton sent a sample of the paper to Clara so that she could decide what decorations would harmonize. The staircase and all the interior woodwork was imported from England. When the house was demolished, the staircase was purchased by M. H. Leitner of Sussex, Wyoming, and some carved figures made from its wood are probably the last trace remaining of that wonderful house.[13]

When Ted and his wife visited in August of 1880, they were, in Moreton's words, "amused and delighted at the house. . . . I had talked of it to them all up the road as a 'log house' which indeed it is, and Sam Ashton said with true British intolerance of his room, 'I did not think there was such a pretty room out of England!!'" In the same letter he could report that the piano was on its way to the house from the railroad at Rock Creek.[14] Returning one afternoon unexpectedly,

Moreton was nonetheless served a fine meal, which he described to Clara to show that conditions were not primitive:

> Green pea soup
> A white fish from the river
> Roast beef of our own growing
> A willow grouse — half pound
> Cabinet pudding
> A pint of champagne

Moreton justified the large expense of the household thusly: "You see at this distance from the rail, not only are wages high but the cost of everything is greatly increased."[15]

One can see that their existence was hardly Spartan. But there was more. The telephone was rare in this era, and not everyone thought it was necessary. Indeed, in 1876 the chief engineer of the British Post Office had remarked rather grandly, "The Americans have need of the telephone, but we do not. We have plenty of messenger boys."[16] Yet, the Frewens, ignoring their countryman's wisdom, had installed a telephone, which connected the ranch house with the Frewen store some twenty-four miles away. This was a particular construction problem, as the insulators took a long time coming out from Chicago. While a working telephone in this wilderness seems a surprising thing to us, it was even more astonishing to the Indians. Moreton was amused to write to Mr. Jerome about an occasion when one band of Sioux was at the house and another was at the store. Wolf's Tooth was put on the telephone at the store to speak to Plenty Bear at the house. He heard the familiar voice come over the line, and Frewen, who was watching, said, "I thought he'd have a fit. They think us mighty medicine men, and treat the telephone with immense respect."[17]

The store at Powder River crossing was a boisterous establishment, presided over by William E. Hathaway. It consisted of one long, low building that housed the store, saloon, and living quarters; in addition, there were stables, a blacksmith shop, and some dugout cabins. The buildings were located on the south side of the Powder River, across from the military reservation (Frewen's authorization from the government for the use of the buildings on the reservation had contained a prohibition against maintaining a saloon). Hathaway provided whiskey, prostitutes, tobacco, and conversation. The bar was shoulder high, and men were requested to deposit firearms behind the counter on entering. The barroom doubled as a dormitory when the weather made it impossible to travel.[18] There were two or three bedrooms, and one guest noted that they were "rough and ready," with no sheets on the beds.[19] By the end of May 1879, Powder River had its own post office.[20]

Moreton was full of dreams about the future of the range. "This range is such an exceptionally good one," he said, "that our 3 year old beeves will be quite fat January, February and March next, bar accidents. The local merchants, Denver with 40,000 inhabitants, Leadville with 35,000 more, promise to pay almost famine rates at that time, as Colorado has suffered from an awful drought and loss." According to his calculations, the income should amount to £6,000 per year (clear). This was to become a familiar theme in Frewen's writing. In the fall of 1880 he boldly predicted that in two years, "we shall have all we want," although he lengthened the time horizon to six years when he wrote a few days later to Leonard Jerome. While the time predictions would change, Moreton never lost his conviction that soon — very soon — he would be enjoying the prosperity that had thus far eluded him.

The style with which Moreton approached his work was not everywhere appreciated. He had staked out a great barony for himself, and this was resented by some. In a letter to the *Leader,* one wrote, "The 'B.S.', which upon translation means British Subject, who is located on Powder River, it is said, points with his dexter finger and claims, presumably by right of conquest (?) all the county from the old post of McKinney to the Big Horn Mountains, thence north and west to Crazy Woman's Fork, and has hoisted the 'Union Jack' over his tent. However, . . . my Briton is being elbowed, and will be crowded . . . ." The writer also questioned whether an alien (i.e., a British subject) could be postmaster, obviously referring to the Powder River post office.[21]

The Cheyenne papers enjoyed poking fun at the abundance of titles among the guests coming and going from the Powder River. In one piece, it was suggested that the legislature should introduce titles of nobility, which would be conferred based upon the number of cattle a person owned. Those without cattle would be referred to as "Mudsills," ineligible for office, except the post office at mail time. Then someone with one hundred head would be called a "Grub," while someone with fifty thousand or more would be a Cattle King, entitled to be addressed as "Your Mawgesty," with corresponding dignity to wife and child. There were numerous titles to fill in between.[22] While much of this was good fun, there was annoyance behind it, too.

The ranch was the center for numerous hunting parties from England, and Moreton regarded the big house as a mere "shooting box," since all of the ranch business was conducted eighteen miles down the river at the cow camp. His hope was that someday it would become quite as ordinary to see a shooting box in the Big Horns as to see "a river in Norway, or a forest in Scotland."[23] Of course, this activity was expected to operate according to the strict rules of the sporting class. When Texas "skin hunters" appeared on the range, killing elk and buffalo, Moreton was quick to write to the secretary of the interior requesting help in eliminating this threat to the game animals.

Nor did he exempt his countrymen from his crusade to limit the killing of big game animals. Early in 1880 William A. Baillie-Grohman wrote an article in *The Field* extolling the virtues of hunting in the

Rocky Mountain west and bragging on his bag of four hundred animals in a period of four months. Frewen immediately took up his pen to attack this "wanton slaughter," protesting the effect on the breeding stock and the waste of meat, since the inhabitants of Wyoming were dependent on wild game for food. He pointed out that the territorial law prohibited killing of elk, deer, mountain sheep, or antelope, except for food. Mr. Baillie-Grohman was quick to reply, giving Moreton the opportunity for the public exposure he reveled in. Baillie-Grohman asserted that the American ranchman subsisted wholly on beef, and this called forth Frewen's denial that any rancher would consider eating an animal worth £6 ($29). Baillie-Grohman also noted that the venture was not without risk to him personally, since he had been "surrounded" by Indians, who had just succeeded in butchering "a lot of troops" some two hundred miles away. This permitted Moreton to wax dramatic, saying the circumstances were little cause for Baillie-Grohman to consider himself a hero. "Because one man kills another at Newcastle, I in London should hardly return thanks for my deliverance from peril." It was all great entertainment.

In order to keep the wrong sort from coming out to hunt, Moreton concocted an "Indian scare" letter, which he sent home to the newspapers in England. He warned that it would now be "madness" to make an attempt to come to the region, as Sitting Bull, with three thousand warriors, was crossing and recrossing the border, making buffalo scarce. He expected trouble from Sioux, Cheyenne, Arapahoes ("hitherto peaceable"), and Bannocks, and he solemnly advised that "hunting and being hunted are vastly different things," urging his countrymen to wait for a more convenient season.[24] Of course, much of this was pure embellishment; Moreton wrote Clara that he hoped this would scare the hunters away.

He felt differently, of course, about his own invited guests; a buffalo hunt the following year, which Moreton described to Clara, illustrates the sporting rules he lived by. He had accompanied a group of visitors into the mountains, where they happened upon a herd of the great beasts. "It is a beautiful broad valley stretching a mile of bright green turf between two dark pine woods, and sloping away far above timberline, two ranges of snow capped mountains show up 'sublime in barrenness.' In the bottom, not a quarter of a mile from where we are standing a large herd of buffalo, nearly a thousand we guess them."

At this point, Sam Ashton was all for stalking them with rifles, but Moreton resisted the idea, because, he said, "a first encounter with these grand beasts is always a green spot in a sportsman's memory." He persuaded them to leave their rifles with the pack train and trust only to their revolvers and their horses' speed. Frewen was riding Walnut, which he claimed was much the fastest horse in Wyoming, and he loaned this mount to Ted, while he stayed with Mrs. Ashton and the pack train to observe the fun. There shortly arose a "great commotion." "Ted on 'Walnut' makes all the running and in half a mile I see him well among the herd and at his fourth shot a big old bull comes down heavily and is dead before Mrs. Ashton and I come up. Sam is a mile away in difficulties with a wounded bull, his six shooter empty and the great beast very furious, so he is glad as I gallop up with his rifle and bull No. 2 gets his *coup de grace*."[25]

The following month another hunting party got into serious trouble with a grizzly bear. W. C. Alston, a burly Scotsman (who later was the partner of Thomas W. Peters in a ranch on the Powder River), made up a hunting party with Major Lewis Lovatt Ashford Wise. The hunters stopped at the ranch house, which Wise called a "palace," and there met their guides; Wise was to work with Oliver P. Hanna, the pioneer from the Big Horn country. The party had considerable success, and late in September they killed a buffalo bull as bait for bears. This strategy was successful, and Wise wounded the bear that was drawn to this bait. The two men then foolishly followed the wounded animal to thick brush, where at times they had to crawl on hands and knees, coming upon the bear when he was only eight yards away. Both Hanna and Wise fired again, but the dying animal charged Hanna, clawing and biting him before Wise could reload and fire again, driving the animal away. Wise took Hanna back to camp (but not before blazing the trees to mark the bear's location) and later recovered the skin from the eleven hundred-pound animal.[26] Moreton remarked that Wise had behaved "quite as he should," although he thought Hanna would always be lame.[27]

Still, not all the folks in Wyoming understood the distinction Moreton made between the hunting he provided for his own guests and the prohibitions he wanted to impose on the so-called "hide hunters" and others. A resident of Fort Fetterman complained in the fall of 1879 that three or four English lords and army officers were slaughtering game for the fun of it.[28] Forever insensitive to such matters, Moreton dashed off a letter to the newspaper (unsigned, but unmistakably his), telling of the large party staying with him, including Charles Fitzwilliam (son of Lord Fitzwilliam), Hugh Lowther (later Lord Lonsdale), Lords Caledon and Rodney, and others. A prairie fire had swept down on the party, burning Lady Lowther's effects before they could be rescued. It is doubtful if the rustics in Cheyenne appreciated the gravity of the loss.[29]

Certainly, the locals in Wyoming found it difficult at times to identify with the lifestyle of these strange people, some of whom seemed to have far too much money. When Hugh Lowther became impressed with the work of a waiter at the Railroad Hotel in Cheyenne, he offered the man a year in England on his estate. The next year, the man returned, bemused by his experience but glad to be back home. When his neighbors carped, Moreton assumed they were just jealous because he had "the best range and the largest herd." He personally pretended to care "but little" about the talk, but it "worried" Dick. Moreover, he sniffed, one must understand that "being a gentleman is much against one here, as in the colonies generally."[30] Horace Plunkett also commented on the animosity that the westerners felt toward the foreigners, and he, too, attributed it to resentment over a difference in social position, coupled with national pride.[31]

Moreton did tend to regard himself as a sort of arbiter of proper society in Wyoming. One day he entered the Railroad Hotel in Cheyenne and spotted the entry "Lord C. Beresford, Ireland" on the register. (The name was well known to the Frewen family; Lord Beresford had been the messenger from the Prince of Wales, sent to challenge Lord Randolph Churchill to a duel in the Aylesford affair.) Rushing into the dining room and not finding Lord Beresford in the establishment, he asked the clerk the identity of the guest who had signed the register, whereupon he was referred to "a miserable little counter stripper who had not even the impudence to brazen it out." Before the man's fellow travellers Moreton proceeded to administer "a tremendous talking to," from which he derived great satisfaction.[32]

The environment was also one of his many interests. He noted the scarcity of timber in the valley, and when he heard some of his hands cutting trees, he ran to stop them. He admitted that when they first arrived in the Powder River country they had been more wasteful with the timber, but now he was more careful of "the beauties of light and shade and green foliage."[33]

It was a beautiful land, but the realities of Wyoming weather did weigh on cattle operations. It was two hundred miles from the ranch to the railhead, and the roads were passable only in reasonably good weather. Often could be heard the litany, "the roads are in an awful state." In the fall of 1880 there was word that snow had drifted to eleven feet on parts of the road between Fort Fetterman and Rock Creek, creating the real possibility that there would be no wheel traffic for the remainder of the winter. Of course, the owners of the ranches in the area left for the winter, but if they got too late a start, the journey was a difficult one. In 1880, the first bad storm struck when the winter stores were not yet at the ranch house, and it was necessary to pack them in by mule.[34]

Another ranching operation was about to start nearby. In May 1879. James Boothby Burke Roche, who had accompanied the Frewen brothers on the hunting trip the previous fall, returned to Cheyenne with his younger brother, Alexis Charles Burke Roche (then twenty-five years old).[35] Alexis Roche would go into ranching in the Powder River country in partnership with Horace Curzon Plunkett (the son of Lord Dunsany) and Edward Shuckburgh Rouse Boughton (then twenty-one, the second son of a baronet). Both Plunkett and Boughton came to the Powder River in the fall of 1879. Moreton claimed to have arranged the partnership of the three men and said condescendingly that he was "in a way" responsible for Roche's "good behavior."[36]

Plunkett, who would loom large in Moreton's future, was only a few months younger than Frewen, a younger son of Baron Dunsany of Dunsany Castle. The family, originally Danish, had settled in County Meath in the twelfth century and became among the largest landowners in Ireland. Although we do not know precisely why Horace decided to come to Wyoming, one account attributes the decision to the family malady, tuberculosis, which caused him to choose a drier climate. According to this story, the choice was between South Africa and the Rockies.[37]

In any case, Horace came to Wyoming, started ranching with Roche and Boughton, and in 1884 organized the Frontier Land & Cattle Co. (with a capitalization of $1,500,000); Plunkett became president at a salary of $3,000 per year. Andrew Gilchrist was vice president and general manager, while Boughton, the largest investor, was treasurer. Relationships with his partners and investors were rocky. Plunkett called Boughton "useless," and he did not approve of Roche's character. On one occasion, Roche acknowledged that he had made a "fearful mess" of the business of buying cattle.[38] Of Gilchrist, Plunkett said, somewhat condescendingly, "He was, I believe, a private in the Life Guards, who has built up a considerable fortune from nothing."[39]

Horace followed the same schedule as other British landowners in the West; he would spend his summer on the range, leaving by the end of October, and by early December he would be back in Dunsany. Remarkably unflappable, he could respond with great equanimity to the literary barbs thrown at him by the Frewens, and his partner Alexis Roche (who stammered) once said of him, "P-P-Plunkett is the s-s-strangest being you ever met." Another described him as a thin, spare man with a prominent nose and keen, kindly eyes, but with a limp. Horace was critical of the Frewens for failing to understand the westerners' feelings about them, but he fared little better in forming friendships in the West, among either men or women (according to his own testimony, on occasion he sought out the company of willing women, but only for "health's sake").[40]

Although the Frewens had been engaged in a flurry of activity, the cattle industry around them had been growing even faster than they. In the middle of 1880, the *Leader* commented that three or four years earlier, a herd of three or four thousand would have been large, and only four or five in the territory were that large; now six, eight, or even ten thousand head was an average sort of herd, and at least seven were larger than that, headed by the Swan brothers, with forty-five thousand head. The Frewens did not even make the list.[41]

In these Wyoming beginnings, if fate did not always smile as sweetly on Moreton as he had hoped — and often it did not — he was little dismayed. Already his restless mind was casting about for other projects to make his fortune. Some of these projects were connected to the ranching business, others were not. And all of them excited him.

Notes to Chapter 3

1. Frewen to Clara Jerome, May 29, 1880, Frewen Papers.
2. Frewen to Clara Frewen, May 13, 1882, Frewen Papers.
3. The agreement in the Frewen files, although signed, is not dated; it probably was executed late in 1880. Frewen Papers.
4. *Cheyenne Daily Sun,* April 13, 1879.
5. *Cheyenne Daily Sun,* May 1, 1879.

6. Andrews, *Splendid Pauper,* 47. John Hunton gives Foley's name as Sam. Flannery, *John Hunton's Diary,* vol. 3, 22.

7. Earl of Lonsdale to Shane Leslie, December 18, 1930.

8. *Cheyenne Daily Sun,* May 1, 1879.

9. *Cheyenne Daily Sun,* April 29, 1879.

10. *Cheyenne Daily Sun,* May 9, 1879.

11. Frewen to Clara Jerome, July 11, 1880, Frewen Papers.

12. Frewen to Clara Jerome, July 25, 1880, Frewen Papers.

13. Lott, "Diary of Major Wise," 90. Although the name of the Sussex post office has been attributed to Frewen and his native Sussex, it appears to have been named for Sussex County, Delaware. See Mae Urbanek, *Wyoming Place Names* (Boulder, Colorado, 1967), 192.

14. Frewen to Clara Jerome, August 3, 1880, Frewen Papers.

15. Frewen to Clara Jerome, September 17, 1880, Frewen Papers.

16. *Across the Board* 22(3) (March 1985), 59.

17. Frewen to Leonard Jerome, February 5, 1881, Frewen Papers.

18. Thelma Gatchell Condit, "The Hole in the Wall," *Annals of Wyoming* 29(1) (April 1957), 44–45.

19. Lott, "Diary of Major Wise," 87.

20. Daniel Y. Meschter, *Wyoming Territorial and Pre-Territorial Post Offices* (Cheyenne, 1971), 15.

21. *Cheyenne Daily Leader,* September 4, 1879.

22. *Cheyenne Daily Sun,* August 14, 1881.

23. Frewen to Clara Jerome, July 17, 1880, Frewen Papers.

24. The letter appeared May 31, 1879.

25. Frewen to Clara Jerome, August 15, 1880, Frewen Papers.

26. Lott, "Diary of Major Wise," 102–103.

27. Frewen to Clara Jerome, October 13, 1880, Frewen Papers.

28. *Cheyenne Daily Leader,* September 18, 1879.

29. *Cheyenne Daily Leader,* September 23, 1879.

30. *Cheyenne Daily Sun,* June 16, 1881.

31. Frewen to Clara Jerome, May 2, 1881, Frewen Papers; and Plunkett diary, July 21, 1881.

32. Frewen to Clara Jerome, July 5, 1880, Frewen Papers.

33. Frewen to Clara Jerome, February 21, 1881, Frewen Papers.

34. Frewen to Clara Jerome, November 28, 1880, Frewen Papers.

35. *Cheyenne Daily Leader,* May 27, 1879; and L. G. Pine, *Burke's Peerage* (London, 1953), 788–89.

36. Frewen to Clara Jerome, July 12, 1880, Frewen Papers.

37. Margaret Digby, *Horace Plunkett, an Anglo-American Irishman* (Oxford, 1949), 21.

38. Plunkett diary, January 26, September 1, 1881.

39. Digby, *Horace Plunkett,* 29.

40. R. A. Anderson, *With Horace Plunkett in Ireland* (London, 1935), 1; and Plunkett diary, May 9, June 6, 1881.

41. *Cheyenne Daily Leader,* July 9, 1880.

· 4 ·

Diversions of One Sort or Other

*I*n the spring of 1880, Moreton was already dabbling in a mine in Leadville, and he had obtained the opinion of "a great mining authority" on the subject. This unidentified expert told Frewen that it would be "criminal carelessness" to do less than his "very utmost" in the matter. How perfect it would be if this were the "bonanza!"[1] But after a trip to Leadville in July, Moreton concluded that the whole thing was "a perfect illusion . . . the company is a 'bogus' one, and the pretended million dollar transfer is simply an imprudent stock jobbing advertisement."[2] Possible litigation clouded the situation, and he ruefully remarked, "I fear me it will only land me in an expensive lawsuit and I shall come off a wiser but not a richer man."[3]

At the same time, he decided to investigate the possibility of making another fortune, this time in coal. On a trip to southern Idaho, he located a coal deposit, which he felt certain would compete in San Francisco with coal being shipped all the way from Pennsylvania. "It has been located by an old man and three sons, who are simply waiting for a capitalist to come to develop it," said Moreton.[4] A few days later he was on his way to the seam to collect samples for analysis, and he told Clara to get him the address of a prospective investor. This was not to be a minor undertaking; he had in mind building a railroad to the Central Pacific mainline forty miles to the north of the deposit. He thought it could all be done for £100,000 ($483,000). Already, he was contemplating negotiations with the railroad for a preferential freight rate. "If the quality is good, it should be worth millions," he concluded. We don't know if he meant millions of pounds or dollars, but in this case, as in so many others, it doesn't matter.

Only three miles from the coal deposit, he found that the river, swollen from melting snow, had become a torrent. Undaunted, he camped that night on the river bank, arose the next morning before daylight, swam the river with a pick and two sacks, walked the three miles to the coal bed, "and having got about 40 pounds of coal, got safely across with it by swimming again, water so cold and running like a mill race."[5] He left two men to work on the project, and he was briefly encouraged by the analysis of the coal he had brought out (36 percent fixed carbon). But, unfortunately, this project to extract Idaho coal was to walk off stage after this brief scene, never to return again.[6]

There was no lack of other projects, however. In the spring of 1881, Moreton was captivated by the idea of a refrigeration plant atop Sherman Hill, between Laramie and Cheyenne. The idea had come to him as he was pondering the perennial problem of the vagaries of the cattle markets. Looking for some means to keep the meat from spoiling while waiting for prices to improve, he heard that a butcher in Cheyenne had succeeded in keeping several beeves in good condition in a shed for several months without refrigeration. If this could be done in Cheyenne, how much better it would work in a place where the average temperature was below freezing! Such a place was near at hand.

Atop the divide between Cheyenne and Laramie was Sherman station, the highest point on the transcontinental line, named for General William Tecumseh Sherman (the general once said he personally selected the station to be honored with his name, in preference to a small "water station" in Nebraska).[7] At an elevation of 8,242 feet above sea level, there were few nights there, even in summer, when ice did not form. And so the idea was formed: the animals would be slaughtered outdoors in the winter and allowed to freeze, then stored in the packing house (without any ice) until the meat could be moved by refrigerator cars to the east, and thence by refrigerator ship all the way to England. The experiment would involve a mere two thousand head in 1881 but could be expanded to fifteen to twenty thousand the following year![8]

The Sherman operation would permit the cattleman to avoid sending cattle to market in September and October, when prices were low. Moreover, shipping live cattle from Wyoming to Chicago cost ten dollars a head, with attendant shrinkage from the journey. Butchering could be done at Sherman in October, and the meat could be kept there until May (when prices would improve) without the need for ice (because of the low natural temperature). Shipment of meat in quantity at low fares negotiated with the Union Pacific would permit delivery to England at a freight cost of only two cents per pound, making it possible to compete successfully in London.

With his customary enthusiasm, Frewen declared that this would "revolutionize the stock industry." He proceeded to raise money, and by the fall of 1881 he was busily buying a ranch near Sherman for holding the animals, negotiating freight rates with the railroad, and supervising construction of the packing house, which consisted chiefly of one building within another. He hired James East, a well-known contractor, to begin construction, which was hampered by the "breezes" that blew so steadily in that place.[9] The first cattle were purchased in October, and although they soon broke the fence down and some escaped, Frewen was still optimistic.

Yet success eluded him. The following year, some cattle were butchered there, and Moreton even commented that someone else was building another packing house — he thought "a dozen" would be up shortly. The Cheyenne *Leader* sent a reporter out to see the operation and to write a story about it. The steers were shot two at a time and butchered, with two men working on each carcass. The capacity of the operation was said to be four thousand sheep and one thousand beef animals. Nevertheless, the export connection was never developed, and the idea did not take off. Already in the spring of 1882 Moreton was thinking that the packing house would fit better with his much grander export scheme, about which more later.

Meanwhile, Dick had an idea of his own. He conceived the notion that money was to be made by opening up Yellowstone Park as a tourist attraction — the park was virtually inaccessible at the time. He approached Horace Plunkett, their near neighbor in the Powder River country, and suggested establishing a stage line from the Utah Northern railroad to the park, which would be served by hotels and boats. Plunkett thought the idea might be profitable, and the two met with Wyoming governor John W. Hoyt in September 1881 to discuss the possibility of a monopoly franchise. Plunkett, disgusted by Dick's domination of the conversation, later remarked that neither he nor the governor could get in a word! Still, the idea continued to tantalize Plunkett until his father told him he was out of his depth.[10] Nothing came of the scheme, although the park did become the tourist attraction that had been forecast.

One of the stranger ideas to interest Moreton was the Texas bat caves. In the spring of 1881, he was getting ready to go to Texas to investigate the caves, which, he had learned, had been the source of raw material for saltpeter for the Confederate government's munitions industry during the Civil War. "What a funny subject to write to dear you about," he said to Clara, "but Peruvian guano is now selling in England for £15 a ton, and we could ship and sell this at a profit for £8, so that if it is nearly as rich, here is a fortune for sure."[11] Later in the year, Dick, who had been conned into participating in this venture (as he did in most of them), would report that he thought they could sell the bat guano for £8 or £10 per ton.

The two brothers had a third partner in the bat caves venture, young Captain Edward E. Shearburn, another Englishman, who may actually have furnished the original inspiration for the venture but in any case would be the source of much trouble. Plunkett had met him in June 1881, and recorded the story Shearburn told him; it is impossible to know how much he believed. The captain had served with the IX Lancers in the Afghan fighting, where he charged with 120 men seventeen times against 10,000 of the enemy. His horse was shot from under him, and his clothes riddled.[12] After losing his money gambling (he was said to have lost £20,000 [$96,000] in one session in Italy), he left the army and came to Wyoming.[13] While at the Powder River ranch, he was thrown from a horse and injured. For a time Moreton was concerned that he would not survive.[14] Although eloquent enough to impress people in Cheyenne with his response to the Queen's toast, his fondness for gambling continued to undermine his finances.

Dick complained that the new man had not put any capital in the bat caves venture, while borrowed money was costing the venture 18 percent at Stebbins & Post. "He seems to be waiting to see if the thing turns out well before he puts a sixpence into it," Dick said. "If it turns out well he would be quite willing to take a third share of the profits." By the end of 1881, the brothers were having words over him. Dick told Moreton to get Shearburn to "retire" from the partnership, Moreton did so, and then Dick countermanded the deal, producing a typical Frewen confusion!

Shearburn's financial troubles soon involved the Frewens. To tide him over until he could obtain funds from England, Dick had given him a letter of introduction to Stebbins & Post, authorizing him to draw $500. When the captain went off to Texas to work on the guano

project, he wired Stebbins & Post for more money, and after the bank
consulted with the Frewens, more advances were made. Finally, the
Frewens decided to call a halt to the situation. Moreton knew that
Shearburn's share of the bat caves venture would not cover his debts
(leaving aside gambling debts). When confronted with the situation,
the young man "cried like a child," said Moreton. "I will start him
home to England . . . I think money to pay his debts will be forthcoming."[15] For a time, this prediction seemed sound, as Shearburn
had presented a draft on his mother for £500 ($2,400), which was duly
paid in London. But, then, a second draft was refused. When Moreton
asked Shearburn's mother to help cover her son's debts, she demurred,
saying she could go no further in helping him.

Meanwhile, Dick had taken a page from his brother's travelling
book and had gone to Egypt to treat his lungs. Soon, letters were coming from exotic places, such as Luxor and the first Cataract on the
Nile, advising Moreton that the partners had no liability to Shearburn, and that Moreton had acted quite rightly by sending the young
man home without pressing him in the courts. But if the Frewens
had decided not to pursue Shearburn in the courts, Stebbins & Post
did not feel the same reluctance; they had him arrested in Texas.

Here, the story got a bit murky. An early newspaper account
said that Shearburn was wanted for $9,000, but the amount quickly
came down to $5,000 in a subsequent story. Brought back from Texas
to stand trial, Shearburn told his story in court and showed letters
from his mother. The judge also heard testimony from the cashier
of Stebbins & Post, a man named John W. Collins.

The principal in Stebbins & Post was Morton E. Post, who played
a major role in many Frewen activities. Born in New York City in
1840, he was a decade older than Moreton, but they had become good
friends. Post came to Wyoming at the very beginning of the settlement of Cheyenne and was a merchant for a time. Then he went into
the banking business in partnership with William R. Stebbins; the
bank eventually became quite large and rivaled some of the incorporated banks in the city. For a time, Post was also the largest sheep
rancher in the territory, and he also had banks, in various partnerships, elsewhere in Wyoming and in Colorado. He was twice elected
as delegate from Wyoming on the Democratic ticket, serving from
1881 to 1885. Obviously, he did not personally run all of his varied

businesses, and the bank was placed in the hands of John W. Collins, who also lived a multi-faceted life.

Collins may not have been as colorful as Shearburn (of this we cannot be entirely certain), but he was an interesting character in his own right. Morton Post had recruited Collins to be cashier (which was really the chief operating position in the bank), and the choice appeared to be a good one. Collins was well liked in Cheyenne, but soon he was passing the word that he might leave to go into banking on his own. Later, he did just that, becoming president of the Cheyenne National Bank and also a bank in San Diego. Collins hired George L. Beard, a young bookkeeper he had brought into the Post bank, to serve as cashier of the Cheyenne National. Outside the banking business, Collins was in partnership with David Dare in a drugstore and in other enterprises (Dare owned a house in Cheyenne known as "Castle Dare"). Ultimately, Collins's banks collapsed, but before they did, he had induced young Beard to sign some of his notes; when the bank failed, the desperate young man (who was said to own the finest wardrobe in town) shot himself in his room in the Cheyenne Club. Collins also took his own life.

This somewhat extended detour is relevant to our story, because in the Shearburn trial Mr. Collins developed unexpected trouble explaining the Shearburn transaction to the judge. Finally, a recess was declared, and Collins was given time to go check the records at the bank. On returning, he admitted that the bank had given Shearburn only $1,000, and this had been paid by the Frewens! The judge thereupon acquitted Shearburn.[16]

Eventually, the Frewens recovered £1,400 ($6,800) from Shearburn (or his family) in London.[17] But Shearburn did not mend his ways. Two years later, Moreton learned that the young man was in jail in Columbus, Ohio, under an assumed name, "for the same sort of fraud as that on Stebbins & Post." Still later, when Moreton was in Bombay on the business of the Nizam of Hyderabad, he spotted Shearburn in a crowd; Shearburn immediately turned away.[18]

As for the bat caves themselves, an inspection trip lifted Moreton's spirits; he thought the quantity of guano "immense," although not as immense as he had hoped. "A rough measurement will hardly allow that there is more than 4,000 tons in sight." Yet, as always with him, "the best remains!" From another cave, which he had not inspected, he had seen bats swarm "in millions . . . we think untold wealth lies in there." Ten tons would be sent off to London to test the market; "the prospect is certain for a nice round sum £12–15,000 [$58–73,000] and very probably the main cave may discover a vast field."[19] The analysis did show 10 to 12 percent ammonia, and in May he could report that there were orders for two cargoes, which he expected would yield a profit of £5,000 ($24,000).

Nevertheless, the profits proved elusive. The samples Moreton had sent back had not been representative of the deeper deposits, which had less ammonia and more moisture, and Dick became restive. He warned Moreton that, in general, his business methods would ruin everyone in the boat with him, and, in particular, with the "wretched bat caves" there had been a lack of careful planning. He thought that £6 or £7 per ton was the highest price that could be expected. Although he didn't understand Moreton's figures, it didn't seem to matter, as Moreton continued to spend Dick's money anyway![20] In reply Moreton suggested that perhaps Ted could be induced to buy Dick's share, but Dick did not want to expose his other brothers to this sort of risk. Finally, in the summer of 1883, Moreton had to report that while they might make "some" profit, it would be "perhaps not much."[21] Exit bat caves.

In what should have been his major business, riches were not coming as quickly as Moreton had expected. Already, in the fall of 1880, he was predicting that the next year would be their "poor" year, although 1882 would be good, and there would be further increases in the future.

Because the range was so exceptionally good, he expected that the three-year-olds would be fat in January, February, and March. He had his eye on the Denver market, which he placed at 40,000 people, with another 35,000 at Leadville; these places would be paying "almost famine rates" for beef at the end of the winter, permitting him to sell a thousand head at £8 ($39), or possibly $45, per head. Dreaming on, he noted that the debts of the partnership only amounted to £1,100 ($5,300) a year, which would leave £6,000 ($29,000) clear profit.

While Moreton thus dreamed, the entire range cattle industry was already suffering from compression of its range. The inexorable pressure from settlers was continuing to shrink the range available to the cattle industry, and the vacuum into which these herds wanted to move was the Powder River country. This region had the combination of grass, water, and shelter that made it ideal for cattle grazing. The best of it was in the sector from Powder River to Goose Creek — precisely the area chosen by the Frewen brothers. Stearns & Patterson chose a range northwest of the Frewens, while Barton & Dillon and Nichols, Beach & Co. came to the Powder River, the latter two outfits expecting to bring ten thousand head apiece.[22] More were on the way.

Moreover, the weather did not cooperate with Moreton's dreams. The winter of 1880–81 was a hard one. In January 1881, Alec Swan said that there was considerable suffering among animals on the Laramie Plains because of heavy snow, and in late March one of the men from the Searight outfit said that trail cattle were dying in large numbers near Fort Casper.[23] By comparison, some cattle in the Big Horn Basin and in the Powder River country were doing exceptionally well, in spite of the severity of the weather.[24] Soon it became apparent that the trail cattle that had been driven in from Texas the previous year were bearing the brunt of the losses; the native cattle found it easier to cope.[25] This disparity may have accounted in part for the fact that some would report only ordinary losses, while others talked of losses of 25 to 50 percent (later, some operators admitted that they deliberately downplayed the losses of that winter "for business reasons").[26]

Moreton admitted that the winter was "fearful," although he was telling Clara they had lost only twenty head from a herd of ten thousand (which had to be patent nonsense). Yet, others had been hurt much worse than they.[27] While he expressed these sanguine opinions to Clara, Moreton had only a month earlier written to the *Leader*, painting a lurid picture of the losses on the range. He said the cattle were lying dead, not in ones or twos, but in "dozens" in every thicket on the river; no doubt the worst was to come, when the cows began having their calves. It was his opinion that not one cow in three was in shape for maternity. To the north, on the Tongue River, he said entire herds had disappeared, and a herd of Texas cattle on the Piney had lost a quarter of its number.[28]

We must suppose that this dire account was another of his "scare" tactics, to discourage new outfits in the Powder River country. We get a clue of this objective near the end of the letter, where he notes that the losses were the result of the "willful overstocking" that had occurred the previous fall. In any case, his report did not go unchallenged. The following month, the *Sun* printed a rejoinder signed "One Who Knows," charging that Frewen had misrepresented conditions. This correspondent said that at no time had there been more than two or three days when the snow was too deep for the cattle to graze, and that the losses would not exceed 3 to 5 percent. The opinion was ventured that Frewen was just trying to keep stockmen out of the region.[29]

Still, there had been considerable losses. Moreover, the survivors were thin and largely unsaleable, and they did not recover during the summer. Throughout the fall shipping season, the buyers in Chicago complained that the beef were not fat enough.[30] The Frewens could contemplate selling only £3,000 worth ($14,000), compared with the £10,000 ($48,000) Moreton had hoped to gross. "A nuisance," he complained, "I wanted . . . to feel happy and vulgarly rich."[31]

It was more than a nusiance. They were "considerably" overdrawn at the bank, and Ted owed the same bank another £6,000 ($29,000). To add to his woe, Moreton had borrowed £5,000 ($24,000) from Stephen on the security of the Galway properties (they were worth only £400 [$1,400] a year). In March, Moreton explained to Clara that he dared not go to England that winter, because his debts there would have to be paid if he returned, and he did not have enough money to cover them.[32]

Friction between the Frewen brothers had become a problem, and Moreton was searching in earnest for someone to buy out Dick. He seriously contemplated selling off the store down at Powder River crossing and some other things so that he could run the ranch alone. Even without the need for raising money to pay Dick, things were difficult: "Our position is really embarrassing," he said, "we have to pay £600 [$2,900] next month and our spring expenses will be heavy, whereas there will be nothing forthcoming until August at the earliest." To make matters worse, he had to pay £150 ($700) on account of Shearburn's obligations, which Moreton still hoped to recover from the young man's family.[33]

Somehow, they managed to survive the fall and winter of 1881, and Moreton got Dick to set his price for selling out. He estimated that the liquidation of the partnership would leave each of them £6,000 ($29,000) clear on top of their investments.[34] By December 1881, he was contemplating borrowing the money. He ascertained that Post in Cheyenne wanted 12 percent, and he hoped to better that in England.

If he could not go home to England that winter, there were things to be done in Wyoming. There were the wedding preparations, which required a great amount of writing and cabling, and the organization of Johnson County was at last to be completed. Elections were planned, and Moreton postponed his departure for the East until they were over, remarking in his characteristic way, "I am conceited enough to think I, and I alone, am able to carry this election in the direction our interests require."

Renamed Johnson, after Laramie County Attorney Edward P. Johnson (who died in the fall of 1879), the county was finally calling enough attention to itself to get official action. There was even a boom in Buffalo, and a case of "lot-jumping" was reported: the cook at the Occidental Hotel jumped the claim of a Scotsman and successfully defended it with force of arms. (The following month, the cook was reported shot at Crazy Woman, but one must use care in associating the two events in this fast-moving arena.)[35] The population seemed abundant: the census showed 637, but opinions ranged up to 800 — easily qualifying the county for organization.

Accordingly, Territorial Secretary Elliott S. N. Morgan, acting for Governor John W. Hoyt, appointed two cattlemen and one farmer as commissioners to call an election. One of the cattlemen appointed was Thomas Willing Peters, whom Moreton called "Willy," but whom many others referred to as "Twice Wintered," to signify the fact that he had spent a couple of winters in the country — which few of the English and Scottish owners did. Peters was now in partnership with W. C. Alston in a cattle ranch on the Powder River. Although Willy Peters was an early friend of Moreton, the relationship later soured in much the same way as did that with Horace Plunkett.[36]

These appointed commissioners met in the old Occidental Hotel in Buffalo (the building was then only a year "old") and set an election for April 19, 1881.[37] Two slates were run in the election, but there was serious contest only for the post of sheriff; all of the other county officers were selected from the so-called "Peoples" ticket. The three county commissioners who were elected were William E. Hathaway, Henry N. Devoe, and W. E. Jackson (Willy Peters had run on the opposition ticket but was not elected).[38] Hathaway was manager of Frewen's "store" at Powder River crossing, and Devoe would soon become foreman for Peters and Alston; he was named chairman of the board of county commissioners.[39] In the style of a proper Victorian English gentleman, Frewen had put his trusted retainer in office.

The county commissioners met June 27, 1881 and authorized the purchase of the Lone Star Dance Hall from one Ed O'Malley, including the stables and all improvements and grounds, to be used as a courthouse, paying $3,150 therefor. The following month the commissioners authorized the construction of four jail cells.[40]

By 1882, Buffalo was a town of twenty-five houses and one hundred or so souls; it was a somewhat wild place, where one woman claimed that the "houses of dissipation" were in the majority.[41] There was work for the law, and the following year, the district court held its first term in the new county. There were twenty-one indictments, which yielded four acquittals and five convictions. The remainder of the defendants had disappeared, and a newspaper reporter commented that it was little surprise, for the jail was no more substantial than a pasteboard box. While the folks in town were thus about the business of establishing the appearances of law and order inside Buffalo, the Indians were still encamped in the Powder River basin, and one source thought there were fifteen hundred near Buffalo itself. Nevertheless, the two cultures were not entirely separated; three "attractive" squaws had entertained a prominent attorney who was up from Cheyenne for the court term.

To the south, Cheyenne was growing up, too: the telephone had come to town and was available to subscribers. Soon there were telephone numbers going all the way up to 100, although there were gaps in between. Stebbins, Post & Co. had No. 1, and the Cheyenne Club, ever on the leading edge of technology, was No. 76; by mid-April the "directory" had 73 numbers, although some could ring both at a residence and at a business.[42] There was also a stir for a time over Oscar Wilde's tour of the West. He stopped over at the Railroad House, and he might have lectured in the city, but for an unkind article in the *Sun,* which suggested that his underwear was the same color as his tie, socks, and the lining of his hat (they were all a mixture of "burnt siena and pink").[43]

The eighth annual meeting of the Wyoming Stock Growers Association was held in April, and in recognition of the growth of their interests, the Wyoming group invited stockmen from Nebraska and Colorado counties to join. The offer was accepted by the stockmen of Sioux and Lincoln counties in Nebraska.[44] The roundups were also greatly expanded. Now the area north of the Platte had so many herds that Roundup No. 5 was split into two divisions to cover the southern part of the region, and No. 6 was sent into the northeastern part of the territory, along the Belle Fourche River.[45]

While the roundup was in progress on the range, Moreton was in New York for his wedding. The successful conquest of the English Derby by Iroquois was reported in the Cheyenne papers on June 2 (under the headline "The Darby," in reference to the English pronunciation of the word), but the event at Grace Church was not reported until the seventh, after receipt of a telegram from New York (we don't know from whom). After the ceremony, Moreton brought his new bride back to the Powder River.

After so much preparation, the long-expected visit from Clara was thus to take place that first summer of their marriage; it proved to be the only journey of the sort they ever had. Coming west by train, they left the railroad at Rock Creek and completed the balance of the journey by coach. At the store at Powder River crossing they were on the Frewen range, and Richard had sent an open buggy to bring them the remaining twenty miles or so home. Plunkett met them on June 27 and found them so tired from the journey that they could hardly keep awake.

Soon guests began to arrive in numbers, and Clara had no time to be bored with the primitive land. In August, Lord Granville Gordon came with Captain and Mrs. Gaskell, Horace Flower, and Moreton's younger sister Anna Louisa (Louise). The next month Gilly Leigh "and party" came back, followed a few days later by Lords Donoughmore, Fitzpatrick, and Montagu; James B. B. Roche arrived early in October.[46] Soon Clara could tell Moreton that she was pregnant, and the guests were told, too, receiving the news with great high spirits. On a trip to the mountains, Clara became ill and had to be carried across the rough road she had so recently traversed, back to Cheyenne, where she suffered a miscarriage. The Gordon party went home, but Louise stayed with Clara. Moreton sadly took them east to New York. Clara would never again venture to "Castle Frewen," which her husband had built for her on the Powder River.

While Clara was journeying back to New York, it was the shipping season in the West. The Cheyenne papers daily carried lists of the number of cattle cars ordered by the big outfits to transport their beef animals to the Chicago market. The Frewens did not figure in these listings until late September, when they ordered thirty-five cars from Pine Bluffs. Early in October, they realized 3.75 cents a pound on eight carloads, and 3.625 cents on twelve more.[47] This was neither the best nor the worst that was being realized that fall for Wyoming beef, and it was not enough to make one "vulgarly rich."

Still the weather continued to harass them. In November, the Frewens lost 50 head of cattle while attempting to drive a herd of 650 to the stockyards to be shipped. The snow was so deep that twenty horses had to be sent ahead of the cattle to break a trail for them.[48]

In the meantime, Moreton was working on a new deal, this time with Pierre Lorillard IV, whose Derby win had so enlivened the eve of Moreton's wedding. Lorillard, some twenty years older than Frewen, had established the stud farm "Rancocas," which produced his Derby winner, but he had also done many other things. After the death of his father, he bought out the interests of his brothers in the tobacco business and earned a large income from this source, which permitted him to embark on other enterprises. One of the most famous of these was the development of the seven thousand-acre Tuxedo Park, featuring a five thousand-acre game preserve surrounded by an eight-foot fence. Another Lorillard later introduced there the tailless "tuxedo."[49] Only five years after winning the Derby, Lorillard sold his racing horses and retired from the turf, because of unsavory practices he had encountered. At the time, it was said that he lived plainly: "no fifteen-dollar-a-week dry goods clerk in New York City dines more frugally." The *New York Times* can be forgiven this bit of hyperbole.[50]

Lorillard had an eye for the ladies and is supposed to have been in love with Clara (Moreton may have thought so, too; he warned Clara about being seen with Pierre when he was not in town). Pierre's friend of many years was Lilly A. Barnes, who received his stud farm after his death. She was known as Mrs. Allen, and the persistent story was that Lorillard had arranged for another woman to dress as a man and go through a mock wedding with Miss Barnes.

In the spring of 1882, Moreton entered into an agreement with Lorillard for the sale of 6,000 calves (2,000 males and 4,000 females). Frewen agreed to deliver half of these in the spring and summer of 1882, and the remainder in the spring and summer of 1883. The price for the calves was to be set by two appraisers who were residents of Wyoming, one to be appointed by each party to the agreement. Frewen was to run these cattle on his range for five years, for a fee of $1.50 per head per year.

As a part of the general agreement with Lorillard, Moreton also turned over the operation of the big house on the Powder River to Colonel Stuart Taylor, Lorillard's representative in Wyoming. While Moreton was initially pleased to be relieved of the expense of the house, he also remarked that the Taylors were ill-suited to life on the range. "I suppose two people so utterly hopelessly unsuited to this life as the Taylors could not be found *even* in America."[51] The Taylors' relationship with Frewen would soon take a turn for the worse.

Lorillard appointed Thomas Sturgis as his appraiser, and Moreton anxiously waited to learn how much he would get for the calves he was to sell to Lorillard. He expected to get at least $14.50 a head for them, and if they brought as much as $15, he would be able to lay his hands on $90,000, which would greatly facilitate the business of buying out Dick's share of the ranch.[52]

Then disaster struck in the form of a letter from Dick. "A blackguard, disgusting affair from Dick," fumed Moreton. "He will only go on condition he has the entire money *down* immediately." This demand may have been induced in part by Moreton's own ready pen, for Dick complained bitterly about letters Moreton had been writing to Ted.[53] The unexpected new requirement for cash would mean that Moreton would have to borrow the money; with luck, his stringency would not last long, though, for the expected payment from Lorillard would ease the situation. He therefore determined to go at once to Cheyenne to see if Stebbins & Post would lend him the money, failing which he would try in New York.[54] "I have no doubt I can get it inside of 30 days," he said. "Lorillard's first payment on May 31 will leave only a balance of $60,000 owing to Dick. The second payment of say $40,000 due on October 1 I can get discounted in New York at six per cent, and the balance I can afford to borrow at 12 per cent from Stebbins & Post." So the plan was framed.[55]

For a few days the outlook seemed to improve. Poor Dick had a "lung attack" at Cheyenne, and the doctor told him the climate didn't suit him. Also, Dick brought back from there the rumor that Moreton was to get $15.00 for the calves. "A splendid price," he exulted to Clara.[56]

But it was not to be. "The last straw!" cried Moreton on May 21. "I have just seen Davis, who tells me they decided $12.50 for heifers

and $13.50 for steers. The price is a simple scandal; but Davis says
Sturgis will not allow a cent more. If Lorillard compels me to sell
on such figures, it's simply ruin." Morosely he mused that he had only
agreed to the deal with Dick on the expectation of $15.00. "Now, unless
I can borrow the money east . . . and unless also Lorillard will tear
up the agreement, I see nothing clear."[57]

The fact that Moreton could see nothing clear did not mean he
was despondent; it merely meant that he had to change direction again.
This time the new direction involved raising money for a new company, which Moreton would manage. This time he did succeed.

The agreement dissolving the partnership was dated May 17, 1882,
and obligated Moreton to pay Richard $40,000 by the end of May
and a further $47,616.24 by the middle of June. In the same agree-
ment Moreton agreed to pay Stephen Frewen $24,000 (which was
£5,000 sterling at the then current rate) by the middle of June, together
with interest of $1,200, calculated at 10 percent per annum. In addi-
tion, Moreton had to secure the release of Richard's guarantee on
the obligations at Stebbins & Post and I. G. King & Sons in New
York ($18,767.21 and $2,835.94, respectively). The agreement was drawn
and witnessed by Frank A. Kemp, who would play a prominent role
in Frewen's future affairs.

One would have supposed that the dissolution, having been
agreed upon, would surely now be peaceful, but such was not to be.
On June 6, Colonel Taylor wired Moreton at Leonard Jerome's
address in New York City. "Your brother is here annoying me very
much. He says he will assume charge here until all the money comes.
You have put me in very unpleasant position. Everything going wrong
you must take instant action to avoid trouble. Answer at once. Mackintosh will go as soon as your reply is received to his telegram and
explain. Taylor." A second wire went to Lorillard, reporting that Dick
was threatening to stop branding calves unless all his money was paid
by the fifteenth. Apparently assuming that Moreton himself would
now be forced to sell out, Taylor helpfully told Lorillard that if he
could buy the entire herd, he would have a "splendid bargain." Taylor
followed these wires with a long letter, in which he quoted Horace
Plunkett, who said that Taylor was "in the most annoying and irritat-
ing position he ever knew any one to be put in."

While these communications were speeding eastward, Richard
took up pen to defend himself against Colonel Taylor. He offered to

submit his dispute with Moreton to the arbitration clause in their agreement. Nevertheless, he also sent Taylor a check for $7,000, which would indicate that there was a claim in that direction as well.

Despite all these rumblings and cablings, the payment due Richard on June 16 was duly made, and the partnership was dissolved.[58] The last communication in this messy affair was from Colonel Taylor to Moreton on June 19. In it he said, "Your brother knows and feels he has made a very bad bargain." Indeed it was, but it would prove a better deal in the end than Moreton would realize for his investment in the firm.

The day after the dissolution agreement was executed, Richard wrote to Moreton, this time from the ranch, saying, "I nearly if not quite forgive you for the wrong you have done me." Still he had to hash over the past. "I think you must in your inner conscience know that when you accused me of drinking raw spirits, or in fact drinking at all except in moderation, that you know you were accusing me of what you know is not the case. Again, if you think of it what you have said & wrote about my neglecting work & never all last year seeing a calf branded was again untrue. Two of the heaviest days of branding last year I was at Crazy Woman. Now, to another point, as we are parting company, you have always taken me the wrong way." And so on, the frustrations of the past year were poured out. Before he closed this polemic, Richard had talked himself around to the position of offering to stay on if Moreton would let him be the manager. Then he ended by saying he wished they had never gone into business together.[59]

Richard made an interesting observation on Moreton's flair for new schemes. "You can make more money by floating such things as the bat caves or the packing house than you will ever make by running them yourself." He was at least half right—Moreton was not good at running businesses.

The partnership between the two brothers suffered from many handicaps. There were, of course, the volatile personalities that burdened them both and made it difficult to produce consistent results. Also, there were the other "partners," such as young Shearburn, who contributed little and drained the business of both time and money. And finally, there was Moreton's peripatetic lifestyle. Beginning in the spring of 1880, he was on the ranch until early May, when he started his trip to Idaho to examine the coal prospect; by the end of

June he was back in Cheyenne, whence he made a flying trip to Denver to talk about the Leadville situation. He was back at the ranch before the middle of July, having been gone more than two months. There were a number of side trips, but he was in the general vicinity of the ranch until the end of November, when he went east to New York.

The following year saw him at the ranch early, by the first of February, but this was the wedding year, and he had to be back in New York for that event in early June. After a sojourn on the ranch with his new bride, during which time there were guests as well as the distraction of Clara's sickness, he was off again to Omaha by the end of October, back then to Cheyenne, where the packing house at Sherman was intriguing him, finally returning to New York at the end of the year.

The New Year found Moreton on his way to Texas to examine the bat caves, and he returned to New York by the end of January, sailing on a steamer. Then there was a short trip to Pierre Lorillard's horse farm, Rancocas, in Jobstown, New Jersey. By the end of April he was on his way west, going by stages to Chicago and Cheyenne and arriving at the ranch the first week in May. It was back to Cheyenne by the end of May and then to New York again. Starting west again at the beginning of September, he was on the Powder River after the middle of the month but was back in Cheyenne by the first of October. He returned east by the end of the month.

One can only draw the obvious conclusion from all this travelling. There was too little supervision of ranching operations, and far too many other projects being pursued at the same time. Although Moreton was a prolific correspondent, he could not possibly have known what was going on during his long absences. When he had a much larger operation to supervise, he did no better, with predictable results.

Notes to Chapter 4

1. Frewen to Clara Jerome, May 23, 1880, Frewen Papers.
2. Frewen to Clara Jerome, July 3, 1880, Frewen Papers.
3. Frewen to Clara Jerome, May 1, 1880, Frewen Papers.
4. Frewen to Clara Jerome, May 29, 1880, Frewen Papers.
5. Frewen to Clara Jerome, June 3, 1880, Frewen Papers.
6. Frewen to Clara Jerome, July 25, 1880, Frewen Papers.

7. *Cheyenne Daily Leader,* September 8, 1880.
8. *Cheyenne Daily Leader,* October 30, 1881.
9. *Cheyenne Daily Sun,* November 6, 1881.
10. Plunkett diary, September 8, 9, 21, and October 23, 1881.
11. Frewen to Clara Jerome, May 2, 1881, Frewen Papers.
12. Plunkett diary, June 8, 1881.
13. *Cheyenne Daily Sun,* April 6, 1882.
14. Frewen to Clara Jerome, April 20, 1881, Frewen Papers.
15. Frewen to Clara Frewen, January 19, 20, 1882, Frewen Papers.
16. *Cheyenne Daily Sun,* April 13, 1882.
17. Account with James, Son & James, February 15, 1882 to April 4, 1882.
18. Frewen to Clara Frewen, May 18, 1884, Frewen Papers.
19. Frewen to Clara Frewen, January 22, 1882, Frewen Papers.
20. Richard Frewen to Frewen, March 20, Frewen Papers.
21. Frewen to Clara Frewen, July 3, 1883, Frewen Papers.
22. *Cheyenne Daily Sun,* May 6, 1880.
23. *Cheyenne Daily Leader,* March 20, 1881.
24. *Cheyenne Daily Sun,* January 28, 1881.
25. *Cheyenne Daily Sun,* February 10, 1881.
26. *Cheyenne Daily Sun,* June 9, 1882.
27. Frewen to Clara Jerome, March 13, 1881, Frewen Papers.
28. *Cheyenne Daily Leader,* March 2, 1881.
29. *Cheyenne Daily Sun,* April 1, 1881.
30. *Cheyenne Daily Sun,* August 7, 1881.
31. Frewen to Clara Jerome, February 2, 1881, Frewen Papers.
32. Frewen to Clara Jerome, March 26, 1881, Frewen Papers.
33. Frewen to Clara Jerome, April 2, 1881, Frewen Papers.
34. Frewen to Clara Frewen, November 5, 1881, Frewen Papers.
35. *Cheyenne Daily Leader,* March 22, April 14, 1881.
36. Lott, "Diary of Major Wise," 114.
37. *Cheyenne Daily Sun,* March 13, 1881.
38. *Cheyenne Daily Sun,* April 12, 1881.
39. Conditt, "The Hole in the Wall," 43. Devoe became Peters's foreman in November. *Cheyenne Daily Sun,* November 4, 1881.
40. *A Survey of Wyoming County Courthouses* (1972), 53.
41. *Cheyenne Daily Sun,* July 23, 1882, and *Cheyenne Daily Leader,* March 25, 1882.
42. *Cheyenne Daily Sun,* March 26, April 11, 1882.
43. *Cheyenne Daily Leader,* March 25, 1882, *and Cheyenne Daily Sun,* March 23, April 8, 1882.
44. *Cheyenne Daily Sun,* May 3, 1881.
45. *Cheyenne Daily Sun,* April 6, 1881.
46. *Cheyenne Daily Leader,* August 28, September 3, 14, and October 1, 1881.
47. *Cheyenne Daily Leader,* October 5, 1881.
48. *Cheyenne Daily Leader,* November 12, 1881.
49. Dumas Malone, ed., *Dictionary of American Biography,* vol. 11 (New York, 1933), 411-412; and *Lorillard and Tobacco* (New York, 1977), 50.
50. *New York Times,* February 1, 1886.
51. Frewen to Clara Frewen, May 8, 1882, Frewen Papers.
52. Ibid.
53. Richard Frewen to Frewen, April 16, 1882, Frewen Papers.

54. Frewen to Clara Frewen, May 8, 1882, Frewen Papers.
55. Frewen to Clara Frewen, May 13, 1882, Frewen Papers.
56. Frewen to Clara Frewen, May 15, 1882, Frewen Papers.
57. Frewen to Clara Frewen, May 21, 1882, Frewen Papers.
58. Receipt from James G. Kings Sons, New York, June 16, 1882.
59. Richard Frewen to Frewen, May 18, 1882, Frewen Papers.

· 5 ·

The Powder River
Cattle Company, Limited

William Drogo Montagu, Seventh Duke of Manchester, Earl of Manchester, Viscount Mandeville, and Baron Montagu of Kimbolton, was to be the first chairman of the Powder River Cattle Company, Limited, when it came into existence on August 5, 1882. "He is just the chairman I should have chosen," Moreton exulted in his diary. "His is the very name to please the canny North country men I am about to visit; for also he is a DUKE, and they all love Dukes here or elsewhere!"

Unencumbered by an uncooperative brother, Moreton was about to enter into his greatest promotion, this time to secure capital for an even larger cattle operation. In a letter to Vivian, Gray & Co., in London, he touted the virtues of the range cattle business (although he said he did not mean to write a prospectus that "no one will take the trouble to read").

First, he dealt with the remarkable climate on the Powder River. Using as his standard the severe winter of 1880–81 (which, he said, had never been equalled), when "even the buffalo in Montana died," Frewen noted that he had been at the ranch from January until the end of spring and suffered losses of less than 1 percent from all causes. His herd was by then ten thousand head (including Ted's operation), and he confidently predicted that the range would accommodate ten times that number. In a curious perversion of geography, he placed the ranch 150 miles south of Yellowstone National Park, as an added attraction for the investor bent on enjoying the sights while visiting the ranch. Cattle disease was "quite unknown," according to Moreton, presumably because of the "dry bracing atmosphere."

Moreton gave a sort of scorecard for the partnership he had just liquidated. He claimed that the 10,000 head of cattle on the range had been the result of an original investment of $114,000 in July 1879. He said that the partners had taken out a total of $125,000, and that the present value of the herd was $192,000. Stated that way, it was a pleasant enough report card. Actually, Moreton's presentation was more than a bit exaggerated. It is true that there were just over 10,000 animals on the ranch books in the fall of 1882, when they were purchased by the Powder River Cattle Company, but Moreton owned only 6,797 of them; the remainder were the property of Edward Frewen, under the "97" brand.[1]

After a long paragraph about the Sherman refrigeration scheme, Frewen got down to his basic offer. He would take shares for his herd and agree to pay the common shareholders 10 percent per annum, taking one third of the remaining profit for himself. If that weren't enough, he predicted that there would be a "fair" dividend come October. Who could resist such a pitch?

Moreton went to England on the *Servia* in late June 1882 to promote his new company. He was optimistic, perhaps a bit more than usual; he felt his tide was "at the flood" and saw the good crossing weather as an omen of things to come. While idle on shipboard he turned his mind to solving the perennial problem of Conservative politicians in England when running for election: money. To Moreton, the solution seemed obvious. He would organize a fund, which, of course, would be invested in cattle and other "Western investments" under the care of competent commissioners, and the income would permit the party to contest every constituency in every general election.[2]

In London, where he had not been for two years, Moreton spent some time with family and old friends and then met Everett Gray, who had "a few hundred copies" of his letter about the cattle venture. Then on to Lord Wharncliffe, who, besides offering "lots of sound advice," promised to be a large shareholder, as did Alfred Sartoris, who had been on the ship when Moreton came back home. Alfred Urban Sartoris was interesting to Moreton because he was the uncle of Lady Clarendon, but his family was notable in other ways as well. A member of an Italian family originally from Savoy, his brother had married Adelaide Kemble, an opera singer and sister of the famous actress Fanny Kemble. From that union was born Algernon Charles

Frederick Sartoris, who married Ellen Wrenshall Grant, daughter of President Ulysses S. Grant, in a ceremony in the White House in 1874.[3]

Charles Waring gave Moreton advice about snagging some "millionaire Australians" for the board and also pledged himself to buy one thousand shares of common stock. "I will gladly take more, but will take no less," he told Moreton—or so Moreton said.[4] Then a happy chance meeting in the street with Lord Abergavenny (of the famous Nevill family) produced the great good news that his lordship had mentioned the matter to the Duke of Manchester. According to Frewen's report of the conversation, the duke had just returned from the great northwest and was inclined to view with favor all things western.

"Early though the hour," Moreton drove straightaway to see Lady Mandeville, the duke's daughter-in-law, to ask for a letter to His Grace. Lady Mandeville had been a schoolmate of Clara's sister Jennie and was another American who had married into the British nobility. Born Consuela Iznaga, her father was Cuban, her mother American. She married Lord Mandeville in 1876, and when his father died in 1890 he became the eighth duke of Manchester, and she became a duchess.[5] On the occasion of Moreton's unexpected visit to her house, the good lady, "having been dancing through the small hours at Marlborough House," was apparently roused from her slumbers. But he nevertheless secured the needed letter of introduction to the duke, dashed round to the duke's lodgings, and left it with a note asking whether "as time pressed, I might call at three P.M. that day."

At the appointed hour, Moreton found another caller waiting on the duke, with the same errand in mind (for a ranch in Dakota). This did not materially interfere with Moreton's errand, and after a few questions the duke declared himself "quite satisfied." Moreton left with a light heart; the company had a chairman.[6]

The next week he had had enough acceptances for the fledgling board to call a meeting of those members who had agreed to serve. There were the Duke of Manchester, Lord Henry Nevill, William Tipping, Everett Gray, and Charles W. Middleton Kemp. After a "harmonious" meeting, Moreton set out for Dundee to work on securing subscriptions. There he found the town veritably "plastered up with American dividends." Then on to Edinburgh and later to York, where banker William Beckett Denison of Leeds suggested that his son Ernest might be a useful member of the board. Ernest Beckett Denison served twenty years in Parliament, until he succeeded as Baron Grimthorpe; he was a friend of Lord Randolph Churchill and was one of his executors.[7] (In 1866, the Denison family secured a royal license to resume the name Beckett, which confuses references to them; there was apparently no consistency in their own usage of the two names.)

Back in London, Frewen dined with Lord Anson and Anson's brother-in-law Lord Belper, both of whom had subscribed as common shareholders. At another meeting of the board, on August 1, Denison was elected as a member of that august group (he was to subscribe £12,000 to the company). Telegrams from Dundee provided assurance that the region would take up most of the preferred shares.[8] The next day, Moreton thought he had convinced Lord Vernon to take a "big block" of common, but advice from a lawyer cooled his lordship's enthusiasm.

William Mackenzie, a Scottish stockbroker, came down from Dundee with full powers to negotiate for the Scottish preferred subscribers. Six years older than Frewen, Mackenzie was the son of a Scottish minister and had helped support his mother and younger brothers after his father's premature death. He had been one of the founding members of the Dundee Stock Exchange, and he would later be the chief power in the Alliance Trust, which controlled the Dundee Mortgage and Dundee Investment companies. His companies had experience with American investments, particularly in mortgages in Washington and Oregon, and he was also a shareholder, along with the Earl of Airlie and his associates, in the Prairie Cattle Company, which was organized in 1881.[9] A formidable person, he would loom large in Moreton's dealings with the shareholders of the Powder River company.

Mackenzie had several points to press, including the suggestion that the preferred stock be reduced to £75,000 and the common to £150,000. Moreton, seeing the need for growth, refused the reduction, but he suggested an *increase* of £50,000 in the common, to give more comfort to the preferred holders, and in this he was supported by Gray. "A rather bold move," declared Moreton, and an ultimatum to this effect was wired to the north, placing the £60,000 block offered there on a take-it-or-leave-it basis. After a tense period of waiting, the conciliatory reply came: "You are wrong to blame us for erring

on the side of caution, but have it your own way, we will take the
£60,000."

On August 5 the prospectus finally issued, after twenty proofs,
and the first actual subscriptions to come in were from Edward Frewen
and Moreton's friend Mr. Winn; to his amazement, Moreton found
that Lord Rosslyn had applied for 2,500 shares of common. Moreton
passed shares around the family; Ted had 2,000 shares and Clara 320
(according to an incomplete proxy list in 1888). Advertisements were
placed in "all the papers," and press comment was "all favorable."[10]

The next week Horace Plunkett's father, Lord Dunsany, took
a "flier" in the company, and by August 10 Moreton confided to his
diary that the subscription was already "overfilled." So confident was
he that he also recorded his prediction that the £5 shares would be
selling for £15 by Christmas of 1883.

The total subscriptions came to nearly half a million pounds!
Moreton reported that the preferred subscribers only received one
share for six subscribed, while the common subscribers received four
shares for each six subscribed, but this does not tally with the number
of shares finally issued; one must suppose that Moreton's arithmetic
was as faulty as his predictions. When the work of allocation had been
completed, there were issued 10,000 preferred shares of £10 and 40,000
£5 common shares, for a total capital of £300,000 ($1,452,000). William
Beckett Denison remarked ruefully that Moreton should feel flattered
and amused that the people of England would entrust £300,000 to
him, when they would not have spent a tenth of that amount on a
cattle enterprise in their own country![11]

Moreton had negotiated quite a deal, indeed. The basic agreement was contained in a contract between Moreton and Charles W.
Middleton Kemp, as trustee for the corporation to be organized. In
this contract, Moreton agreed to sell the two land filings he had made
(160 acres at the home ranch and 640 acres on Crazy Woman), together
with the improvements and cattle on the range for $257,111, of which
$206,741 was for the 6,797 head of cattle, and $10,000 was for the
refrigerator at Sherman. He was to be paid £12,000 in cash, and 8,000
common shares in the company (20 percent of the total to be issued).
He could not dispose of more than half of his shares during the first
five years. Moreton was to have the position of manager for the company in America until November 1, 1887. He was to receive, as a salary,
one-third of surplus profits, but only after a 10 percent dividend had

been paid on the entire capital of the company (the directors were to be the sole judges as to whether there were net profits for the purpose of this payment).

On November 1, 1887, the property of the company was to be appraised, and if its value exceeded £300,000 ($1,549,000), Moreton was to receive one-third of such excess. Disputes were to be settled by arbitration.

The articles of association of the company provided for two classes of stock, 10,000 preferred shares of £10 each, and 40,000 common (ordinary) shares of £5 each. The preferred shares were entitled to a 10 percent dividend, and that dividend was to be cumulative. The preferred shares were also to be redeemed on November 1, 1887 at £12 per share.

The board was to consist of not more than twelve members, and the first board consisted of only five: the Duke of Manchester, William Tipping, Lord Henry Nevill, Andrew Whitton, and Ernest Beckett Denison. One-third of the board was to be elected at each general meeting of the shareholders.

The duke, not yet fifty-nine, was descended from an old family; an elder branch had been created Dukes of Montagu by Queen Anne, and the dukedom of Manchester dated from its creation by George I in 1719. The family claimed descent from Drogo de Monte Acuto, who came over with William the Conqueror (although this connection was apparently fanciful), and each duke therefore took the name Drogo. The family seat was Kimbolton Castle, the seat of the Mandeville family, who had been ennobled as baron and viscount in 1620.[12] In the Victorian era, the Manchesters had the reputation as leaders of the "fast set," personified by the Prince of Wales. William, the seventh duke, was married to the German-born Countess Louise von Alten (she was for over thirty years deeply engrossed in a torrid affair with Lord Hartington, whom contemporaries referred to as "Harty-Tarty," but in public the duchess and Hartington always addressed each other formally, by their titles. When Manchester finally died in 1890, the lovers married, and since Hartington had by then succeeded as Duke of Devonshire, Louise became the famous "Double Duchess").[13] Manchester has been called a "well-intentioned bore," and Disraeli said he was "silly, but not dull," whatever that can mean.[14]

The Dundee director, Andrew Whitton, was the largest preferred shareholder and a close associate of William Mackenzie; they sat on a number of the same boards together. He managed the estates of the Earl of Wharncliffe, who would also give Moreton a good deal of trouble later.[15] "A typical Scot," he won Moreton's heart when he expounded his philosophy on Moreton's role in the company. "You are manager, sir," he was quoted by Moreton, "and we of the Board would do very ill to fetter you in any way. Go right ahead, buy at your discretion, thus you will do best for the shareholders." Whitton could not know how rashly he was speaking!

Henry Gilbert Ralph Nevill was the son of the Marquess of Abergavenny, a Conservative Party leader; one day he would succeed to the title himself (on the death of his older brother). They were members of the famous Nevill family, from whom the "kingmaker" earl of Westmorland was descended (the earldom of Westmorland was attained in 1571 as a result of the earl's participation in the northern rising of 1569), and were created earl and marquess of Abergavenny in 1874 and 1876, respectively. Henry Nevill's wife has been called London's most celebrated hostess. She was a great friend of Jennie and Randolph Churchill, although she once remarked on the subject of the many marriages of British peers with Americans, "I like Americans very well, but there are two things I wish they would keep to themselves—their girls and their tinned lobster."[16]

It is appropriate to pause and review the complex financial arrangements of the company. We cannot be certain that Moreton was solely responsible for the terms, but we must assume that the general outline was his handiwork. In this deal he was looking in only one direction—up! The company was capitalized with 10,000 shares of preferred stock, which could be bought out in five years, improving the position of the ordinary shareholders, of which Moreton was an important member. No matter that in the meantime the preferred stockholders were to be paid 10 percent on their investment before *anything* could be paid to the ordinary shareholders—there would be plenty to pay both! No matter that the preferred shareholders had preferences in liquidation—who could contemplate such an ugly possibility! (Ironically, Frewen's solicitor would later give his opinion that the buyout provision was illegal under English law, as it amounted to a reduction of capital without going through the formal chancery proceedings, but unfortunately, this view came too late to save him.)[17] Then, there was the matter of the manager's compensation. Frewen was to get nothing if a 10 percent dividend could not be paid. Who could suppose the company would earn so little? After all, he was to receive a full third of the excess — that was the bonanza on which his eyes were firmly fixed.

While the company's beginnings were very grand, it is appropriate to pause and note a small matter of confusion concerning it. The name by which the company was known, in London and elsewhere, was the Powder River Cattle Company, Limited. Since the corporation was organized under the British laws, it was necessary that it qualify to do business in the jurisdictions outside the United Kingdom where its operations were to be conducted. While there was no lack of activity in Wyoming, there is no indication that the company ever qualified to do business there. As a consequence, another company with an annoyingly similar name soon made its appearance. In March of 1882, a Colorado corporation was organized with the name Powder River Live Stock Company, to engage in cattle ranching in Colorado and Johnson County, Wyoming. The incorporators were James A. Brown, James L. Marston, and George R. Buckman, all of Colorado. Since the English company had not registered with the Secretary of the Territory, the Colorado company had no difficulty doing so, with the result that there were two Powder River companies operating in Johnson County for a number of years. There is no indication that this fact was in any way disturbing to Moreton. The Colorado company's charter expired in 1902.[18]

The paperwork out of the way (in England, if not in Wyoming), the board authorized the signing of checks for £32,000 ($155,000), and Moreton immediately sent £17,000 ($82,000) to Stebbins & Post. Three days later he was once more on the *Servia,* headed west to spend that money.

In New York, Moreton tarried only briefly and then went directly to Cheyenne (Clara went to Newport) and sent two men to the corn states to buy cattle. He bought 10,000 cattle, 10,000 sheep, and 200 horses that first week in Cheyenne. "They are all 'laying' for me here, to sell me herds on the range at their book values, and are surprised that I laugh at them," he said. He had offered Plunkett and Roche $175,000 for the EK ranch; when Plunkett countered with $260,000, Moreton called the counter "simply crazy."[19] While in Cheyenne, Moreton also inspected the refrigeration facility at Sherman and saw with satisfaction that mutton placed in it the previous December was still good.[20]

Another sort of deal suggested itself to his fertile mind. "I have perfected, all but, a nice new scheme," he said to Clara. "It occurred to me . . . that probably next year we should want to double our capital and in that case a second range would be necessary. Charley Oelrichs has got an excellent range, as good as ours and much less stocked. . . . Their firm has 8,500 cattle, Draper has 7,500 and Van Tassell has 7,800 on that range, and it will well carry 40,000 more. Here, then is a second base of operations. Charley has bought Harry out, I have bought Draper and expect to get Van Tassell in a day or two." The price was only $600,000, and Moreton expected to make Oelrichs a one-fifth partner of the company in the new venture (he had earlier told Clara he would offer Charley one-third, but his was a swiftly changing world). "The board will ratify the arrangement without doubt," he concluded confidently.[21]

While in Cheyenne, Moreton learned that Morton Post wanted to get $40,000 of common stock in the company at par, but Frewen was unable to get it for him. Still smarting from anger with the Sturgis brothers over the Lorillard appraisal affair, he gloated that Post "does not share that snob Frank Sturgis' view of my purchases. How I will snub them all after next year's dividend."[22]

By the middle of September, Moreton could report that he had "done splendidly" and had a total of 40,800 head for about £215,000 ($1,041,000).[23] But the frenetic purchasing soon drained the cash resources he had received, and when he asked for more, the answer was not favorable. The board would not confirm the Rawhide purchases (the Oelrichs and Draper herds), nor would they sanction any partnership; they ordered him to confine his investments to a maxi-mum of £120,000 ($581,000), including the sum needed to acquire his own herd.

Moreton immediately assumed that some dark force was abroad, seeking to do him harm. "Some cursed rumor like Frank Sturgis put about has probably got across the water," he said, although we are left without a clue as to the nature of the Sturgis rumor. In any case, Moreton had already given company notes for the money, and Harry Oelrichs had already spent some of it, so there was little choice about going through with the purchase. To get over the temporary crisis, he cabled London that the purchases must be completed, but that he would personally repurchase the Rawhide herds from them later in England and make them the nucleus of a new company. The

London business mentality was wearing heavily on him: "I had a million times rather be accountable to a board of Scotch business-men."[24] Alas, this preference would later change for him, as well.

All of his complaining had some effect, for soon Kemp cabled from London to say that $225,000 would be coming but that there would be no more until May. "I'll change their tune when I get home," Moreton fumed. "Meanwhile, by stretching my personal credit I shall manage all right." Two days later, he was still struggling against the strictures imposed by London. "Those wretched people at home, instead of helping . . . are worrying me all they can. I may perhaps have to go to Denver to arrange for help with the banks there, but I expect Post will carry me and when I get home I can twist that cursed Board at my will and pleasure," he said. "You see, Ted and I own more than one third of the whole common stock and I can easily enough among my own friends secure enough help to give us the control if it comes to a general shareholders vote."

The board in London next decided to do something that was again unsettling to Moreton: it sent out its own representative to evaluate his activities. One should not necessarily interpret this action as a vote against Moreton (at least at this stage), since the same sort of "inspec-tor" was sent out by the board of the Swan Land and Cattle Com-pany during the first year of its operation, and that board was cer-tainly not suspicious of Alec Swan at that time.[25] The man selected by the Powder River board for the job was John McCulloch, a Scottish farmer from Dumfriesshire (the county where Mackenzie was born). On Mackenzie's recommendation, McCulloch had been appointed as inspector of loans in America for the Dundee Mortgage Company, one of the Mackenzie group of companies, and had come to the United States in 1880.[26] While he had extensive experience in agricultural arbitrations and had served as director of the Scottish Chamber of Agriculture, his credentials in the range cattle industry seem to have been limited to a 600-mile stage journey he had taken with O. P. Johnston, who then owned a small herd on the Powder River, and a year's supervision of a small herd in Iowa.[27] It is clear the board was selecting a man who was known to them, even if he did not have long years of experience with the Wyoming range cattle industry.

McCulloch met Moreton in Chicago on October 3, and he reached the ranch on the eighth. There, McCulloch spent four days riding the range and inspecting the improvements as well as the live and dead stock. His time on the range was limited; he was concerned about the risk of being snowed in. He stayed in Cheyenne until the eighteenth, watching the beeves being shipped to Chicago.

Moreton did not go to the ranch with McCulloch, choosing instead to stay in Cheyenne, fretting nervously about the outcome of the inspection. "If he is half as much in love with the range as I am, his report will glow."[28] Frank Kemp was with McCulloch and brought him back to Cheyenne on the fifteenth; to Moreton's great relief, he found the "inquisitor" well satisfied.[29]

McCulloch's report was written in Denver on October 20, and it ran twenty-four handwritten pages. He began with a general review of the prospects for the range cattle industry and concluded that the free range was as good an investment as "a first and ironclad mortgage," something his readers would undoubtedly identify with. Beginning on the seventh page, McCulloch finally got down to the specific properties. He described the range of the Powder River Cattle Company rather more expansively than even Moreton would have been inclined to: from latitude 40° to 50° and from longitude 105° to 110°. But when he reduced this fanciful geography to dimensions measuring fifty by eighty miles (the longer distance running north-south) he was more nearly right. While the range was large (he thought two million acres), it was difficult to estimate its carrying capacity, although he hazarded the guess of twenty acres per animal; he felt that increasing the herd up to 50,000 would not entail more than ordinary risk.

On the subject of land titles, McCulloch noted that Frewen had taken out "first papers" on 160 acres where the home ranch was located. Although a desert land filing had been made on 640 acres on Crazy Woman, he did not think the patent would likely issue. The great bulk of the land was being used under possessory rights, and the same was true of water resources, "but as similar interests are so large it would be almost confiscation to disturb them and I have little fear on that score." He did foresee the need for Congress to lease the grazing land, which would involve additional costs for the cattlemen, but with "full equivalent" value in terms of security of tenure.

Taxes were not excessive: the herd was assessed on two-thirds the actual number and at $17 per head. Frewen had paid $2,245 the previous year on only 9,800 cattle, and McCulloch thought he had been "too honest for the surroundings." He noted with favor the annual assessment to the Wyoming Stock Growers Association to be used to hire inspectors.

The house was "necessary," although McCulloch thought a $220 piano "too great a luxury." However, it was there before the company purchased the property. He found the telephone a convenience but not a necessity if one were starting a new ranch.

With respect to the cattle count, McCulloch noted that the records he was shown included no provision for losses, and he recommended improvements in these tallies. He went through the listings of all the herds bought by the company, coming to a total of nearly 34,000, of which about 7,000 were on Tongue River, 8,600 on Rawhide, and the balance on Powder River. In addition there were 450 horses and 8,000 or 9,000 sheep.

Taking all this information into account, McCulloch proceeded to summarize the values of the properties that the company had purchased from Frewen. He thought the cattle worth about $180,000, the improvements on the ranch about $60,000, and the refrigeration operation about $9,000, for a total just under $250,000. While the total was not quite as high as Moreton had calculated ($247,265 versus $257,111 claimed in the agreement), McCulloch advised that the difference was too small to justify a protracted arbitration.

He estimated that the ranches were costing about $30,000 a year to run, and he noted that Moreton's expenses for 9,000 head of cattle were "very heavy," reaching about $14,000 per annum.

Looking at the overall situation, McCulloch expected that the 34,000 cattle would yield 5,000 marketable animals each year at a net price of about $37.50 per head. Deducting expenses of $38,000 and London office expenses of $17,500 would leave net profits of $132,000. From this the 10 percent preferred dividend could be paid. Since only $1,100,000 had been invested up to this point, the remaining $72,000 would represent a 12 percent dividend on the $600,000 of common stock. He felt that an additional 20,000 head would yield proportionately higher returns, leaving $89,000 to be distributed on the additional capital of $500,000, or an 18 percent dividend (15 percent on the average for all common stock). Of course, the herd would continue to increase, so that at the end of five years there would be a very large sum available. Moreton could hardly have selected anyone who would have been a better exponent of his views of the future.

Even before McCulloch's report was finished, there was more trouble from across the water. Everett Gray cabled Moreton in code that the board was dissatisfied, and their confidence "much shaken." Since there were some very large payments coming due on account of his purchases, this lack of confidence came at a very awkward time. He at once began planning to go to London to plead his case in person. A few days later, he was telling Clara he meant to have "an awful row with my own board, and they will see whether they or I have the whip hand."[30] But before he was ready to leave, word arrived that the board was backing down; Moreton was almost inclined to be gracious: "It is quite contrary to all our interest for me to quarrel with my board. . . . Not, however without giving them a piece of my mind."[31]

McCulloch's report was not well received in some quarters in England, and Plunkett later remarked that he collected his money for proving that the English were meat-eating people. Difficulties arose over his compensation, and he brought an action against the company for $3,000 for his services in connection with the inspection trip. Moreton consulted with John Clay in Chicago, who represented other Scottish investors in America, and Clay proffered the services of his lawyer to handle the matter of this "wretched fraud."[32] Later, McCulloch settled and withdrew the action.[33]

Moreton had other problems. The dispute over the Lorillard appraisal and purchase had dragged on, and it was not until the middle of October that Moreton was able to negotiate his way out of it, even enlisting Clara to help with Pierre ("Work on P.L. if you can to sell me Taylor's calves. . . . Tom Sturgis treated me shamefully in this matter").[34] Pierre had paid the appraised value of the calves to Moreton, but the latter was determined to avoid the sale if he could. In an agreement dated November 6, 1882, Lorillard agreed that the calves need not be delivered (in effect, Moreton bought them back, since they were already on his range), and Moreton gave Lorillard his note for $45,000 at 6 percent, payable in one year. In addition, Pierre agreed to pay $15 a head for the calves to be purchased in the following year.[35] It is interesting to note that the agreement was made with the now liquidated firm of Frewen Brothers, although Moreton's note was to be secured by the pledge of £10,000 in common stock of the Powder River Cattle Company.

The negotiation was rendered the more difficult by problems with

Lorillard's man, Colonel Taylor. Taylor had originally offered some of the calves to Moreton, but he then asked to be relieved of the deal because he would get into trouble with Pierre. This Moreton consented to. But then Frewen accused Taylor of advising Pierre that he could get $40,000 from Frewen for relieving him of the contract, and Taylor denied the substance of the conversation, causing Moreton (in his letter to Clara) to call him a "low liar" and "whining cur."

And there seems to have been more than business ethics involved, although we are as usual at the mercy of Moreton's florid prose. "What do you think he does here?" Moreton thundered. "He has a room in the town and he invites little schoolgirls up there for filthy purposes, the Hound. Everybody is talking of it and he boasts of it. I expect he will get shot or thrashed. What a cur." After vowing to tell Pierre that he will not deal through Taylor in the future, he gives us this moral philosophy: "It is not the immorality of the whole thing, so much as the extreme vulgarity that disgusts me so."[36]

Whatever the facts were, there was a strange incident in Cheyenne (where Taylor was living) early in 1883. One Maud Norton, a fourteen-year-old girl who was working for Taylor, reported to the police that she had been abducted on the city streets in broad daylight by a man wearing a star and taken out to Fort D. A. Russell. When the sheriff tried to verify the story, she was unable to identify from among the entire police force the man with a star who had carried her away, nor could she remember the road they had taken or the places they stopped. It is clear that whatever motive she had for making the original complaint had been altered by the time the sheriff appeared.[37]

Having settled the Lorillard problem, Moreton crossed the Atlantic in early November, arriving on the sixteenth. The board had been expanded to seven, adding the Earl of Wharncliffe and John Leng. It met in early January, with Lord Wharncliffe in the chair. Wharncliffe derived his wealth from extensive coalfields on his Yorkshire estate. The earl's family name was Montagu-Stuart-Wortley-Mackenzie. He was well acquainted with Andrew Whitton, and this connection would cause trouble for Moreton later. Although Moreton was initially pleased with the earl ("a capital prompt chairman he made, no excess of talk"), this feeling was not to continue for long; he perhaps should have taken warning from the fact that the Rawhide project was "squashed flat." Moreton professed himself satisfied, as the board approved of other purchases, and he could see an advantage in having operations concentrated on the Powder rather than dispersed to the Rawhide as well.[38]

Early in February, Moreton issued his first report to the shareholders of the company. It was entitled "Free Grazing" and was apparently intended as a marketing piece, as it carried a price of sixpence on the cover. He had thoughtfully advised the *Leader* that it was in preparation (although they did not print his name in connection with this "news item").[39] Inside the front cover was a handsome map showing the location of the company's ranches, on Tongue River, on Crazy Woman, on Rawhide, and on the Powder River and its tributaries.

Moreton reported that the herd, including horses, numbered 39,000 head, acquired at a cost of $1,075,000, or about $27 a head. He thought there should be 9,000 calves branded in 1883, since 8,000 were branded from these herds in 1882; he also expected that 5,000 steers and 1,000 old cows would be sold in the fall of 1883. But expenses would be high—he anticipated a dollar a head.

On the subject of dividends, Moreton did not want to commit himself, but he thought 15 to 22 percent could be paid on the original capital for four years, at the end of which time the capital would have doubled. The report ran sixteen printed pages and included a good deal of Moreton's philosophy about the cattle business. At the end there were appended three pages on the subject of Texas bat guano, in case some of the readers of his report would have an interest in this subject! Since the company did not own the bat caves, this was a curious bit of advertising, indeed.

Even though Moreton was not rich, he still could act as though money did not matter; he was not even aware that the Post bank had credited an item of $35,000 or so to the company account, rather than to his personal account, as it should have. He happily told Clara that he was "better off than I thought, which is an enormous relief!" Then, he added, "This will look very unbusinesslike to you!" Indeed, it was.

Notes to Chapter 5

1. Fred E. Hesse has the annual "book counts" of the Powder River Cattle Company from its inception until 1886; these numbers are taken from that record, which is apparently in the handwriting of Frank Kemp.

2. Frewen diary, June 21, 1882, Frewen Papers.

3. Frewen diary, July 6, 1882, Frewen Papers; and Sir Bernard Burke, *Burke's Landed Gentry* (London, 1930), 1994.

4. Frewen diary, July 18, 1882, Frewen Papers.

5. Ralph G. Martin, *Jennie,* vol. 2 (New York, 1971), 219.

6. Frewen diary, July 20, 1882. Frewen Papers.

7. Churchill, *Winston S. Churchill,* vol. 2, 124.

8. Frewen diary, August 1, 1882, Frewen Papers.

9. W. G. Kerr, *Scottish Capital on the American Credit Frontier* (Austin, Texas, 1976), 20, 21, 169.

10. Frewen diary, August 5, 1882, Frewen Papers.

11. Frewen diary, August 10, 1882, Frewen Papers.

12. The Rev. Alexander Jacob, *A Complete English Peerage,* vol. 2 (London, 1769), 375–76, 386.

13. Martin, *Jennie,* vol. 2, 219.

14. Churchill, *Winston S. Churchill,* vol. 2, 67; and Brian Masters, *The Dukes* (London, 1975), passim.

15. Kerr, *Scottish Capital,* 59.

16. Martin, *Jennie,* vol. 2, 251.

17. Spencer Whitehead to Frewen, February 17, 1886, Frewen Papers.

18. A copy of the charter and amendments for the Powder River Live Stock Company can be found in the Wyoming Secretary of State's office, Cheyenne.

19. Frewen to Clara Frewen, September 8, 1882, Frewen Papers; and William W. Savage, Jr., "Plunkett of the EK," *Annals of Wyoming* 43(2) (Fall 1971), 208.

20. Frewen diary, September 11, 1882, Frewen Papers.

21. Frewen to Clara Frewen, September 13, 1882, Frewen Papers.

22. Frewen to Clara Frewen, October 8, 1882, Frewen Papers.

23. Frewen to Clara Frewen, September 15, 1882, Frewen Papers.

24. Frewen to Clara Frewen, September 18, 1882, Frewen Papers.

25. *Cheyenne Daily Leader,* August 23, 1883.

26. Kerr, *Scottish Capital,* 176.

27. W. Turrentine Jackson, *The Enterprising Scot* (Edinburgh, 1968), 33.

28. Frewen diary, October 11, 1882, Frewen Papers.

29. Frewen to Clara Frewen, October 15, 1882, Frewen Papers.

30. Frewen to Clara Frewen, October 20, 1882, Frewen Papers.

31. Frewen to Clara Frewen, October 24, 1882, Frewen Papers.

32. Frewen diary, October 23, 1882, Frewen Papers.

33. Frewen to Clara Frewen, May 16, 1884, Frewen Papers.

34. Frewen to Clara Frewen, September 6, 1882, Frewen Papers.

35. Frewen to Clara Frewen, October 14, 1882, Frewen Papers.

36. Frewen to Clara Frewen, September 24, 29, 1882, Frewen Papers.

37. *Cheyenne Daily Leader,* January 5, 6, 1883.

38. Frewen diary, January 11, 1883, Frewen Papers.

39. *Cheyenne Daily Leader,* January 18, 1883.

·6·

A (Very Brief) Peaceful Interlude

*O*n April 3, 1883, the board met before Moreton was to leave London for the West. "Most harmonious board meeting," he recorded in his diary. "Now that all purchasing is concluded, there is no possibility of our being at issue." It was to prove a vain appraisal, but that is rushing ahead of our story.

After a Sunday at the Duke of Manchester's estate, Kimbolton, Moreton sailed on the *Fulda* for New York. There he stopped off at Lorillard's stud farm, Rancocas, came back to the city and collected the gossip about the stock market ("almost dead"), and then boarded the train for Chicago, in company with Frank Kemp and Alfred Sartoris. Another stop in North Platte afforded Sartoris a look at the cattle bought there for the company, and then they were on to Cheyenne, where Moreton found so many of his countrymen that he thought the town was literally in the hands of the British.

This happy infusion of British capital was noted at the Wyoming Stock Growers Association meeting, where the cattlemen were told that herds were now selling for 25 percent more than a year earlier, doubtless because of the investment of £6 million of English and Scottish money. The association's membership was now 262 — 53 had been added in 1882, 76 in 1883. Among the new 1883 additions were Moreton Frewen and John Clay, Jr. At this session Judge Joseph M. Carey became president. The association set a total of nineteen round-ups to cover their members' herds, and No. 15 was devoted to the Powder River range, with Fred G. S. Hesse as foreman.[1]

Later in the year, a special meeting of the association considered the problem of cattle thieves operating in the Powder River country. The calf crop had been short, and comparatively few mavericks were returned in the roundups. At the same time, some operators had "established" new brands, which were growing rapidly. In one particular case, a herd of 1,500 was found to be short 90 animals during its passage through the Powder River country; the missing animals were being held in the badlands until the herd had passed by. As a result of the meeting, warrants were issued for ten men (it was noted that this action would require a special term of court, as the jail was too small to accommodate all of them). Ominously, the ten were all foremen or assistants on ranches in the area and were "well known."[2]

Meanwhile, the Powder River country was becoming more settled, at least in its major town. Early in 1883, word got around that a new bank was coming to Buffalo, in the form of a partnership between Post's partner William R. Stebbins and John H. Conrad of Ft. McKinney, to be known as Stebbins, Conrad & Co. In Cheyenne, Stebbins & Post had just completed a new bank building, an impressive two-story stone structure with a corner entrance between stone pillars, but within a few months the Stebbins brothers (William R. and C. M.) sold their interest in the Cheyenne partnership to Post; the two groups were thereafter separate in banking in Wyoming.[3] But the appearance of a new bank apparently did not entirely erase the frontier spirit of the town. One correspondent complained that there were a dozen saloons and no church in Buffalo![4]

In Powder River company affairs, the board had questioned the wisdom of managing the Rawhide ranch so far from the company's other activities. Moreton thereupon enlisted Rensselaer Schuyler Van Tassell to manage the Powder River cattle on the Rawhide range for ninety-five cents a head, although he expected to have E. W. Murphy sufficiently trained to take over management in a year. The deal with Van Tassell was terminated at the end of the year, but not because of a change of manager. Moreton realized that the Rawhide range was getting crowded, and early the following year he told Van Tassell that he was going to move many of the female stock to Powder River and the steers to the Hanging Woman range in Montana.[5] It was to be the first, but not the last move for the Powder River herds.

In early 1883, the Powder River company acquired a herd from Van Tassell, and with it a brand that would give its name to a Wyoming town: the J-rolling-M brand. Originally named after Jim Moore, the brand came into the hands of the Harris brothers after the demise of the Powder River Cattle Company. They founded the town of Jay Em, which has recently been listed on the National Register of Historic Places.[6]

Van Tassell, who gave his name (although unwillingly) to the town of Van Tassell, was an interesting person in his own right. It is said that he ignored the railroad station bearing his name and continued to freight his supplies from Cheyenne. In December 1886 he married Louise Swan, daughter of Alexander H. Swan, and the proud father of the bride gave them a handsome stone residence in Cheyenne. Unfortunately, the financial collapse of Swan the following year left the builder of the house unpaid, and it was acquired by David Dare, becoming known as "Castle Dare." (Van Tassell bought a suitable replacement from Governor Moonlight).[7]

Although not permitted to buy much for his own company, Moreton couldn't resist dabbling in the cattle market. On behalf of his good friend Algernon James Winn, whose ranch on the Nowood was about sixty miles from the Powder River headquarters, he bought first a trail herd for thirty-three dollars a head, and then a range and herd on the Sun River in Montana for thirty-four dollars a head. These transactions required Moreton to make a trip to Denver with his banker friend Morton Post, but this was a small price in return for "many kindnesses in days long gone by."[8]

It was May 19 before Moreton arrived at his ranch on the Powder River, and there he found things going "most smoothly." He was off to Crazy Woman almost immediately, to "inspect" the work on the desert land entry he had filed on there; he expected to grow five thousand bushels of oats for horse feed on this property.[9]

A week later, he was off again, looking at a new acquisition. He had found a ranch located in a small valley on Crazy Woman, two miles wide and eight long, between perpendicular cliffs. The two ends could be easily fenced, forming an enclosed range large enough to carry 800 head of cattle. Of course, so small a herd meant little to an operation of 40,000, but Moreton had a special need for this valley. He wanted to use it to segregate purebred cattle, then on the Rawhide, from the rough range animals, quite rightly believing that better breeding stock would improve the quality of the herd. He would have both Shorthorns and Sussex cattle on the range.

There was another advantage to the canyon ranch; it was cheap: for $1,300 he could obtain the entire valley. (Of course, since he was not acquiring any land title, and in light of the decision on fencing being handed down in the Cheyenne court — of which more presently — the deal may have been fully priced after all!). There was an inter-

esting bonus to the purchase: a small herd of buffalo stayed permanently in the little valley, and Moreton hoped to keep them there on
his "private" range.

Horace Plunkett had a similar enclosed range, and Moreton went
over to see it first hand. "What a park he has got!" It was grand,
perhaps 10,000 acres.[10] (Plunkett also had an interest in wild animals;
he had two mountain lambs "a fortnight old," and they were allowed
to jump through open windows on the ranch.)[11] At the end of May,
Moreton purchased the new range from Bob Stewart and proceeded
to add two miles of fence to complete the enclosure.

In a letter that June to Thomas Sturgis, secretary of the Wyoming Stock Growers Association, Moreton complained that the
Indians had lived on beef all winter and spring. There had been two
cases of cattle stealing at or near Buffalo.[12] (The year before, the
Indians had obliged him by killing a deer — a tame one that Moreton
had sent to the ranch from Antelope Springs!)[13] And in an effort to
secure the help of the military, he complained in a letter to General
Howard, who commanded the district of the Platte, about the Crows
and "these annual picnics among our ranches." A group of Crows was
then in camp on the south side of the Tongue River, where there were
no buffalo, obviously to prey on cattle.[14]

A copy of Moreton's letter was published in the *Omaha Herald*,
and it was reprinted in Cheyenne, where it generated a good deal
of interest. The *Leader* reported that Pratt & Ferris had lost cattle in
the Powder River country, and Henry C. Lowell had reported losses
to the Crows in the Big Horn country and that there were sixty lodges
on Little Powder River and thirty on the Belle Fourche River. Cowboys at the Sturgis ranch complained that the Indians boldly came
to the ranch and appropriated all the food they had. In one case, it
was learned that a band of Sioux from the Pine Ridge reservation
in Dakota was carrying a pass from the agent there, Dr. T. V. McGillicuddy, entitling them to a thirty-day hunting trip. Red Cloud actually
went on a visit to the Wind River reservation, having crossed Wyoming to get there.

The editor suggested that the root of the problem was the inadequate level of rations and the self-dealing of the agents, which forced
the tribes to become beggars or thieves. When the Bureau of Indian
Affairs received complaints regarding these matters, the agents on
the reservations were asked for their advice. McGillicuddy, who had

been frequently investigated for alleged wrongdoing, responded that he couldn't keep the Indians on the reservation and offered the comment that losses to Indians was just one of the risks of the cattle business — like a bad winter.[15] His explanation for the short rations was the fact that he had far more Indians in his care than the government assumed when rations were provided.[16]

Wanton killing of wild game had subsided; the hide hunters had disappeared from the area, although one person noted that it was almost too late for the game.[17] As a reminder that there were still violent forces in the country, Moreton told Clara that two Texans had been shot in the store, one dying and the other badly wounded. The next day, he thought both would die. "No loss, anyhow."[18]

The roundup was in progress. Spring runoff from the mountains had raised the streams to unusually high levels; Moreton and his hands determined to let the horses swim across, but, to protect their clothes, they stripped naked and put their clothes in waterproof saddlebags. Frewen was on Walnut, and all went well until they were half way across, when "the old horse goes down like a stone, and we are both lost to sight for a few seconds." Moreton was washed off the horse to fend for himself. To avoid getting hit by the horse's legs, he swam away from the animal, and Walnut came back ashore on the side they had just left. Naked, shivering Moreton was on the other bank. Eventually horse and rider were reunited with the help of a cowhand, but the saddlebags proved not to have been waterproof after all![19]

As the roundup continued, Moreton soon learned that there had been severe losses through the winter. About 500 head of sheep were gone, or about 8 percent of the 6,000 or so the company owned, and he expected the calf brand would "fall rather short. . . . This is a great nuisance."[20] Still, he hoped the board would let him have the rest of the capital to invest (£24,000), so he could "swell" the dividend, but he doubted they would agree.[21] He was right; early in August he reported "a civil letter, too, from our worthy chairman, but the brutes won't send me the balance of the uncalled capital."[22]

By this time, his euphoric predictions about the dividend were evaporating, and he was anxious about how large it might be. Certainly it would not be 20 percent, but perhaps 10. Soon he learned that the directors were sending Andrew Whitton out to inspect the ranch, and Moreton, glad for the chance to romance the old Scotsman, hoped he could "enthuse old Whitton to pay 18 percent."[23] "He will be much interested and return to Scotland as enthusiastic as I am about Powder and its prospects." Undoubtedly, Moreton was nervous about Whitton, not only because he was the largest preferred shareholder (Moreton said Whitton held 20 percent of that class), but because of his supposed influence over Lord Wharncliffe. If he could make a good impression on Whitton, it would be good for the value of the shares, as Moreton now expected to sell all that were unencumbered.[24]

The early roundup returns from the Tongue River range were good, again fueling the enthusiasm that was never far beneath Moreton's surface, but by October, he was talking about the need for the shareholders to be satisfied with "a moderate dividend." A few days later, he admitted that the dividends would be "a disappointment to us all."[25] So bad was the "gather" from the Rawhide range that he was considering having the men rework the country to look for more animals. Still, there was some good news. The prices in Chicago were relatively good, and the Powder River stock netted $55 a head, so that Moreton could once again dream briefly of a 20 percent dividend. Barely two weeks later he was doubting whether 15 percent could be reached, considering the poor returns from the beef roundup.[26]

Moreton contented himself with favorable comparisons between his company and those of his neighbors, who had much worse problems. "Poor Harry Oelrichs and the Sturgis outfit nearly gave their cattle away!" Yet, the "disappointment" dividend he expected was still 10 percent; it was nearly the end of October before he conceded that 5 percent would be "the outside." The trouble, of course, was the scarcity of animals. "Our total sales will barely reach 4,000 head, instead of some 7,000, as I had intended," he told Clara.[27]

Nor was Moreton the only Frewen worried about the dividend. Ted wrote with the sad news that his rents had fallen off £6,000 a year, and he was anxious to know what the Powder River Company dividend would likely be.[28]

As the sobering news settled in, Frewen began to cast about for ways to reduce expenses on the ranch. He decided to pay off the Tongue River outfit and to run that range as an outpost of the Powder River operations.[29] Later, he would ponder moving from the home ranch itself.

There was also some carping from London. Kemp referred to

the sheep and the refrigerator project as "experiments," and Moreton immediately challenged the label. He reminded the directors that there were already a quarter of a million sheep in the territory, so that could hardly be called an experiment. In the case of the refrigerator at Sherman, he chose a comparison farther away: the Victoria Meat Company was an "immense success." The poorer showing for the Sherman facility he attributed to the fact that Frank Kemp had been called home to England, and the meat was kept too long, losing its color and its juices.[30]

As always, when trouble loomed, new ideas provided the needed antidote to the pain. Inspecting the land he had enclosed on the Tongue River, Moreton conceived the idea of showing Whitton the area, and "if he agrees with me, we will make 3 or 4 farms of it and bring out the farmers from England." In the middle of August, he was happily surveying ditches to convey irrigation water to the property.[31]

Moreton was also confronted with a domestic dilemma. Clara, who was in England, was once again pregnant and soon to be delivered — with Moreton generally making later predictions than she. But the impending appearance of Whitton on the range made it difficult for Moreton to break away and rush to her side, and he finally decided not to do so. Hugh Moreton Frewen was born on October 9, 1883.[32] Moreton was on his way east (though not yet homeward bound) when a cable reached him on October 16 with the good tidings.[33]

Whitton finally did arrive, in the middle of September, and he was "very much pleased" with his trip, if we are to believe Moreton, who recorded the astonished "Wonderful, Wonderful" as each vast stretch of grazing land came into view. The traveller stopped by Plunkett's EK outfit and then went to see Moreton's new canyon ranch, with which he was "delighted," according to our not quite impartial reporter.[34] The canny old Scot told Frewen that "he would not dare to put in any report how highly he thought of the business, or no one would believe him."[35]

Whether Moreton believed all that he had enthusiastically told Clara about Whitton's visit, we cannot know, but before long it was painfully clear that Whitton was less than completely satisfied. He had quickly learned that fully £1,900 ($9,000) had been lost on the packing house venture, and the sheep operation did not gain his approval, either.[36]

Even though things were not first rate on the range, it was heartening to hear that some major shareholders seemed to be happy with their investment. One of these, Alan Gardner, had dined with Pierre Lorillard, who ventured the opinion that the Powder River Cattle Company would make the fortunes of all its shareholders![37] Another shareholder, Charles E. Lyon (second only to Moreton in size of holding) had written to suggest a trip for shooting, as well as business.[38]

Earlier in the year, the Scottish representative of the preferred shareholders, William Mackenzie, wrote to Moreton to ask his advice about the Swan holdings in Wyoming. Swan had been in Glasgow negotiating for the establishment of a company, and Mackenzie wanted to help him if the values were as they were represented.[39] Swan already had a large operation in Wyoming by the time he visited Edinburgh in 1883. In December 1882, Alexander Swan had sold the National Cattle Company and the property of the partnerships Swan & Frank and Swan, Frank & Anthony to the Swan Land and Cattle Company, Ltd., thus organizing Wyoming's grandest cattle company in the wake of the largest cattle sale the territory had ever seen. The capitalization of his Wyoming companies was nearly $1,900,000 (the Cheyenne newspapers said $2,500,000), and his range was a solid block of about 4.5 million acres on which 87,500 head of cattle grazed.[40]

The new Swan company soon became involved in a major controversy, which had begun in a rather innocuous way. A farmer named Michael Odder, who had patented 160 acres from the government in 1877, cut a fence that he claimed was on his property. The fence had been built by the Swan interests, and the company promptly sued him for $960 in damages. Originally, the report had been that "some miles" of fence had been cut, but the amount sought in damages and the size of Odder's farm make it more likely that something considerably less was involved.

This simple argument soon escalated into a full-scale war on the fencing practices of the range cattle industry. The managers of the big outfits were strangely ambivalent on the subject, although all of them apparently had some fences on public lands. They made the frequent comment that fences were a danger to cattle during bad storms, as the animals tended to bunch up along fences and freeze to death, rather than drift to a sheltered spot. They claimed, however, that they fenced strictly to protect themselves and that they would much prefer that there were no fences. Particularly in the areas where cattle drives were frequent, if a fence had been constructed on one side of the driveway, the rancher on the other side was forced to erect a fence to keep the cattle from grazing his range as they moved across. The smaller stockmen, on the other hand, were insistent that they needed the protection afforded by fences, since they did not have the manpower to control their herds and keep other herds off their range.

To the government, of course, there was no such thing as "their" range; all use of the public domain was unauthorized trespass and was tolerated only so long as the land was not harmed. Certainly, anything that hindered the taking up of land under the public land laws was contrary to government policy. Nevertheless, Judge M. C. Brown, the U.S. attorney for Wyoming, moved cautiously (he owned a brand himself). He asked Washington for advice, noting that the Swan case was not exceptional; one individual had reportedly constructed fifty miles of fences and cut one thousand tons of hay annually from the enclosed public land.[41] The requested advice was not long in coming: the Department of the Interior ordered Brown to move against those fencing the public domain.[42] In the ensuing case of *U.S. vs. Swan,* et al., Chief Justice Sener ruled in August that the fences must come down.[43]

Michael Odder had brought down a giant, but he could not stay to enjoy the victory. Apparently mentally disturbed as a result of the dispute, he and his wife had already sold the 160 acres to Colonel Elias W. Whitcomb in April, and Whitcomb resold it to Alexander H. Swan in June; the Swans could then rebuild the fence on their own land.[44]

The subject of the public lands was also debated in London. A letter published in the London *Times* early in 1883 pointed out that the "grazing rights" the companies were boasting about were nothing more than "trespass" on the government lands not yet taken up by settlers.[45]

The troubles of the industry were not limited to illegal fencing, or to inclement weather, of which there was plenty; cattle thieves also contributed their share. The stock growers association was becoming increasingly concerned, although Moreton thought the stealing was still on a very small scale. Nevertheless, he meant to root out the thieves before they could "secure imitators." Unfortunately, security on the ranges was limited, especially in the winter. "Except myself and just we few Britishers, not a boss ever comes near his range, let alone live on it." More truthfully, Moreton himself only stayed west during those winters when fear of creditors kept him from England. Nor was cattle theft solely the province of free-lance rustlers. Frewen complained that the roundups were being conducted in a "slovenly" manner, so that there would be more strays available for stealing. Cowboys were carrying short-handled branding irons under the flaps of their saddles, and he suggested that it should be illegal to carry an iron with a shaft under four feet. He was aware of so-called "maverick" brands (he mentioned the Young brothers), and he threatened to have his men brand any such animals with the "76" whenever they were found.[46]

The humorist Edgar Wilson (Bill) Nye chose the topic for one of his letters to the editor (later he managed the Laramie *Boomerang*). "A poor boy can in a few years, with an ordinary Texas steer and a branding iron, get together a band of cattle that would surprise those who figure simply on the ordinary rate of increase," he said. "Men soon learn that it is possible and even frequent for a cow wearing a 'Z' brand to be the fond and loving mother of a calf wearing the 'X' brand, and vice versa. Sometimes a calf will develop a brand that has never been in the family before. . . . I have read a good many agricultural and scientific works on the subject, but they throw no light. They do not explain how Texas steers can multiply themselves with elegance and preciseness. They are painfully and criminally silent on the subject. They do not recognize the Texas steer in fact, or the possibility of his replenishing the earth. They do not seem to look to him as a multiplier."[47]

Moreton was not laughing. He identified the proprietor of the 17 Mile Ranch as a major culprit. According to Moreton, the only cattle the man had ever acquired lawfully were four milk cows bought in 1881, yet he had just sold a herd of cattle! The work had apparently been accomplished by a hired hand, who in his "leisure hours" branded animals found on the range.[48] Early the next year, Moreton thought that conditions had improved. He commented that "our good men have stood solid and the whole gang who made the Sweetwater country their headquarters have been dispersed."[49]

Then there were also con men around. Shades of the Shearburn case, another Britisher, Chandos Pole, was borrowing money on the strength of a connection with the Powder River Company. Moreton had to wire the bankers in San Antonio to warn them and was thinking of advertising in the newspapers. In disgust, he said, "We claim that Americans sell us all their worthless securities, but it is free trade in return, we send them all our high class criminals."[50]

If the industry and the company were having troubles, Moreton's personal finances were in even worse shape. With no payment in sight for the year's work, he had to find the means to pay his own not inconsiderable expenses. "I shall have to plot and scheme so much, darling, to pay our way this winter." There was that big debt to "old Pierre," and also one to the Post bank in Cheyenne. Pierre proved to be a gentleman in the matter: when Moreton offered to pay him a high rate of interest in exchange for an extension, Pierre "absolutely refused to take more than six percent," which was the original rate in the note.[51]

Moreton was also burdened with a contract he had signed with Plunkett & Roche the previous year. Having failed in his effort to buy out the EK spread, Moreton agreed to buy EK cattle delivered to Chicago in 1883 at five cents per pound. Since he was contracting for cattle in Chicago, there could have been no thought of expanding his range operations—it was merely a speculation on cattle prices, and a poorly timed one, at that. The price to Plunkett turned out to average six dollars a head more than Plunkett would have been able to realize in the Chicago market. Moreton was determined to get out of the deal, saying that it was "in form and substance so illegal that it might well suggest to any suspicious shareholder doubts as to my own bona fides."[52] The deal was not so clearly illegal; foolish it certainly was.

Plunkett was not responsive to Moreton's early efforts at negotiation, which opened with typical Frewen finesse: Moreton told Plunkett that the company had repudiated the contract! This only made Plunkett more determined to press for the redress due a gentleman and a man of honor.[53] Finally, in an "unpleasant, but perhaps satisfactory and quite amicable interview," Frewen agreed to take personal responsibility for the unfortunate commitment, since it could not be "foisted" on the shareholders.[54] It was agreed that the matter should be arbitrated, with W. C. Alston as Plunkett's arbitrator and Willy Peters as Frewen's.[55] Joyfully anticipating the results of the arbitration, Moreton considered this problem at an end, since any payment the arbitrators might agree on would only come at the end of two years, "by which time, if it does amount to two or three hundred pounds, I shall not feel it."[56] When Plunkett sold the cattle in the fall, the contract proved to be worth $6,000 to him.[57]

While Moreton was thus experiencing new trials and testing new associations in his incorporated state, Richard was also branching out in the cattle business. Using his brother's model, Richard organized the Dakota Stock & Grazing Company, Limited, to buy the Hat Creek Ranch of N. R. Davis & Co. in the Dakota territory, for $500,000, payable in two installments a year apart. The ranch was supposed to have over 17,000 cattle on a range rather grandly described as "over 600 square miles, or thereabouts." Sensitive to the value of the right name on the prospectus, the board included, in addition to Richard Frewen, the Earl of Dunraven as chairman, and Lord Castletown. The total capital was set at £250,000 ($1,208,000), in 50,000 shares of £5 each. Charles W. Middleton Kemp was secretary of the corporation, the same office he held with the Powder River Company. But Dick's deal included no nonsense about not being paid as manager, so he did not follow Moreton's example blindly.

The season's work complete in the West, it was time for the journey home. After stopping three nights in New York with Leonard Jerome, Moreton sailed on October 31 aboard the *Servia,* arriving in time for the board meeting on November 20, before the Duke of Manchester departed for Berlin.[58] According to Moreton, Whitton's earlier concerns had been overcome and his "very favorable" report was received by the board with "great satisfaction."

Moreton enjoyed the role of expert, whose advice and influence was sought. Lord Wharncliffe stopped by to urge Moreton's assistance in setting up a nephew in the West, and a clergyman came on a similar errand for his son.[59] There was also much shooting and endless rounds of parties.

Then, in January of the new year, the board met on two consecutive days, the directors being unable to understand the accounts for the year. Kemp had not "digested" the accounts, according to Moreton, although it was apparent even to him that the dividend could not be more than 5 percent. Frewen dined with the Duke of Manchester, whom he described as "a nice old gentleman, but has no natural business aptitude, and as chairman is too much inclined to allow us all to wander from the point."[60]

At the end of January, Moreton submitted his own report to the shareholders, who by now had received Whitton's report and the official accounts. As he would do many times in the future, Moreton glibly explained away the lackluster results. He blamed the weather for the losses the company had suffered, but pointed out that the Powder River range had fared better than those of competitors in the region. Even though 2,400 of the cows purchased the previous year had not been bred (they were on the trail, without bulls), there was a 60 percent calf crop from the remainder. The "book count" for the herd had increased about 10 percent to 49,000, after allowing for a "standard" 4 percent loss for the year.

He complained that the board, exercising the discretion given it by his agreement, had valued the cattle at $28 per head, even though he told them that no "transfers" of good cattle in Montana or Wyoming had been made at less than $35 per head; he was inclined toward a value of $36, which would make the total value of the cattle herd £365,000 ($1,763,000).

Frewen overlooked a couple of problems with this type of analysis. In the first place, nearly 20,000 of the animals in the herd were calves or yearlings and not likely to bring the same price as mature animals. Moreover, considering the difficulty he had encountered in rounding up saleable beef, the "normal" 4 percent may have been an inadequate reflection of actual losses.

Taking the value of £365,000 for the cattle, and adding appropriate sums for horses, sheep, and improvements, Moreton came to a total asset value of £387,000 ($1,869,000). Considering that £276,000 ($1,333,000) had been invested by the shareholders, there was an unrealized profit of £111,000 ($536,000) before the payment of the dividend. He concluded with the opinion that he could liquidate the company in the spring for his values. When he had given this analysis to the board in January, he said they were "incredulous." No doubt they were!

He felt compelled to comment on what return could be realized in the cattle business, since the current year's dividend was so meager. We need not bore the reader with his calculations, but he reckoned that a 27 percent dividend could be paid year after year, merely by selling the natural increase of the herd. "If then," he lectured, "though we have at hand the means of paying 27 per cent dividends, we yet prefer to pay much smaller dividends and carry our profit largely forward, I hope Shareholders will recognize that the present is seedtime, the harvest is ahead."[61]

The long-awaited dividend was not 20 percent, nor 18 percent, nor 10 percent, but 6 percent, the lowest of the nine largest cattle companies. At the end of February, Moreton received his payment, which amounted to just under £2,400 ($11,600) on his 6,892 fully-paid shares (less deduction for capital calls).[62]

A list of western cattle companies prepared in Dundee includes results for the year 1883, ranging from the mammoth Prairie (with 129,000 head) and Swan (109,800 head), having £500,000 to £600,000 capital, down to the Western (31,000 head) and Arkansas (24,000 head), with capital in the range of £180,000 to £240,000. The Powder River was in the middle of the group in size, although not in dividend payments; the Prairie paid 20½ percent and the Texas paid 12½ percent, while four others paid 9 to 15 percent. Only the Hansford and the Powder River paid as little as 6 percent on ordinary shares.

It was in 1883 that Moreton finally settled Clara in a house of her own in London, at 18 Chapel Street (later changed to Aldford Street), Mayfair, which he took on long lease from the Duke of Westminster. Moreton's grandniece, Anita Leslie, says that Papa Jerome "bought" the house for Clara. In any case, Moreton had soon mortgaged it. It was there that her son had been born, and it was there that she would entertain interesting guests. One of these was Milan Obrenovich, King of Serbia, who had won independence for his country from the Turks and had married the daughter of a Russian colonel. Later, he divorced Queen Natalie, and soon after, he was forced to abdicate in favor of his teen-age son. To Paris he fled, and there met Clara Frewen, in town for a visit. When Clara returned to London — Moreton was of course travelling — the king followed. Showering the Frewen children with gifts, Milan pursued Clara, offering to take back the throne if she would be his queen. While he languished in the neighborhood, boxes of gardenias (her favorite flower) were delivered every day.[63]

Jennie thought Milan's table manners were not nice, and Queen Victoria absolutely refused to receive him (she disapproved of divorced monarchs), although he did meet the more tolerant Prince of Wales. Moreton, when he returned, took the king shooting! In his autobiography, he devoted four pages to the exiled king and his stories, and included a photograph of him, as well; he admitted that the king was "an almost daily visitor" at the house.[64] An explanation for this remarkable tolerance is difficult to find, even considering the somewhat flexible rules of the day, unless one accepts the conclusion of Anita Leslie. She flatly stated that Moreton was too confident of his own amatory prowess to be jealous. He was "consistently unfaithful" to his wife, according to Leslie, who quoted him as saying, "Every woman I have ever enjoyed has been completely paralysed by the vigour of my performance."[65]

In any case, Moreton's *business* performance was less than stellar in 1883, but this did not depress him for long; he already had some new ideas that would guarantee success for the future, and he launched himself into these new fields with great vigor in 1884.

Notes to Chapter 6

1. *Cheyenne Daily Leader,* April 3, 4, 1883.
2. *Cheyenne Daily Leader,* November 24, 1883.
3. *Cheyenne Daily Leader,* February 4, April 5, July 3, 1883.
4. *Cheyenne Daily Leader,* November 15, 1883.
5. Frewen to Resselaer Schuyler Van Tassell, February 8, 1884, Frewen Papers.
6. Urbanek, *Wyoming Place Names,* 108, 207.
7. *Cheyenne Daily Sun,* December 10, 1886, May 28, 1887; and William H. Barton, "David Dare and the American Dream," *Annals of Wyoming* 41(2) (Fall 1979): 12.
8. Frewen diary, May 12, 1883, Frewen Papers.
9. Frewen to Clara Frewen, May 22, 1883, Frewen Papers.
10. Frewen diary, June 1, 1883, Frewen Papers.
11. Frewen to Clara Frewen, May 29, 1883, Frewen Papers.
12. Frewen to Thomas Sturgis, June 9, 1883, Frewen Papers.
13. Frewen to Clara Frewen, April 29, 1882, Frewen Papers.
14. Frewen to General Howard, August 9, 1883, Frewen Papers.
15. *Cheyenne Daily Leader,* September 7, 1883.
16. Flora Warren Seymour, *Indian Agents of the Old Frontier* (New York, 1941), 318–20.
17. *Cheyenne Daily Leader,* February 27, 1883.
18. Frewen to Clara Frewen, June 6, 7, 1883, Frewen Papers.
19. Frewen diary, June 7, 1883, Frewen Papers.
20. Frewen to Clara Frewen, July 16, 1883, Frewen Papers.
21. Frewen to Clara Frewen, June 14, 1883, Frewen Papers.
22. Frewen to Clara Frewen, August 4, 1883, Frewen Papers.
23. Frewen to Clara Frewen, August 27, 1883, Frewen Papers.
24. Frewen to Clara Frewen, August 4, 1883, Frewen Papers.
25. Frewen to Clara Frewen, October 1, 7, 1883, Frewen Papers.
26. Frewen to Clara Frewen, August 31, September 17, 1883, Frewen Papers.
27. Frewen to Clara Frewen, October 24, 1883, Frewen Papers.
28. Frewen to Clara Frewen, August 10, 1884, Frewen Papers.
29. Frewen to Clara Frewen, October 14, 1883, Frewen Papers.
30. Frewen to the Directors of the Powder River Cattle Company, August 19, 1883, Frewen Papers.
31. Frewen diary, August 16, 1883, Frewen Papers.
32. Andrews, *Splendid Pauper,* 82.
33. Frewen diary, October 16, 1883, Frewen Papers.

34. Frewen diary, September 16, 1883, Frewen Papers.

35. Frewen to Clara Frewen, September 17, 1883, Frewen Papers.

36. Frewen to the Earl of Wharncliffe, undated Tuesday, 1884, Frewen Papers.

37. Frewen to Clara Frewen, August 17, 1883, Frewen Papers.

38. Frewen diary, July 22, 1883, Frewen Papers.

39. William Mackenzie to Frewen, February 21, 1883, Frewen Papers.

40. Harmon Ross Mothershead, *The Swan Land and Cattle Company, Ltd.* (Norman, Oklahoma, 1971), 19–26.

41. *Cheyenne Daily Leader,* January 16, 1883.

42. *Cheyenne Daily Leader,* January 20, 1883.

43. *Cheyenne Daily Leader,* August 24, 1883.

44. Laramie County Clerk, deeds dated April 7 and June 7, 1883.

45. *Times,* February 13, 1883.

46. Frewen to Judge Joseph M. Carey, August 9, 1833, Frewen Papers.

47. *Cheyenne Daily Sun,* February 4, 1880.

48. Frewen to Thomas C. Sturgis, August 10, 1883, Frewen Papers.

49. Frewen to William Mackenzie, February 12, 1884, Frewen Papers.

50. Frewen to Clara Frewen, May 18, 1884, Frewen Papers.

51. Frewen to Clara Frewen, May 7, 1884, Frewen Papers.

52. Frewen diary, October 4, 1883, Frewen Papers; and Savage, "Plunkett of the EK," 209.

53. Plunkett diary, August 2, 21, 1883.

54. Frewen diary, August 2, 1883, Frewen Papers.

55. Plunkett diary, August 21, 1883.

56. Frewen to Clara Frewen, August 20, 1883, Frewen Papers.

57. Plunkett diary, October 10, 1883.

58. Frewen diary, November 20, 1883, Frewen Papers.

59. Frewen diary, November 21, 1883, Frewen Papers.

60. Frewen diary, January 12, 1884, Frewen Papers.

61. Moreton Frewen, "Report of the General Manager, Mr. Moreton Frewen, to the Shareholders at their First Annual General Meeting, held February 26, 1884," January 28, 1884, Frewen Papers.

62. First Dividend Warrant, February 29, 1884.

63. Andrews, *Splendid Pauper,* 145–46.

64. Frewen, *Melton Mowbray,* 115–18.

65. Anita Leslie, *Clare Sheridan* (New York, 1977), 11.

·7·

To Superior and Beyond

*M*oreton Frewen once wrote, "I wonder whether I am as happy as I think I am. . . . From living at a critical time much with Dick, whose nature it is to find the dark lining in the silver cloud, I reacted violently into the other extreme, with the result that I am by custom which has become a second nature, sanguine and enthusiastic—to I suppose a ridiculous extreme."[1] This was a remarkably candid analysis.

A new project to inflame Moreton's imagination required the cooperation of governments. His objective was to ship Wyoming cattle all the way to England, and to do so he had to overcome the restrictions on importation of live cattle into that country. He immediately began a frontal attack on these impediments, enlisting in his cause F. R. Lingham, who was a leading exporter of live cattle from Boston to Canada. A great, blond ex-lumberjack, Lingham became a faithful follower of a number of Frewen schemes.

In January, after seeing an unfavorable letter on cattle shipping in the *Times,* Moreton at once set out to persuade that powerful newspaper to "change front," as he put it. He telegraphed ahead to schedule an interview with Chenery, the editor, but failed to get it right away. After securing an introduction, he set off again but ended up with "only a subeditor, who evidently was not equal to the responsibility." Whenever someone did not agree with him, he often thought him "unequal" to the task.

Nevertheless, his letter to the *Times* did get printed in late January. Another letter was printed a few days later in the *Morning Post,* which also ran a news article on the subject. But Moreton lamented that they were not favorably impressed by his recommendations.[2]

By mid-February, he got his friend Albert Grey to introduce him around at the House of Commons, where a bill was drafted, .and Moreton also put in some time with the owner of the *Telegraph*, who is supposed to have promised support. A week later, an hour with Lord Carlingford produced the assurance that the government would use the proposed powers "to the utmost," if they were enacted by parliament. Moreton commented rather ungraciously that his lordship was "a nice looking old gentleman, but he does not impress me as being a large minded or over-active man."[3]

A cloud appeared on the horizon in the form of reports of foot-and-mouth disease in Texas, which would surely stir opposition to importation of live American cattle to England. Moreton speculated that the story was likely a "canard" started by the "Chicago dressed meat ring."[4] Ironically, his own actions had contributed to the disease scare. In the summer of 1882, Dick bought forty-eight Shorthorn bulls in Lexington, Kentucky; they stopped at the St. Louis stockyards on the way west, and by the time they reached Waterloo, Nebraska, they were sick. Fourteen subsequently died of splenic, or Texas fever. When he learned of the sickness, Moreton wired Sturgis for help; the territorial veterinarian was dispatched to investigate, and his report was communicated to the newspapers in August. The matter was also discussed in the veterinarian's report at the Wyoming Stock Growers Association convention the following April. There was therefore ample publicity given to a proven case of disease.[5]

Still, the all-important bill did pass second reading in the Commons.[6] And Moreton did not neglect the Lords. Half an hour with the Duke of Richmond sufficed to modify his opposition to the proposal, and word soon reached Moreton's ear that the bill was "safely conducted" through that house.[7]

This hurdle safely behind him, Moreton attended the company's general meeting, which he said went off fairly smoothly (no thanks to Ted, who had caused some trouble, which at this distance cannot be further discerned).[8]

Then west again. In April, he set sail, taking the *Servia* for the fifth time. A week with Leonard Jerome in New York let him gather news of the stock market: Northern Pacific was only twenty-three, and he wished he had the money to buy it. New York generally was "flat and woebegone, never was there such a shrink in values."[9] Then, in early May he was off to Ottawa to see his friend Lord Lansdowne, who was Governor General, and John Henry Pope, the Canadian Minister of Agriculture, to pave the way for the cattle trade.

According to Moreton, Pope considered the project "sound, and of great benefit to Canada" and promised to establish an inspection bureau at Sault Ste. Marie to accommodate the importation of the American cattle. The minister promised to help as soon as the British parliament passed an appropriate enabling act, and the Governor General sent Moreton a letter of encouragement, saying "It is a big thing and worth turning trouble for."[10] "I have seen them in Canada," he reported back to Clara. "It seems perfectly certain that my great project is to be put in execution this year."[11]

With this encouragement, Moreton next addressed a personal application to Lord Carlingford in London, asking the British government to let the cattle in free of restriction.[12] Later in the month, he heard from England that the bill had passed the Lords, and he expected to hear any day that "the coast is clear." Then, the news came from Tom Sturgis, secretary of the Wyoming Stock Growers Association, that the Canadian Cabinet had decided to allow the Wyoming cattle to pass through Canada in bond. Two days later, Moreton was confidently predicting the first shipment to Liverpool by the end of August.[13]

While confident of the future of his new venture, Moreton was at the point of giving up on another. He told Frank Kemp to try to sell the boiler at Sherman, and Kemp suggested that a better price would result if the entire refrigeration facility were sold as a unit.[14] Moreton told him to go ahead, hoping the machinery and building would bring $6,000 (the company had paid him $10,000 in stock and cash for it); unfortunately, Kemp had to report later that he had been unable to sell either the boiler or the entire facility, although the Wyoming Meat Company might later make an offer.[15] Three years later, when Horace Plunkett was manager of the Powder River Cattle Company, he had a lumber merchant measure the buildings for sale as used lumber.[16] Plunkett called the Sherman operation "Frewen's folly," but it had been an exciting dream while it lasted.

Out on the range, reports of cattle conditions north of the Platte were favorable that summer, although there were some disturbing incidents that foretold trouble on the range. One cattleman had driven a herd onto the Powder River range and then offered them for sale, at what Moreton called a 50 percent premium over the high prices of 1882. Frewen rejected the offer (and solicited the agreement of his neighbors to do likewise), whereupon the man turned the herd loose on the range. Frewen and his neighbors resolved that they would do their utmost to prevent him ever seeing his animals again.[17] Another case involved a neighbor, Chauncy Stoddard, who let his herd drift onto the Powder River range and did not participate in the roundup to recover the "drift," thereby leaving them to graze on this new pasture.[18]

Later in the year the cattlemen in the north organized themselves to control as best they could the influx of animals. As secretary of the group (they called themselves the "League"), Moreton wrote to one man as follows: "The Powder River stockmen consider their position as jeopardised by your reported intention to move in cattle onto their range. You were informed earlier in the year, by Mr. Kemp that in the event of your settling there you would not receive those neighbourly offices which are customary, and without which the business cannot be carried on successfully. I have now to inform you that if you insist on moving in we shall oppose your interest by every legal means."[19]

The cattlemen also turned to the legislature to protect their interests. At the session in the winter of 1884, the territorial legislature decided to institutionalize the roundup system by enacting it into law. The Buffalo *Echo* was opposed to the resulting maverick law, claiming that it was, in fact, an association law and that it therefore discriminated against the small stockmen, who were not members of the association. The secretary of the association had tried to counter this argument by pointing out rather lamely that there were eighty members of the association who owned fewer than one thousand head, and one with only twenty-five.[20]

As finally enacted, the law provided for the election of foremen for the roundup, the election to be carried out by the Wyoming Stock Growers Association. The foreman was to be in charge of the sale of mavericks, and he could retain 10 percent of the sale price as his fee.[21] Actually, the law as enacted was more favorable to the small stockmen than the bill as first introduced. Originally, the bill had included a presumption that illegal branding had been done by the owner of the brand and required that those bidding to purchase mavericks post a $3,000 bond.[22] Of this bill, W. H. Holliday of Laramie said it was the first instance of a law that "declares that a man shall be pronounced guilty until he has proved his innocence."[23]

Moreton was hotly opposed to the new law, and he decided to enlist the help of Alec Swan. The letter he wrote to Swan was one of the usual Frewen pieces, ranging from the polite to the nearly rude. He started off by referring to the matter as a "delicate topic" and then charged that Swan's foreman had bought mavericks for fifty cents a head, implying that they may well have been Powder River animals. Swan, who had just returned from the British Isles, prepared a frosty reply, in which he denied the allegations in Frewen's letter and noted that he had opposed the maverick bill, but that it had passed over his objections. Then he closed by saying, "I do not take exception to your letter from the standpoint that it is meddling with your neighbors' business, but allow me to ask you what side of the Bill you take, as I am entirely unable from your letter to discern whether you are for it or against it."[24]

With its new authority, the stock growers association prepared for its annual meeting, which would be the grandest ever: only the opera house would be large enough to accommodate all who were expected. There were then 145 members, and another 72 had applied for membership; 152 visitors came to observe the proceedings, and representatives from Montana and Dakota were added to the executive committee of the association.[25]

At a meeting later in the year, the grateful association honored secretary Thomas Sturgis for his many services to the industry, giving him a silver punch bowl and a pair of eight-candle candelabra from Tiffany's (the bowl was valued at $3,500 and the candelabra at $1,500).[26]

Such happy signs of internal contentment did not obscure some new public relations problems. It was the practice of the big outfits to discharge their range hands at the end of the season, and the Cheyenne papers had noted that Fred Hesse had settled up with and laid off twenty-six men in the first week of December 1883.[27] Now, however, the newspapers were suggesting that these men should be retained on the payroll to look after the stock during the winter.

New on the public relations scene was the cattlemen's own newspaper, published in Cheyenne, the *Northwestern Live Stock Journal*, owned by its editor, Asa S. Mercer, and his partner, S. A. Marney. The partners came to Cheyenne in November 1883, having bought the necessary equipment on credit, and were soon claiming fifty thousand weekly circulation. This new competition was not welcomed by the other Cheyenne papers, who criticized Mercer for his failure to discuss the bad news about the livestock business.[28] Mercer was supposed to be a great grandson of a man who once owned one hundred acres in Manhattan, which were soon to be reclaimed at the end of a ninety-nine-year lease; one cannot be sure whether the story was seriously reported or not.[29] There was considerable glee at the other papers when Mercer got into a fistfight with Marney in the office, which soon involved Mercer's wife and two children (each sibling armed with a rock). In the melee, Mercer's wife struck the unfortunate Marney with a majolica spittoon, shattering the spittoon and knocking him senseless.[30]

Change was not confined to the cattle industry. In Cheyenne, the introduction of a settled time zone created a brief stir, as railroad time disappeared. Residents were told to set their clocks back three minutes, as the trains would now arrive and depart on meridian time.[31] The availability of both gas and electric lighting made it necessary for the city to decide between these two sources of illumination for its streets. R. S. Van Tassell opened up the first livestock feeding operation designed to serve the local market; cornfed beef had never before been sold in Wyoming.[32]

Late in 1882, a fire had damaged the Cheyenne Club, briefly disconcerting a few residents (including one gentleman who was forced into the street with no protection other than "that afforded by nature and curtailed nocturnal garments"), and providing a convenient excuse to enlarge premises that were already "too small."[33] At a cost of $10,000, a new addition was opened in 1884. In addition to the usual comforts, the Club included a post office for members, a splendid dining room thirty feet square, and fourteen bedrooms, all lighted by electric lamps. There were then 170 members, half of them resident in Cheyenne.[34]

In June, Lillie Langtry came through Cheyenne on her way to Denver, in the "Manitou Marble," a special excursion coach (dingy outside, elegant inside). A few days later, she returned to Cheyenne with Harry Oelrichs (who had been a "former acquaintance" in New York City) and visited Harry's ranch, seven miles from the city. The railroad coach had already been renamed the "Jerome Marble" by the press, thus associating it with Moreton's father-in-law, who was thought to have paid the tab for it. We are relieved to learn that Harry provided Lillie with suitable floral remembrances, for he was later involved in an action by a New York florist seeking payment for the balance due on an account of $503.90 for the period August 17, 1880 to March 1, 1884, for bouquets, corsages, and other collections of cut flowers "of a daily character," when Lillie was in America.[35] Unfortunately, Harry's monopoly of the lady's time was interrupted by the appearance of Freddie Gebhart, who was so loathed by Moreton. Public notices do not tell us if Moreton met the lovely Lillie on this occasion, but we must assume that he did, for he had arrived in Cheyenne from England on May 21.[36]

The territory was filling up. There was a government surveying party in the Big Horns in 1884, and a petition signed by nearly four hundred resulted in the organization of Fremont County that year. Crook County was also to be organized the next year, with Sundance as its seat. The cattlemen in the latter county, ever jealous of grazing lands, had been unsuccessful in having the county seat placed at Sand Creek, which would have kept it off the range.[37]

In Johnson County, Buffalo had about five hundred people in 1884, or double its size of a year earlier. The new courthouse was expected to be finished by the end of the year, at a cost of $31,650. A problem had cropped up over the title to the city lots, however. The former commander at Fort McKinney, Major Verling B. Hart, had filed on the Buffalo townsite in 1877; he had since died, and his widow now owned the entire town! At first, Mrs. Hart had proposed to sell lots at ten dollars each and to donate land for public purposes. However, after the patent issued, it appeared that the donations would no longer be forthcoming, and the lot sizes were shrinking. As a result, some disgruntled settlers mounted an unsuccessful challenge to the patent.[38]

The wild character of the area had still not noticeably improved, and in December a grand jury in Buffalo turned its attentions to the vices of the city and its environs. The opinion was expressed that gambling was taking place on roundups, and the grand jury held that this should cease. Moreover, the "practice of fornication" in Buffalo was said to threaten the peace and quiet of the city. There is no record as to what local action, if any, was taken on the jury's recommendations, although the stock growers' meeting in the spring did discuss the gambling issue, without taking action on it.[39]

On the Powder River company range, work was progressing on land filings. Moreton anticipated that a large number of settlers from

Kansas would be entering the territory. To protect the company from this incursion, and to secure valuable land, he proposed to spend as much as £1,000 on filings and irrigation works in 1884.[40] It was necessary to prepare the irrigation ditches before final proof could be made. It was also a requirement of the Desert Land Act that the filings be made in the name of individuals, and there was an acreage limit for each person. The company therefore "arranged" to have the filings made. Moreton said he had located 2,000 acres that could be filed on. Although clearly against the intent of the Desert Land Act, this method of filing by the big cattle companies was apparently the custom during the later period of the range cattle industry.

The filing at Crazy Woman had been made by Moreton himself, and to do so he had to declare his intention to become a U.S. citizen; we do not know if that was a pro forma intention or a real one. In order to prove up on the desert land entries, it was necessary to give evidence that water had been brought onto the land. We thus have a rare instance of formal record of the Powder River ranching operation. Frewen's affidavit supporting the Crazy Woman filings testifies that 2 acres of vegetables were planted and irrigated in 1884, and 120 acres were planted to hay. The following year, wheat, oats, and hay were raised on both sides of the Middle Fork of Crazy Woman, with yields of twenty-one bushels of oats and twenty of wheat, and half a ton of hay per acre.[41] The irrigation ditches constructed in connection with the land entries consisted of one, modestly named the "Moreton," to serve 400 acres and another, named "Dick," to serve 600 acres.[42] Both water rights are still valid, representing the sixteenth and eighth priorities, respectively, on that stream.[43]

The canyon ranch that Frewen had bought from Bob Stewart was filed on by one of the company's employees, named William Clarkson, who had agreed to transfer his rights to the company. But in this case, he would probably have to be paid $250 or so to do it. Fred Hesse had also made a filing, but this was for himself, not for the company.[44]

The Tongue River filings were made by Charles Carter and a man named Warren (both company employees), but there were conflicts between these filings and a preemption claim. Eventually, a relinquishment was secured from the preemption filer, and both Warren and Carter signed agreements to transfer the land to the Powder River Cattle Company when title was received from the government.[45]

While this system of acquiring land seemed to work in practice, Moreton became uneasy about the possibility that one of the filers might decide not to reconvey; there would obviously be no legal way that a conveyance could be forced. He told Dick that good relations had to be maintained with Fred Hesse, especially because of the effect on the filings.[46]

Back home, creditors were getting restless. Some sharp correspondence passed between Moreton and Vivian, Gray & Co., regarding his failure to make payment on a loan that he had secured with some of his shares in the company. He complained about the tone of the firm's demand, saying that he regretted the expressions in their telegram. The response was cool: "As you have left without complying with my request to repay the whole of the loan, I do not think the regret can be very great." (He still owed £683, to which the interest had been added; the collateral was 963 ordinary shares.) They went on to point out that their usual rate was 10 percent, and that it was "utter folly" to loan "for a long time" at 6 percent. Undoubtedly, their annoyance was increased by the knowledge that Moreton had recently obtained additional money from "another quarter" but still had not repaid their 6 percent loan.[47]

Moreton was also trying to sell some of his shares to cover his cash needs. In June, Vivian, Gray & Co. wrote to say that the British public were "utterly disgusted as a rule with American securities, and above all American management," so that there had been no buyers. The price was only 4½ on the ordinary shares, while the preferred shares were going at 11¼.[48]

And still the British government had not acted on the import scheme that would save everything. Nevertheless, even though he had not broken through the government red tape, Moreton claimed he was already getting some benefit from the prospective movement of cattle overseas. In one case, he had threatened to export a herd rather than settle for less than four cents a pound, and the buyers met his price. By the end of August, he could exult that "the papers are full of me. . . . The English press neutral, the Yanks and Canucks d-----g me freely."[49]

Back on the ranch, while awaiting the expected good news from Canada and England, Moreton committed to his diary his analysis of the presidential race then going on. Blaine had sewed up the Republican nomination, "a triumph for politicians of the most venal order," according to Moreton. He claimed that Blaine had been "mixed up with every important steal of the last twenty years."[50] Needless to say, Moreton was a Cleveland man.

After the roundup at the end of June, Moreton was back at the home ranch on the Powder River, to find that one of his guests had killed a bull buffalo within a mile of the house. Already, these magnificent animals were becoming scarce, and he remarked, "I doubt whether we shall ever again see the grand old beasts near the house."[51]

Notes to Chapter 7

1. Frewen diary, June 8, 1884, Frewen Papers.
2. Frewen diary, January 19, 1884, Frewen Papers.
3. Frewen diary, February 22, 1884, Frewen Papers.
4. Frewen diary, March 10, 1884, Frewen Papers.
5. Frewen to Thomas Sturgis, July 13, 1882, Frewen Papers; *Cheyenne Daily Sun,* August 9, 1883, and *Cheyenne Daily Leader,* April 3, 1883.
6. Frewen diary, March 23, 1884, Frewen Papers.
7. Frewen diary, February 21, 1884, Frewen Papers.
8. Frewen diary, March 2, 1884, Frewen Papers.
9. Frewen diary, April 26, 1884, Frewen Papers.
10. Marquess of Landsdowne to Frewen, June 12, 1884, Frewen Papers.
11. Frewen to Clara Frewen, May 16, 1884, Frewen Papers.
12. Frewen to Clara Frewen, May 16, 30, 1884, Frewen Papers.
13. Frewen to Clara Frewen, June 19, 21, 1884, Frewen Papers.
14. Frank Kemp to Frewen, May 29, 1884, Frewen Papers.
15. Frank Kemp to Frewen, June 18, 1884, Frewen Papers.
16. Plunkett diary, November 6, 1887.
17. Frewen to Frank Lusk, April 16, 1884, Frewen Papers.
18. Frewen to Stoddard, June 6, 1884, Frewen Papers.
19. Frewen to Mr. Tomkins, August 16, 1884, Frewen Papers.
20. *Cheyenne Daily Sun,* January 20, 1884, and *Democratic Leader,* February 16, 1884.
21. *Laws of Wyoming, Eighth Legislative Session, 1884* (Cheyenne, 1884), 148–52. The law was approved March 6, 1884.
22. *Cheyenne Daily Sun,* January 26, 1884.
23. *Democratic Leader,* February 28, 1884.
24. Frewen to Alexander H. Swan, August 14, 1884, and Alexander H. Swan to Frewen, August 25, 1884, Frewen Papers.
25. *Cheyenne Daily Sun,* April 8, 1884, and *Democratic Leader,* March 29, April 8, 1884.
26. *Cheyenne Daily Sun,* October 16, 1884.
27. *Cheyenne Daily Leader,* December 6, 1883.
28. *Cheyenne Daily Sun,* February 4, 1885.
29. *Cheyenne Daily Sun,* April 23, 1886.
30. *Democratic Leader,* July 18, 1884.
31. *Cheyenne Daily Sun,* April 30, 1884.

32. *Democratic Leader,* November 19, 26, 1884.
33. *Cheyenne Daily Sun,* December 8, 9, 1882.
34. *Cheyenne Daily Sun,* April 19, 1884.
35. *Cheyenne Daily Sun,* December 30, 1885.
36. *Cheyenne Daily Sun,* May 22, June 3, 9, 1884.
37. *Cheyenne Daily Sun,* August 23, 1884, and *Democratic Leader,* November 16, 1884.
38. *Democratic Leader,* May 6, 1884, and *Big Horn Sentinel,* August 29, 1885.
39. *Big Horn Sentinel,* December 13, 1884.
40. Frewen to Charles Fitch Kemp, June 8, 1884, Frewen Papers.
41. Affidavit of Frewen to the Land Office, September 29, 1886, Frewen Papers.
42. "Water and Ditch Claim," April 16, 1884.
43. *Tabulation of Adjudicated Water Rights of the State of Wyoming, Water Division Number Two* (Cheyenne, 1963), 117.
44. "Mr. Kemp's Notes as to Land Titles," December 3, 1884.
45. Frank Kemp to Frewen, June 7, 1884, Frewen Papers.
46. Frewen to Richard Frewen, December 12, 1884, Frewen Papers.
47. Vivian, Gray & Co. to Frewen, April 29, 1884, Frewen Papers.
48. Vivian, Gray & Co. to Frewen, June 5, 1884, Frewen Papers.
49. Frewen to Clara Frewen, August 28, 1884, Frewen Papers.
50. Frewen diary, June 8, 1884, Frewen Papers.
51. Frewen diary, June 27, 1884, Frewen Papers.

· 8 ·

Envoy Extraordinary

$\mathcal{A}$t the end of June, bad news arrived from England. "No hope of lake route opening this summer," the cable said, and Moreton made the operator read it three times to make certain he had got it right. There was only one thing to do: he must go at once to England "to show cause why these barbarous and fatal restrictions should be removed."[1]

Time was short, since he reckoned he needed permission by the first of August, so a man was sent to fetch Fred Hesse so he could be told of Moreton's imminent departure; there was difficulty finding Fred in the dark, but by midnight he arrived. Then the long ride to Rock Creek to catch a freight train to Cheyenne—no time to stand on ceremony—where the help of Tom Sturgis (of recent ill repute) was enlisted. That worthy set to work, writing a "requisition" for the Governor of Wyoming to sign under the Great Seal of the territory, and a second "letter of credit," authorizing Frewen to represent the Wyoming Stock Growers Association on a mission of importance.

The latter credentials, bearing the seal of the association and countersigned by association president Joseph M. Carey, introduced Frewen as the bearer of a formal application from the governor for the release of the cattle of the territory from restrictions imposed upon their entrance into Great Britain, and as the representative of the association to make any explanation that might be necessary. Sturgis described the association as having four hundred members who owned two million head of cattle, worth (with improvements) $100 million. Of Frewen, he said, "His cattle interests in the Territory are very large, and his personal acquaintance with the stock business is so intimate that no one could be better qualified to give to you the minor details you may require." It was a fine endorsement and could not have been better written by Moreton himself.[2]

A wire to New York to reserve a cabin on the *Alaska,* and then he was on the train east. There was just time in Chicago to make a call or two (he always seemed to have someone to call when passing through any moderately large place), and on to New York, only to find that the *Alaska* had gone. Nevertheless, he was soon on the *Aurania,* bound once more for the home country, an uneventful crossing, except for the last two days spent running through heavy fog (a bad omen?).[3]

In England, he soon located the difficulty. Real or fancied fear of disease in the imported animals had been stirred up by an unfortunate outbreak of Texas fever, followed by expert advice from the Treasury Cattle Commission, "locating disease wherever it can," according to Moreton. "In legislation, it is a mistake to be influenced by reports of specialists; professionals read all things through professional spectacles, they live and live only appeals to the fears of those more ignorant or more honest than themselves."[4]

After a number of hurried meetings to collect support, it looked as though the desired end was in sight; a meeting was arranged, subject only to the attendance of the Canadian High Commissioner, Sir Charles Tupper. Moreton naturally believed that there would be no difficulty from that quarter, considering all the work he had done in Ottawa (Landsdowne had asked Lord Carlingford to "do all he could to meet your wishes. This I fear all I can do"),[5] but when Tupper cabled home for instructions, Pope responded that nothing should be done that would jeopardize Canada's favorable importation rights. The High Commissioner was unwilling to judge whether the proposal would jeopardize the Canadian position and therefore declined to attend, "and so the trade is lost for this year."[6]

In an attempt to salvage things, Moreton sought the help of Lord Lorne, who had preceded Landsdowne as Governor General of Canada, but late in July a response from that quarter warned that unless Frewen could reassure the government of Canada on the disease question, the cause was lost. "Her position is too strong." And he had no hope of himself exerting Imperial influence: "My role is only as a collapsed colonial to back Canada's expressed wishes."[7] Frewen sent Lingham to Canada, to bend the ear of anyone who would listen.[8]

The Canadians soon made their opposition explicit, and in writing. Frewen secured a copy of a letter dated September 27, 1884, from the Marquess of Landsdowne to the Earl of Derby, in which the entire subject was reviewed in detail. The first priority with Canada, said Landsdowne, was to preserve its own preferential access to the British market. Although the Minister of Agriculture had no evidence to show that there was actually infectious disease at the present time in Wyoming, Montana, and Colorado, still there was pleuro pneumonia in Illinois. To aid in analysis of this risk, the Canadian consul in New York had contacted a professor at Cornell University. The professor pointed out that the infection in Illinois was very near the Chicago stockyards, "the greatest cattle entrepot of the West." In light of this threat, the Canadian government was proposing even stricter regulation of its border with the United States. (Indeed, Quebec province did quarantine Wyoming cattle, although the Wyoming Stock Growers Association vainly reassured Moreton (as their representative) that there was no disease in the territory, despite the presence of splenic fever in eastern Nebraska.)[9]

Two other arguments had been made for the export scheme. The first was that it was impossible—and therefore a waste of effort—to regulate the U.S. border, since it was continually being crossed by both cattle and buffalo. Next, there was the somewhat tangential argument that Wyoming and Montana were virtually isolated from the eastern states, and that cattle traffic was always in the easterly direction, not toward the West. The official Canadian response to these arguments was that, first, the territory immediately north and south of the border was not occupied by cattle ranches, nor was it true that large herds of buffalo frequented these districts. Unfortunately, no evidence was adduced for these statements other than the determined opinion of the minister himself. On the matter of the insularity of Wyoming and Montana, Landsdowne presumed that there were surely breeding stock moving from east to west.

The Canadians proffered one final carrot. If a state or group of states were to adopt and enforce effective quarantine regulations, the case would be "entirely altered." However, the governor general noted that no state had in fact taken such precautions, and the U.S. federal government was without power to force them to do so.

Moreton made one final effort by asking the speaker of the House of Commons whether it would be possible to propose a direct routing for the cattle, via the Lakes and through Portland, Maine, or Boston. The speaker responded that the application would, of course, be carefully considered, but Boston would not likely be approved, because a cargo from that port had contained pleuro pneumonia as recently as June (no similar case had been discovered in cargoes from Portland since 1879). In short, it was not auspicious.[10]

These setbacks did not depress Moreton for long; he merely extended his time prediction to the following year. "If I can help in England, we see our way next spring to such a coup in Canada as will bring the Canuck farmers to terms. That old villain Sir John M!" The last reference was to Sir John MacDonald, the Canadian prime minister, whom Moreton had tried to enlist in the cause, pointing out the great profits that would accrue to the Canadian railroads from the shipment of the American cattle.

Before leaving England, Moreton had lunch with his good friend Gilly Leigh (it would be their last meeting), and by early August he was back in New York, en route to Montreal. There, Pope told him, "they are going to shuffle those Canucks," although one wonders whether that is a faithful representation of the assurances given by the minister. After more press interviews, he was on his way back to Cheyenne before the middle of the month. At the end of August, he was in St. Paul, trying to get support from the Northern Pacific, in expectation of freight from the transfer of the cattle to Canada for export. A vice president of the line advised Moreton to look at the new railroad development then taking place opposite Duluth at Superior, as a location for transfer stockyards. Acting on that advice, Moreton was at Superior early in September.[11] Almost immediately, he had transferred his affections to that place. "I somehow think our fortune will really date from this spot, not dear old Powder. . . . Six lines of rail, all will be completed this year, converge here and the bay itself is the most prodigious harbor in the whole world. . . . We have selected the place for the stockyards. The 320 acres will cost us about £2,000 [$10,000]. We think we can ship the whole way to Buffalo from here and when those beasts of Canadians allow — the whole way to Montreal without transfer and very, very cheaply."[12]

A month later, he wrote to John Clay to ask him for a full assessment of the Superior situation, saying, "The railroad syndicate who have bought up the town site in Superior have decided to take me in on the 'ground floor'. . . ."[13] (We do not know what Clay responded, but it must not have been as favorable as Moreton could have wished, because he later told Dick not to be concerned about Clay's opinion.) Despite the disaster of their previous partnership,

Moreton had enlisted Dick in his Superior project. Dick sent F. R. Lingham to get options on five hundred or one thousand acres to test the price situation, or as Dick put it, "to find out how the cat jumps." Lingham responded that there were no solid blocks of ownership, and it would be hard to get options on even one hundred acres; he did send the particulars on one piece that might be had at $200 to $300 per acre.[14]

Moreton had taken some shares in the land development syndicate, and Dick wanted some, too, although he had to borrow money on the shares of his company (which could pay no dividend). Dick wanted to participate in the project, but he also remembered their past dealings: "I hope we may be able to find each of us enough to do without coming into contact, but if not, why I will clear out," he said.[15] Eugene Jerome, one of Clara's relatives, was also involved in the project.[16]

Moreton's plans for Superior were fulsome, including a hotel and a bank. Richard talked to a prospective partner for the bank (they were contemplating a private bank, not a national), and suggested they might each put up $25,000 toward the capital. "We must run it in a very conservative way and keep large balances in hand," he said, although one must question whether the word "conservative" had any meaning for Moreton.[17]

Moreton authorized Dick to go to New York to negotiate with the Superior syndicate. Unable to get any explicit instructions from Moreton, Dick wrote saying that he was intending to buy 200 or 300 acres in different parts of the town at $250 per acre but not to give any pledge as to future improvements to be made on the land (the syndicate had been making noises about requiring $1 million in improvements). He also wanted the right to sell the land after it was fully paid, another point the syndicate was resisting (they wanted to restrict resale of the land until improvements were made). He was prepared to offer the bank and a hotel. "Now if they won't agree nearly to this, I shall throw the game up," he concluded.[18] When these terms were laid on the syndicate negotiators, Dick and young Jerome laughed heartily at their chagrin.[19]

The syndicate was not amused. Dick acknowledged, "There is no doubt that my humour or ill humour was a little too much of a good thing for those people in Wall St.," he said on his return from New York. Moreton, however, did not want to lose the deal; "I think we shall make a mistake if we hold out too long, for there is likely to be a boom in the spring that will harden their hearts," he said.[20] Dick contritely suggested that Moreton could go back to the syndicate and lay the blame on him, telling them that his brother's manners were "somewhat blunt" but that "nothing was meant."[21]

It was well that Superior looked promising, because in November, Moreton was ready to admit that times were not "ripe" for the export trade. Although he intended to work hard on it during the winter, he was prepared to settle down and feed stock at the Superior location, rather than using Superior as a way station for exports.[22] Soon he had Lingham building stables for 500 head to be fattened there that winter.

In no time, he had translated the expected cattle feeding operation into expected dividends. "I think we shall have no difficulty in paying a ten per cent dividend on the six months ending last July and another ten per cent up to December during next April out of sales of cattle we are feeding, and again a ten per cent up to June next in June; this arrangement of dividends twice a year will make us popular and I want very much to get support and a fresh issue of capital."[23]

It was heartening to dream about paying dividends twice a year, but the reality was that no dividend could be paid at all unless expenses were cut. This reality necessitated some painful choices, and it was during this summer that Moreton made up his mind to give up the old home ranch he had first built in 1879. Now that the Northern Pacific had been built into Montana, a ranch headquarters on Crazy Woman would be thirty miles nearer the rails and would be only twenty-five miles from Buffalo, the county seat. He could run the telephone line from there into town, a distance of only ten miles from the store at the Powder River Crossing. (Of course, there had been no county seat in the region in 1879, and no railroad to the north.) Moreover, the old ranch had some shortcomings that Moreton had not owned up to before: the water was so bad that he could not grow hay there, nor could he raise a garden. Finally, the thoroughbred cattle were up on the canyon ranch on Crazy Woman and would be "so interesting a family to look after." These were the rationalizations; there was also the practical imperative: "The truth is it is a very considerable and not quite necessary expense to the company, and the waste and worry connected with it annoy me. I can have a couple of rooms built

and locked up for me at Crazy Woman and I do not think that I ought
to spend something like a thousand a year keeping up a house which
I am in occupation of so short a time."[24]

The thought was wrenching to him. "It quite goes to my heart
to dismantle that, the first fortress of civilization in this savage west,"
he said. Three weeks later, he was considering moving even farther
north, to the Tongue River, whence he could reach the railroad in
a single day. This curious loosening of his deep attachment to the
old ranch was a symptom of later thoughts; it was not a large step
to contemplate giving up western management altogether.

While Moreton could wax sentimental about the Powder River
country, he could also be pragmatic about it. As early as the spring
of 1883, when he was asked for advice on ranching, he replied that
Wyoming was getting too crowded, that Montana would be a better
location. "Here in Wyoming we have too many companies, Greek
is forever meeting Greek and high prices are the result."[25]

Moreton's neighbor Horace Plunkett was also having concerns
about overcrowding on the Wyoming ranges. He had just incorporated, and was for the first time faced with the need to provide
regular dividends, if the shareholders were to be happy. Although
there had been a good calf brand, the ranges were definitely finite,
and Plunkett told Moreton that they must sell off some of their female
stock to limit the increase; otherwise the winter would take the increase
from them. It was a sober prophecy that would come true before
long.[26]

The numbers of cattle shipped also told the story of overstocking. Tom Sturgis told the *Democratic Leader* that there had been 157,000
head shipped from Wyoming in 1882, only 117,000 the following year,
and the 1884 totals were not expected to exceed 100,000, below the
125,000 in the years 1879 and 1880.[27]

Moreton was dismantling other dreams, too. By the end of
November the Texas bat caves had been sold; Dick was happy for
the help it gave his situation ("it must nearly clear us").[28] By the following fall, the last shipment of guano had been sold (a total of 513
tons at a bit over £7 per ton), and Moreton was served up a bill for
his share of the loss on the bat cave operation. It amounted to nearly
£1,300 sterling ($6,300).[29]

The Frewen brothers didn't need more bills to pay. Dick, who
at this time seems to have been a sort of free agent for Moreton in

Cheyenne, wrote that "money is very tight here. When I say very, I mean very." His finances had become so tight that the Post bank was returning his checks unpaid. "Poor Dick is low and says he can pay no dividend and is too poor to go home this winter," Moreton sadly told Clara.[30]

Dick warned of another potential problem, this time with Frank Kemp, the assistant manager in Wyoming. "I hear Kemp is too fond of blackguarding you behind your back, and making out that he could do the work a good deal better," said Dick, adding that Kemp should have been kept as bookkeeper, rather than made assistant manager. Moreton responded with thanks for the warning. He intended to return Kemp (a "quarter bred" chap) to the books. "I don't like him, I never did, because he like his worthy brother is a snob, not merely a cad."[31] (The "worthy brother" was, of course, Charles Fitch Kemp, manager of the company in London.) Maybe Moreton had never liked Kemp, but it was only two short years earlier that he had told Clara what a "jewel" Kemp was![32]

It was not only the English who were causing Moreton trouble in the West; there now appeared a scion of good American stock, none other than Lawrence, the son of Uncle Lawrence Jerome. No stranger to trouble, young Lawrence had been indicted for larceny and receiving stolen goods a few years earlier. At that time, the charge was not pressed, since Jerome was of "good antecedents" and "well connected," although he was doubtless "technically guilty."[33] Lawrence had come west looking for work, and Moreton told him to "move on at once." "Imagine how hopeless he must be," Moreton said, "to come up here to ask employment of me and to commence at my own doors as it were, drinking, gambling, running into debt and being knocked down by a cowboy!!" We do not know which of the sins thus enumerated counted most against young Lawrence in Moreton's book, but obviously he was disgusted.[34] A few days later, Frewen advised Clara that Lawrence ("that person") had gone up to the canyon ranch and would return soon to the home ranch. "He has sunk oh, so, so, low," he added.[35]

But there was more. "Fancy that brute, telling a lot of infamous women in Buffalo that he was the great train robber Doc Middleton." Young Lawrence had thus chosen to impersonate a premier horse thief. So convincing was the story that these women repeated it; the news soon reached the ears of the law, whereupon Lawrence was arrested but, to Moreton's chagrin, he was released "upon his explaining to everyone that he was your brother and my brother in law." Aside from borrowing money all over the country, he had taken a rifle belonging to another and pawned it in Buffalo, and he had bought a horse for $60 on credit, which he had quickly resold for cash. "I wish they would hang the cur," Moreton concluded.[36]

Moreton arrived back on the Powder River on September 12, and left the ranch again on the seventeenth with the Ashtons, who were on their way south to the railroad, en route to New Zealand. He was thus away from the ranch when Gilbert Leigh of Stoneleigh died. Heir to a barony and member of parliament from the family seat of South Warwickshire, Leigh was a small, wiry, red-haired man who wore an eyeglass. A dear friend of Moreton's (they had been in Acacia Lodge together), he had been in that first group to visit Wyoming in the fall of 1878.[37] He returned again to hunt, and his name first appeared in the ranch visitor's book in October 1879. Back again in the fall of 1884, Leigh was with a party in the Big Horns, near Ten Sleep Canyon. Moreton told Clara that Leigh "left camp for a stroll" and walked off the sheer wall of the canyon, falling to his death below. Moreton's telegram to Lord Leigh stated that his son had shot a wild sheep and had fallen when trying to reach it. Leigh left camp on September 14, and his body was found only on the twenty-first, after a week's search. Moreton wrote to Clara from Cheyenne, "I have just heard this terrible news of poor dear Gilly's death." Gossip had been circulating that in the interval between the accident and discovery of the body, poor Gilly had starved to death; this rumor was scotched by W. H. Grenfell, who had been with the party that finally found the body and saw that Leigh had fractures of the skull, back, thigh, and leg; he concluded that death was instantaneous.[38] Leigh's brother came to Cheyenne to get the body, and Moreton at once made plans to return to England, saying, "I should like to follow so old a friend to his resting place."[39]

There then developed an embellishment of this tragic story, which has taken on a life of its own. According to this tale, Leigh's body could not promptly be taken away because of poor travelling conditions, and so it was preserved frozen in the unheated back room of a cabin until spring. It is a colorful story, but quite fanciful. The body was taken to Rock Creek, where Horace Plunkett met the remains on October 6, and was shipped east to England.[40] Moreton was present at the interment (his brother Edward was a pallbearer).[41] Moreton wrote many doleful words on the occasion of Leigh's death (including a piece for publication in the *Herald*), and the English papers were lavish in their praise of his courtesies to the Leigh family, but it was poor old brother Dick who found the money to pay the expenses Gilly had incurred on his last hunting trip.[42]

Since he was thus called back home, Moreton could meet with the board of the company in November, and there he heard the reading of a "very unpleasant" letter from Andrew Whitton, who had been west again in June (but had not seen Moreton).[43] According to Moreton, Whitton's letter to the board contained "a number of very absurd reflections upon my management." While he defended himself against these charges, he surprisingly did urge the board to get other managers, because his own time was being taken up by the Superior project.[44]

Whitton raised another point that disturbed Moreton considerably. Since the company had not been able to pay dividends of at least 10 percent, it was suggested that the shortfall should be recovered at the end of the five-year period (with interest) and paid to the shareholders before Moreton should be able to share in profits.[45] Early in November, Moreton took this matter to Spencer Whitehead, his solicitors; these gentlemen gave him their advice, and, incidentally, opened an account with him for their fees and costs, which would run many pages and cover several years. The dispute would not go away easily.[46]

The idea of running such a farflung, strange business from London was probably always a bad one, even in good times, but when the business was in trouble, it was a disaster. While Moreton struggled on with the board, others watched from the sidelines. A year later, Horace Plunkett commiserated with Moreton over the problems of dealing with the London office. It was "ludicrous," he said, to attempt to manage such a complex business from London, with only occasional "visitations" from abroad.[47] Unfortunately, Horace would not be so understanding of Moreton's problems when he was in charge in Wyoming and taking orders from the London office.

Although dealing with company affairs was not a happy diversion for Moreton, other things were. There was still time to help with family affairs. The "Kid" (brother Stephen) was full of enthusiasm to be sent to Bechuanaland, where there was a "filibustering" expedition, but his colonel would not recommend him; he accordingly appealed to Moreton. Clara was thereupon induced to write a letter to the prince. The word came back that he would be "too happy" to help and would write to the Military Secretary. Moreton noted in his diary, "these little confidences attract him more than anything."[48] Perhaps the prince tried, or perhaps he did not; unfortunately, the colonel (a "brute") so blocked the matter with red tape that it could not be done.[49]

In November, Moreton hosted a dinner for Sir John MacDonald, the Canadian premier (the same "old villain"), whom he now described as "a delightful old gentleman, and the image of the late Beaconsfield." Sir John is supposed to have promised that he would "endeavour to contrive" some legislation on cattle exports that would be helpful.[50] At the end of the year, Moreton lunched with Horace Plunkett and his father, Lord Dunsany, and was pleased to learn that Horace had unfurled the banner of free imports in Ireland, although he admitted that "there is much work — perhaps years of it" before success could be assured.

The lure of politics was becoming greater, and Moreton was uncertain which party to join. He dined with W. H. Hurlbert, of the *Herald,* who advised him to wait, but always to remember that the union with Ireland should be repealed! Moreton had an article entitled "Progress to Poverty" published in the *Fortnightly,* which he hoped would enhance his image and perhaps contribute to success in the Superior project.

In December the board met again, and Moreton tried for a dividend of 7½ percent but did not prevail; the payout was set at 3 percent, although an additional 7 percent would be paid in June if the feeding operation permitted, making a total of 10 percent (all of which the directors proposed to relate to the year 1884).

When the accounts for the new year were finally prepared and forwarded to the shareholders, they showed that £16,600 ($80,000) had been earned, on sales of nearly £34,000 ($164,000). The displeasure of the board was apparent in the opening sentence of the directors' report: "The Directors regret that Mr. Moreton Frewen, the Manager of the Company in America, has been unable to make a more satisfactory realisation of the Stock."[51] After paying the preferred dividend of £10,000 pounds, there remained only £6,800 in the dividend account that could be made available for ordinary shareholders, only enough to pay 3 percent.

The report quoted Frewen's explanation of bad weather and noted that the company had gone into the fattening business, both at Superior and at Stromsburg, Nebraska, for which expenditures of about £5,500 had been incurred. Moreton hoped to realize $45 per head, after expenses from this venture. (There were 550 head at Superior and 1,065 at Stromsburg.)

The assets on the balance sheet included a total of £316,000 ($1,526,000) for cattle, valued at $28 per head, which was the value used by the board for the 1883 accounts. The previous year, Moreton had predicted a total calf brand of at least 10,000 for 1884; yet there were actually *fewer* calves branded in 1884 than in 1883 (9,187 versus 9,824). Simplistically, this equates to only a 41 percent calf crop, if there really were 22,270 cows on the range at the beginning of 1884, as the books say there were. One must therefore doubt the other figures for the herd, which are also book counts. Only 4,301 animals were sold in the year, which again seems low in relation to the supposed herd size. The herd is supposed to have increased to 54,581 from 49,113 the previous year, but the proceeds do not argue for any increase at all. The Rawhide herd was actually a little smaller than the year before, and all of the increase was attributed to the Powder River, where there were supposed to be 37,700 head.

In his report to the shareholders, Moreton took up most of the space with glowing predictions about the feeding operations. Finally, he came around to an evaluation of the company's properties. He analyzed the situation both in terms of unit value and in numbers. The cattle had been purchased at $17 per head, whereas now they were "quoted" at $33; 42,000 had been purchased, now there were 56,000. Of course, $33 per head was not the amount shown on the balance sheet (it was $28 there), but also the quantities were not exactly correct (aside from the general questions on book count). It is true that 42,000 had been purchased before the current year, but an additional 2,800 were purchased in 1884. Moreover, Moreton always conveniently forgot about natural losses, even "book" losses; these amounted to 2,200, effectively reducing the comparison to a herd of 54,000 related to purchases of about 47,000. This was not a terribly robust record. In one respect, he seems to have learned a lesson; there were no predictions of 27 percent dividends for the future.[52]

The Scottish investors again prepared a summary statement of the affairs of western cattle companies at the end of 1884, and the poor Powder River continued to lag the field. The Swan, with over 120,000 head of cattle, had managed a dividend of 10 percent on its ordinary capital, against the sorry 3 percent for Powder River; all of the big outfits paid 6 percent or better.[53]

Notes to Chapter 8

1. Frewen diary, July 28, 1884, Frewen Papers.
2. Thomas Sturgis to the Lord President of Her Brittanic Majesty's Privy Council, July 1, 1884, Frewen Papers.
3. Frewen diary, July 28, 1884, Frewen Papers.
4. Frewen diary, August 14, 1884, Frewen Papers.
5. Marquess of Landsdowne to Frewen, July 3, 1884, Frewen Papers.
6. Ibid.
7. Marquess of Lorne to Frewen, July 24, 1884, Frewen Papers.
8. *New York Times,* July 24, 1884.
9. Thomas Sturgis to Frewen, August 4, 8, 1884, Frewen Papers.
10. Arthur Peel to Frewen, October 8, 1884, Frewen Papers.
11. Frewen diary, August 29, 1884, Frewen Papers.
12. Frewen to Clara Frewen, September 3, 1884, Frewen Papers.
13. Frewen to John Clay, October 8, 1884, Frewen Papers.
14. F. R. Lingham to Richard Frewen, November 25, 1884, Frewen Papers.
15. Richard Frewen to Frewen, November 14, 1884, Frewen Papers.
16. Richard Frewen to Frewen, November 5, 1884, Frewen Papers.
17. Richard Frewen to Frewen, November 7, 1884, Frewen Papers.

18. Richard Frewen to Frewen, November 15, 1884, Frewen Papers.

19. Richard Frewen to Frewen, November 18, 1884, Frewen Papers.

20. Frewen to Richard Frewen, November 27, 1884, Frewen Papers.

21. Richard Frewen to Frewen, December 5, 1884, Frewen Papers.

22. Frewen to Richard Frewen, November 4, 1884, Frewen Papers.

23. Frewen to Clara Frewen, September 12, 1884, Frewen Papers.

24. Frewen to Clara Frewen, September 7, 1884, Frewen Papers.

25. Frewen to Pell, May 12, 1883, Frewen Papers.

26. Horace C. Plunkett to Frewen, November 8, 1884, Frewen Papers.

27. *Democratic Leader,* August 2, 1884.

28. Ian Mackintosh to Frewen, October 31, 1884; and Richard Frewen to Frewen, November 29, 1884, Frewen Papers.

29. Account with Wyllie & Gordon, London, October 15, 1885, Frewen Papers.

30. Frewen to Clara Frewen, September 12, 1884, Frewen Papers.

31. Frewen to Richard Frewen, November 27, 1884, Frewen Papers.

32. Frewen to Clara Frewen, April 29, 1882, Frewen Papers.

33. *New York Times,* November 22, 1881.

34. Frewen to Clara Frewen, September 7, 1884, Frewen Papers.

35. Frewen to Clara Frewen, September 12, 1884, Frewen Papers.

36. Frewen to Clara Frewen, September, 1884, Frewen Papers.

37. Andrews, *Splendid Pauper,* 66; and Frewen to Clara Frewen, September 1884, Frewen Papers.

38. W. H. Grenfell to Frewen, October 10, 1884, Frewen Papers.

39. Frewen to Clara Frewen, September 24, 1884, Frewen Papers.

40. Plunkett diary, October 6, 1884.

41. Andrews repeats the "frozen body" story, *Splendid Pauper,* 86–87. The funeral was described in a long article in the Manchester *Guardian,* October 29, 1884.

42. Fred G. S. Hesse to Frank Kemp, November 5, 1884, Frewen Papers.

43. Andrew Whitton to Frewen, June 23, 1884, Frewen Papers.

44. Frewen diary, November 11, 1884, Frewen Papers.

45. Frewen to Richard Frewen, November 4, 1884, Frewen Papers; and Stibbard, Gibson & Sykes to Spencer Whitehead, Esq., December 8, 1884, Frewen Papers.

46. "Mr. Spencer Whitehead Costs Charges and Expenses in the Matter of Mr. Moreton Frewen and the Powder River Cattle Company, Limited," November 5, 1884 to July 27, 1886, Frewen Papers.

47. Horace C. Plunkett to Frewen, August 17, 1885, Frewen Papers.

48. Frewen diary, November 11, 1884, Frewen Papers.

49. Frewen to Richard Frewen, November 17, 1884, Frewen Papers.

50. Frewen diary, November 28, 1884, Frewen Papers.

51. *Report of the Directors and Statement of Accounts to November 30th, 1884* (London, 1884), Frewen Papers.

52. "Mr. Moreton Frewen's Report to the Shareholders of the Powder River Cattle Company (Limited)," March 17, 1885 (London, 1885), 21, Frewen Papers.

53. Jackson, *Enterprising Scot,* 94–95.

· 9 ·

Sniping From The Sidelines

Writing in Superior early in 1885, Moreton confided to his diary, "I have had, God knows, two anxious years, and until I came here did not see my way out of the wood; now if I can only get help and some money, I am sure I do." At least he was not discouraged.

The general meeting of the company was held January 15, 1885, and the shareholders could not have been too pleased with him, considering the 3 percent dividend in prospect, compared with the 27 percent or so he had so glowingly predicted a year earlier. Nevertheless, after the meeting, irrepressible Moreton thought they had been "not unreasonable," and that there was a feeling that, while they were disappointed with the dividend, he was disappointed, too, "plus all the work." Whether any disinterested shareholder actually felt that way, this was surely his conception of how they *should* feel!

Certainly, there was one shareholder who was not so sanguine about Moreton's relationships, especially those with the board. After the meeting, Lord Wharncliffe tried to give Moreton some advice. There had been difficulty over the expenses that Moreton was incurring at Superior, and Moreton was apparently not particularly forthcoming with explanations; this is not hard to imagine, considering his euphoric attachment to that location. The earl reminded him that his figures had been misleading, and urged him to send over a detailed account comparing the expenditures with the original estimate (something Moreton was never much interested in doing).

Then there was the matter of loose business practices, including a power of attorney that Moreton had given Lingham. Wharncliffe reassured him that no one was questioning Lingham's integrity, but that it was not "business." "One must always be more careful about other people's money than about ones own even," said he. Since

Moreton so seldom had much of his own to be careful about, this was not particularly persuasive advice.

Finally, the earl expressed sorrow over conflict at the board level and the breach that had now opened between Frewen and Everett Gray (we have no details on its origin). He hoped this could be papered over. In a "private" comment, Wharncliffe tried to explain why he could not always favor everything Moreton wanted to do. "My position at the Board is always a source of a certain amount of conflicting feelings," said he. "For yourself personally, I have no sentiments but those of real attachment, and true friendship. I am most happy and proud to recognize in you and your charming wife warm friends. But . . . when 'on duty' . . . the man must be put aside for the Director. The board have been very much irritated this year, and set against you by what you call your 'want of discipline' and my efforts have all been directed to peacemakings so far as my sense of duty allowed to do this. I have been occasionally successful, and I softened matters down, and on Thursday I strove to shield you from attack. I hope that you will now make my position a little easier, and regain the confidence of the Board."[1] Later, the earl would have cause to be less friendly to Moreton.

Another sign of trouble brewing appeared a few months later. Moreton had proposed that the company borrow £25,000 ($121,000) to continue to expand, and William Beckett Denison, the banker, himself also a large shareholder, sharply disagreed: "The working of the Company has been hitherto so utterly disappointing and the expectations originally held out have been so far from being realised that, as a large holder of common stock (I believe the largest except your brother), I should much prefer to have my money invested in the Co. safely returned to me, and I have little doubt that if the alternative were offered to the holders of common stock of having the amount of their investments repaid them, or of putting out more money — whether in the shape of fresh money or of foregoing dividends *again* for the purpose of further extensions, they would one and all prefer the former."

Lord Wharncliffe was also opposed to the expansion proposal. "We have exhausted all our share capital," he said, "and the placing of debentures is not practicable in the English market. So there is no point in talking about the extension of our corn feeding operations. We have not got the money." He reminded Moreton that the feeding operations were much less profitable than the shareholders had been led to expect. Therefore, there could be little hope of getting the shareholders to commit new funds to something of such "doubtful value." He suggested that the only prudent policy was to keep the herd at the level it was when the company was formed, and to pay annual dividends from the sale of marketable animals.[2]

Nor was Denison optimistic about the feeding project at Superior. "I am afraid that whatever efforts your sanguine nature may lead you to recommend for adoption, will be met by some new combination on the other side, and that, somehow or other, your fat stock will be beaten out of the markets in the same way that your lean have been."[3] It was an amazingly good analysis by someone not intimately acquainted with Moreton's businesses.

Given troubles with the board in England, Moreton anticipated a better climate in the West. By the end of January, he was once again on the *Servia,* westward bound. He did not know a soul aboard, which must have made for a very trying experience for him. Then the ship encountered a fierce storm. "Ports stove in, boats swept away, bridge skylights smashed, main salon flooded up to the tables while we were at breakfast, and in the midst of all this turmoil and fury of waters, the steam steering gear broke down and for ten minutes we were swept from stem to stern, lying broadside on to the waves." There were four days of these trials, but our Moreton says he did not even become ill; he thought it "comical" how scared many of his shipmates were. "There was a general hunt for hymn books 'and suchlike' all over the ship!!" A group of the grateful passengers (including Moreton) raised £162 in recognition of the work of the captain and crew in this crisis.

After telling Clara this exciting story, he quickly came back to the stark reality. She must continue to try to cultivate important people in London, "because I am sure to have more trouble with my board."

He was met by Lingham in New York, and after seeing the Jeromes, they went west. The weather was still not cooperating, and the train was snowed in on the way across Michigan. They finally reached Superior on the fifteenth, having taken a week to come from New York.[4]

In Superior, he found all was going well. A buyer representing the Marquis de Mores made an offer of five cents a pound for the cattle, and after quibbling briefly over a quarter of a cent, Moreton made the sale. "A splendid sale," he said, "entirely corroborating all I have thought of this place for feeding. . . . Well, it is an enormous smack in the face for my damned board, altho we can afford to take no notice."[5]

On to Cheyenne, where he reported that losses had been small there, "awful though the winter has been elsewhere." This was his favorite formula for dealing with trouble — by comparison, things were worse somewhere else. The *New York Times* reported that the winter of 1884–85 was the worst since Lewis and Clark came west, although the *Times* correspondent thought most losses in Montana were of cattle brought from other states, who had not had sufficient opportunity to acclimate. It was also reported that Indians (Cheyennes, Crows, and Piegans) had burned extensive areas in the Powder River and Tongue River regions, forcing the ranchers to relocate their herds.[6] And Jim Winn of the Big Horn Cattle Company reported that there were seventy-five families of Crows camped in the Big Horn region, and Washington was no help getting them to move back to the reservation.

After a long talk with Hesse, Moreton said he was generally satisfied, but Plunkett noticed that the hard times had dampened even Moreton's spirits.[7] Moreton and Hesse went over the expenses and effected some deep cuts, which Moreton felt must detract from getting the work done. We do know he was seriously considering a plan to get rid of the management position. He wrote to Wharncliffe to suggest that he find a suitable man, who would report directly to the board, at a salary of £1,000 a year.[8] He did not go to the ranch, but instead returned to Canada, where he dined with "dear old Sir John Macdonald" who was "kind and judicious." By the end of March he was on his way back to England.[9] While there, he offered the manager's job to Horace Plunkett at £1,000 per annum. Plunkett declined, for reasons of health.[10] (This offer is particularly interesting, in view of the fury with which Moreton attacked Plunkett's appointment later!)

In April 1885, Moreton gave up the manager's position in America, to be replaced in that role by Thomas W. Peters, his friend Willy. The agreement giving up the managership was not put in writing at that time (this would be the source of some minor disputes later). Frewen agreed to pay Peters's compensation of £1,000 from his own pocket (since the company would otherwise be incurring an additional cost for a manager's salary). The agreement was for the balance of the five years yet to run on Frewen's contract. Provision was also made for the possibility that Peters might resign or be dismissed; in that event, F. A. K. Bennet (from London) could be appointed, or Hesse and Murphy (foremen in Wyoming) could be appointed jointly. Moreton was still obligated to pay the salary, whether or not he had consented to the change in manager.[11] Willy Peters accepted the position on the condition that Moreton would assist him with the job, and the latter readily accepted; that harmony was soon broken. (Moreton later asserted that he always assumed he would pull the strings from off stage.)

While Moreton was thus handing over management in the West, Dick was representing the family at the annual meeting of the Wyoming Stock Growers Association in Cheyenne. There were 360 members and 75 additional applicants. Dick Frewen rose to champion the cause of the nonresident members. The Wyoming members, of course, were effectively captives of the association, since the legislature had made it a part of the state government. But the members in other states and territories had no way to challenge the assessments made by the association, and Frewen suggested that there should be a committee to do this. Moreover, said Dick, the treasurer should make a detailed accounting of expenditures, not merely saying that $50,000 had been spent. In typical Frewen style, he commented that he did not care to remain in an association where the executive committee had such unlimited power.

There was a distinctly measured response to these complaints. Judge Carey, the chairman, noted for the benefit of the assemblage that many of the expenditures were made "in a secret way" and therefore should not be made public! This answer seemed to satisfy everyone, including the representatives of the press (it seems the investigative reporter had not yet appeared on the scene).

The following day, Dick again returned to the fray, complaining that he had been railroaded the day before. He then offered a resolution to limit assessments. The judge opposed the resolution from the chair, and was often applauded during his remarks. As nothing further was being done on the resolution, Dick asked what disposition was to be made of it; Colonel Babbitt moved that it be tabled, and the motion passed! Nevertheless, in the evening session, Dick again raised the subject, and after some amendment, a resolution on assessments was finally passed.

There was other business before the association in addition to Richard Frewen matters. It had become a matter of concern that mavericks were being bought at bargain basement prices; there were specific examples where the Swan outfit had bought some for prices ranging from $.50 to $2.50. (This was, of course, the complaint Moreton had addressed to Alec Swan earlier.) The association finally decided to set a minimum of $10 per head, and Swan agreed to reimburse the association for the difference between what he had paid and the average cost per head of $13.23 for all mavericks sold during 1884. The matter of gambling on ranches, which had been raised by the Buffalo grand jury, was discussed but then laid on the table.[12] An executive session of the association was attended by representatives from both Cheyenne newspapers, who were pledged to secrecy; however, both newspapers published the proceedings after they heard about them from "street gossip."[13]

Colonel Babbitt proposed a committee of five to revise the maverick law. This was opposed by Herbert Teschemacher, who noted that the last legislature referred to the bill before it as having been drafted by three thieves; the Babbitt proposal would open the door to a charge that the three thieves had increased to five. The proposal was lost.[14]

The cattle industry was much discussed in the press, and not all comments were favorable. Earlier in the year, the Cheyenne papers carried stories of the supposed efforts of the big outfits to keep the little stockman out. It was said that George Sailor of Medicine Bow had had his 1,000 head of cattle run off his range by the big outfits. In the Powder River country, cowboys ("intensely English") told a prospective settler that he was on the Frewen range, although he was thirty-five miles from Frewen's "castle." Moreton's efforts to get American cattle admitted to England had drawn the attention of the national press. The Chicago *Breeders Gazette* accused him of exaggerating the number of cattle in the West, contending that there really was no surplus available for export. Another Chicago paper maintained that Frewen had "right and fact and fiction on his side."[15]

While some of the stories about the actions of the big outfits might have been fictional, the death of Si Partridge was real enough. Partridge lived at Old Fort Sanders, and was reportedly lynched for horse stealing by fifteen men. The *Boomerang* commented that the responsibility for the killing "rests with those who will give nothing up."[16]

To underscore its serious intent in the fencing controversy, the federal government detailed troops to assist the government land agents in removing illegal fences, but the *Sun* commented that "most" cattlemen had acquired title to large tracts and would thus be "undisturbed." This reference may have been directed primarily toward the Swan, which had reported 600,000 acres of freehold land in April.[17] The Powder River company, of course, had no land of any significance.

There was an ugly incident in September that had no connection with the cattle industry, but which focused the attention of the nation on the savage forces lurking just beneath the surface of this new land. In Rock Springs, the Chinese population was expelled from the town in an orgy of violence that Governor Francis E. Warren called "the most damnable atrocity and brutal outrage that ever occurred in any country." But the Rawlins *Journal* deplored the uproar that resulted from the "silly gabble of the philanthropic baby press of the East."[18]

While these events were afoot in the West, Dick Frewen and Eugene Jerome were still trying to strike a deal with the syndicate at Superior. In a meeting in New York, a verbal agreement had been reached. But when Jerome produced a written document (Dick had already gone west), the other party refused to sign. Finally, Jerome accepted the best arrangement that he could get agreement on and waited nervously for Moreton's response. The syndicate agreed to sell up to three hundred acres with three-quarters of a mile of waterfront at $320 per acre. They also offered bonuses of free land in return for permanent improvements beginning at $100,000. One hundred free acres would be provided in return for improvements costing as much as $500,000.[19]

Land development at Superior might be attractive, but there were doubts cropping up about the feeding operations, and not just from shareholders in England. Plunkett had been to Superior, and he was not convinced that it would succeed as a feeding operation in competition with feedlots in Nebraska and Iowa. While he acknowledged that Moreton had secured low freight rates to transport both the cattle and their feed, he was not convinced that the Superior operation could afford the burden of having to haul the feed in, rather than having the cattle stop on the way to be fed in the corn belt states.[20]

Wharncliffe had come to the same conclusion about Superior; moreover, he thought the weather was too cold there, compared with

Nebraska. Finally, there was little hope of farming in Superior to grow feed, since the available land had been largely bought up by speculators. "We shall make very little profit out of our cornfed cattle," he said, "but I believe that we should have done worse, had we not tried the experiment."[21]

Moreton was already casting his eyes in another direction. Dick had been sent north to reconnoiter the ranges of Montana and western Canada. He wrote from Ft. McLeod to say that the mosquitoes were worse than any he had seen in India or Africa, but that the cattle looked as good as he had ever seen on any prairie, and that there was a "goodish" lease he would like to get for a Canadian range. The situation was not without difficulty, however; cattle could not be brought into Canada from the states unless a duty of 20 percent was paid, or unless they were held in Canada for two years before sale. He doubted that money could be made if duty had to be paid, even though prices were high, and suggested that Moreton try to get Ottawa to waive the duty before bringing in any cattle.[22] Dick's report had the desired effect; in less than two weeks, Moreton told Clara that he meant to stop in Ottawa to see "dear Old Sir John" about a lease in Canada![23]

He then proceeded to England, in company with some of his own cattle, which had been loaded at Superior. Late in July, the steamer *Croma* docked in the Thames with one hundred head of cattle on board. The majority had been born in Wyoming in 1881, but a few came from Oregon, having walked from there to Wyoming. The press reported Moreton's estimates of the economics of this trade, but the sad truth was stated tersely in a clipping he saved. Entitled "The Cattle Trade," it said, "Our market today is overdone with beasts. This, combined with the extreme heat and the large number on offer . . . has caused depression of the gravest kind."[24]

We do have some data on the costs and realization from the *Croma* shipment. It was a split shipment, twenty-five head for Moreton's personal account, and seventy-five head for the company. The company was charged a total of nearly $2,500 for feed and passage, including shipping charges from Stromsburg to Superior for the animals from that location. Seventy-two head were killed in London, from which the company realized just under $6,200, leaving a margin of $3,700 to pay for the cost of raising the animals. Against that realization had to be offset the amount that could have been obtained by selling the cattle in Chicago or some other American market. In any case, this was the only shipment the company ever made. This was not the importation that Moreton had been urging, since the animals had to be killed on arrival. There was still no legal way to import live animals.

The dispute between Moreton and the board over the proper interpretation of their 1882 agreement had taken a nasty turn. The board had already advised the shareholders that they intended to declare an additional 7 percent dividend related to 1884; this dividend would be paid from the increase of the herd, not from sales of cattle. Moreton was opposed to this dividend, because he saw it as a way of avoiding the obligation to pay him one-third of the increase in the herd at the end of the five-year period. In effect, the board could ensure that the common shareholders would always get a full 10 percent dividend before any profit split was made with Frewen (indeed, Andrew Whitton had already declared that Moreton should be paid nothing until the common shareholders had received their full 10 percent dividends). Moreton went to his solicitor, Spencer Whitehead, for advice, and the latter employed a barrister, Montagu Cookson, Q.C., to render an opinion. Cookson recommended that Frewen seek an injunction against the board's action.[25] Frewen read this opinion to the board at the meeting in which he gave up the manager's position.

After much needling by Moreton's solicitor, the company's solicitors finally wrote to say that the board was going to declare an additional dividend of 6 percent (not 7 percent, as had been threatened) out of the increased value of the herd, but that they did not intend "at the present" to give notice of the dividend to the shareholders. Spencer Whitehead thereupon replied that this action would bring an immediate request for arbitration.[26] Meanwhile, Moreton was sounding out possible friendly replacements for some of the directors.

But even such a good friend as Lord Rosslyn could grow weary. "For myself I wish that I had never heard of a horned beast," he said to Moreton. "I will tell you a story. I telegraphed my factor, 'Buy all horned beasts.' The message arrived, 'Bury all horrid beasts.' I wish we could."[27]

By this time, the harmony between Moreton and Willy Peters had entirely evaporated. Peters had told the board that the feeding operation was an "utter failure," and he had recommended against the Alberta lease, thus drawing forth an anguished letter from Moreton which began, "What are you driving at? I fear you will upset the coach for me." After arguing that the Alberta project was the only hope for paying off the preferred shareholders in 1887, Moreton offered to come at once to take over the reins again, which he now said he had given up only because of his wife's "condition."[28] (Clara's "condition" was the impending birth of Clare, born September 9. Moreton told Lord Rosslyn that she was "not beautiful, but of size and ferocity indescribable!")[29] Peters replied coldly in October with some complaints of his own. He felt aggrieved that Moreton had arrayed himself in opposition, although he still expected that in the end Frewen would find cause to thank him for his work. This was not to be.

Although Wharncliffe did not entirely agree with Peters's assessment that the cattle feeding operation had been an "utter failure," still he thought that the prudent course was to pay dividends from sale of culled animals, and he thought Peters quite qualified to decide how much the herd should be reduced by such annual culling.[30] Peters had by this time become quite a thorn in Moreton's side. Near the end of October, Murphy told Moreton he did not know how much longer he could stand Peters, who was "meddling" with every aspect of the business. Murphy thought the company could have made $30,000 to $40,000 by feeding the cattle, but Peters would not agree.[31] Of course, neither Murphy nor Lingham were making it easy for Peters to succeed. Although Lingham thought Peters was beginning to see some of the errors of his ways, he still wrote Frewen, "I think it would be as well for Murph and I to let him get well stuck in his own mud. I think the swelling is going down in his head."[32] On the other hand, Plunkett thought Peters would make a good manager if he were kept on.

Moreton brought Lingham over to England from Superior to argue his case, and this annoyed Wharncliffe, who warned him that the expense of the trip would not be paid by the company if he had any voice in the matter. The earl sternly scolded Moreton for his attacks against directors Henry Nevill and Whitton, threatening him with exclusion from further board meetings if he could not refrain from such outbursts.[33] Two days later, the earl did relent and agreed to see if a board meeting could be called to hear Lingham's arguments. "But," he added, "*money* is the one thing to be considered first."[34] Indeed it was.

The following month another scolding came from Wharncliffe,

this time because of Moreton's active pen. He had collected an impressive book of clippings from his efforts to secure importation rights
for live cattle, and he had also had time to write a number of letters
to the editors urging the coinage of silver (in addition to gold). But
in the fall of 1885 he decided to take up the pen to write about the
western ranges of the United States.

In August, the *Economist* carried the news that President Cleveland had issued a proclamation against illegal fencing of the public
domain. Following the appearance of that article, there was a letter
to the editor of the Edinburgh *Courant* pointing out that the Prairie
Cattle Company (which had been mentioned in the article) was not
in fact the subject of specific government action on fencing. Moreton
could not resist the opportunity to get into the argument. He proceeded to take Cleveland to task for having abandoned the states rights
principles of the Democratic party and thereby adopting instead the
position of the Republicans. On the subject of land titles, he said,
"I have always believed the Western land titles . . . were a snare and
a delusion, merely 'titles' till some one arrived to question them." After
declaring that the cattle business was in a "crisis," he urged anyone
having cattle to market them, since the prospect was for extremely
low prices until the grassfed cattle in the U.S. had been brought to
market.

Wharncliffe told Moreton that such statements would surely
injure the market for cattle company shares and suggested he be more
politic, although he ended, "Pray accept this letter in a most friendly
spirit."[35] Frewen responded that he had only *initialed* the letter he sent
to the newspaper (of course the editor well knew what name went
with "M.F."). Then he lamely argued that true panics arise from lack
of knowledge, and that the shareholder would be better prepared for
the coming crisis having read the helpful knowledge in his letter![36]

A few days later, the earl told Moreton, "My present care is the
Pref. dividend, which must be met, if the company is to remain
solvent."[37] Here for the first time was the specter of the preferred shareholders, whom Moreton had included in the capital structure so that
they could be bought out within five years. Now, the situation would
be very different if the money could not be found to pay their dividends. Instead of being bought out, they could be running the company!

In Wyoming, there were ominous signs that the industry was

not doing well. Scanty recoveries of saleable animals heightened the need to remove every source of expense, and the feeling was widespread among the big operators that cattle rustling was a major expense. In September 1885, the executive committee of the stock growers association drew up a formal list of those who were considered rustlers of mavericks and other people's cattle. The "blacklist" already existed in substance (Frewen mentioned it the previous year), but this one was printed and issued from the secretary's office. It carried the names of twenty-eight men, under headings listing six different classes of offenses, including branding mavericks, horse stealing, and cattle stealing; ten of those on this famous blacklist were from Johnson County.

Conditions on the range were bad. In contrast with the optimism Moreton had felt in the spring, Fred Hesse now estimated that the loss from the last winter had been 15 percent; the calf brand was about 1,000 short of the prior year's total.[38] The winter of 1885 was not starting out well, and in December, the *Big Horn Sentinel* reported that large numbers of range animals had been driven to the town by the cold weather, in search of food and shelter.[39] The *Sun* reported that cattlemen in the Powder River country were driving their stock into the mountains, as there was no range at all on the prairies.[40] Dick wrote to say that there was "not a blade of grass on Powder or Crazy Woman" and that the only hope was to move the cattle to the British North West (Canada). (He was still without money, and although he was thinking of going home to England, there was the dilemma that "one can't live in England without some, and I have absolutely none.")[41]

On his way home in the fall, Horace Plunkett reported that the range had not recovered at all; the cattle were scattered, even over on Jim Winn's range on the Nowood. He recommended that in the spring the roundup should concentrate strongly on the fringe ranges, as the cattle would be all over other ranges.

While things were bad in Wyoming, Superior was not a great success, either. Lingham saw not "a shadow of a chance" of a common dividend, since only 2,400 steers had been taken from the range, together with 600 cows to be fattened, and it was too late to gather any more cattle. He hoped that the hayfields at Superior would yield a good crop the following season (he expected to plant 500 acres), but they were not ready for 1885 feeding.

Both Plunkett and Sturgis had set up feeding operations, but they had chosen the corn country for their locations, at Blair and Gilmore, Nebraska, respectively. Frank Kemp went to see them and found them in "splendid" style. Sturgis could feed 3,250 head of cattle at Gilmore in eighteen minutes.[42]

Later in the spring, Horace Plunkett suggested cooperative management of their two outfits, and Moreton agreed. Plunkett wanted to take some of the grazing load off the Powder River range by keeping the northern cattle off that range and sending the female stock and bulls into the mountains. He also wanted cooperation on wages. A final point of annoyance was some claim jumping by Peters's men, although Plunkett supposed that it was not in fact authorized by Peters.[43]

The joint operation with Plunkett's EK outfit went very well. In a report to Frewen, Plunkett flatly stated that without this cooperation there would have been a regular disaster, although conditions were still bad. The calf crop was short, and the drought was an additional burden. Plunkett was particularly critical of the horses of the 76 outfit, which he thought were largely Murphy's "bargains in horseflesh." He was concerned about the herds: "I fear losses from all causes on all ranges are much larger every year than we ever would allow." Although both he and Frewen shared this as an opinion, he said gloomily, "We are nearing a strong documentation." He was correct, of course. When the time came to liquidate the big herds, they were not there.

Plunkett promised to help the Powder River Company in any way he could (because it was near his own range, and he feared disruption in the event of a failure). He felt that it could pull through, although it could never pay 40 percent, or even 20 percent dividends. He had also been drawn into the difficulties that Dick's company was experiencing, and he had thereby earned that volatile Frewen's displeasure (as he would one day earn Moreton's as well).[44]

In early November, Wharncliffe once again tried to reason with Moreton, telling him that it was unreasonable to assume that the company could sell £15,000 of debentures to raise more working capital, and warning him that there would be trouble if shareholders did not receive their dividends. He acknowledged that there was little prospect for Moreton to divide any profits at the end of five years.[45]

Wharncliffe was growing uneasy about his private correspondence with Moreton and finally urged him to write an official letter to the board.[46] Moreton promptly composed a comparatively contrite letter to Charles Fitch Kemp, in which he asked to be allowed to see reports from the West so that he would be in a better position to communicate with shareholders, who contacted him "almost daily." Kemp was obviously suspicious of this request, seeing in it an opening for Moreton to be in direct communication with the field operations (besides, if the shareholders wanted to know something, they could be referred to the company). Frewen gave assurance that he only intended to communicate at "home"; he could not resist needling Kemp with the share price, which was under £3.[47]

Despite his statements to Fitch Kemp, Moreton was not without access to western information. Frank Kemp had written that Peters had filed desert land entries on the "rest of the River," and Moreton promptly wrote to Wharncliffe, quoting "a most reliable source" (perhaps to avoid betrayal of Fitch Kemp's brother—actually, Murphy passed on the same information later in the month) and warning the earl that these filings would cost $75,000, which would be "clean thrown away," since the land could not be proved up (i.e., irrigated) as required under the act.[48] Wharncliffe replied coolly that he was sure Peters and Kemp had received good legal advice. Moreton responded the next day, "You are not a lawyer," and went on to give the earl his own legal opinion as to the futility of the filings! (He thought the land was timbered within the meaning of the act and therefore not subject to being filed on.)[49]

Dick was a continuing source of information to Moreton, and he was now consistently urging that his brother "sack" Peters and take back the management of the ranch. He was longing for closer association again—claiming he was now older and could get along—and he had now hatched the idea of moving the headquarters of both ranches to Chicago. It is not clear what this would accomplish, particularly since he was consistently critical of the Cheyenne offices as being too far from the range. He also reported that Peters had moved into new offices in Cheyenne, with a private office for himself, while Frank Kemp had to share his office with others.

There was continuing trouble over a herd of cattle Murphy had sent north to the Powder River, and ultimately to a new range in Montana. Kemp had accused Murphy of falsifying the book count, because he had tallied 4,000 cattle and they were short on delivery. Murphy told Moreton that the exact count was 4,158, but that he had given the round figure to Kemp, remarking ruefully, "as you told me not to be *accurate* about it, so I did as I have told you." When the herds came down the trail to Hesse, he had them counted, and his total was nearly 1,000 short of Murphy's tally. Dick expected that poor Murph would get fired for his trouble, but he was inclined to accept Murphy's version of the story (Dick was right about the firing: Murphy sent Moreton the letter [appropriately written on pink paper] in which Peters terminated Murphy's employment with the company).[50] While Dick was very negative about Peters, he did think Hesse would work well with Moreton if Peters were removed.[51]

Moreton was not keeping up with the demands of his creditors. To pay his expenses, he was obliged to borrow money where he could; there was £2,000 from Wharncliffe's nephew and £4,000 from Charles E. Lyon (in addition to £2,000 borrowed previously from Lyon).[52] The money he had borrowed from Pierre Lorillard had now grown from $45,000 to over $50,000 and the £400 he paid in late 1885 did not even cover the accrued interest.[53] At the end of the year, he had to renew his notes with the Post bank, paying interest at 20 percent on principal of $96,000. Post expressed the forlorn hope that Moreton might raise something to apply to the indebtedness.[54] Frewen's friend C. E. Lyon also had to write, expressing his disappointment for the lack of payment on the £4,000 he had loaned: "If you can't pay, of course, you can't and I must somehow make the best of it."[55]

With all of his troubles, Moreton still had time to contemplate a political life. He wrote to Lord Rosslyn that he was off to Barrow-in-Furness, where he had a project of "huge size" to work up; that project was to stand for Parliament. Unfortunately, he soon learned that his constituents were, as he told Lingham, "Socialists." *St. Stephen's Review* reported that he had retired from the contest, saying, "He is strong on vaccination, the Barrow people are not; he dislikes free schools, the Barrow men don't. These little disagreements ruffle the mind of Moreton Frewen." Other press reports ungraciously quoted constituents who attended the Liberal association where Moreton was "on approval." Moreton had treated the assembly to some of his original thinking, and one constitutent commented, "It's positively disgraceful that every fad and hobby should be trotted out," while another said, "He's neither one thing nor the other." Parliament would have to wait.

As always when trouble was particularly vexing, there was a new idea to distract Moreton from depression. W. H. Cruikshank of the Chicago, St. Paul, Minneapolis & Omaha Railway wrote to Dick suggesting that the iron ore in the Duluth area could be developed if fuel for the purpose could be obtained from peat bogs. He thought the resource could be acquired at not more than seventy-five dollars per acre. Dick promptly gave the letter to Moreton.[56]

Moreton's deteriorating situation with the board reached a climax on November 11, when he formally demanded that the arrangement with Peters be terminated, effective July 1, 1886. He went on to argue that winter feeding was the only way that the low prices of September and October could be avoided; Peters, of course, was totally opposed to winter feeding. Moreton also wanted to sell some of the breeding stock to raise money to finance the feeding operation, but to do so he had to move this stock some distance away from their range (so that brands would not be confused). For this purpose, he had recommended moving part of the herd to Alberta, and here again Peters was opposed. Moreton closed by declaring that he had hoped to spend more time at home but would consent to go to America the following year to manage the ranch.[57]

The response of the board was delivered in a letter from Fitch Kemp on November 26. Kemp said the board intended to enforce its agreement with Moreton, including his obligation to pay Peters's salary for the remainder of the five-year period. After assuring him that the board entirely approved Peters's policies, Kemp closed by saying, "The Directors have no intention of proposing to ask you to go to America next year."[58]

Although the company's accounts would not be completed until the following February, they would then show that a total of 4,569 head of cattle were sold, a couple of hundred more than the previous year, but less than £29,000 ($140,000) had been realized from the sales. The most sobering information was the calf brand total, which was only 7,805, or nearly 1,400 fewer than the previous year. The book count for the herd at the end of the year was 48,550, about 6,000 fewer than 1884, as a result of a 5 percent loss provision and a special reduction of 7,000 in the Rawhide herd.[59] The value of the herd on the balance sheet was therefore reduced from £316,000 ($1,529,000) at the end of 1884, to only £282,000 ($1,365,000) at the end of 1885, although Moreton would contend that this reduction properly reflected only a drop in value per animal (he estimated £1 per animal), not reduced numbers.[60] Nevertheless, after expenses of £12,000 in Wyoming and £2,000 in London, there was £14,000 ($68,000) to carry to the dividend account; at least the preferred dividend could be paid for another year. Unfortunately, this sum did not exist in cash. There were certain deferred items on the balance sheet for the feeding operation at Superior, and Moreton himself owed the company over £800 ($3,900), which he presumably did not have the means to pay even if he were inclined to do so.[61] The stage was set for more difficulties in the new year.

On November 28, Wharncliffe wrote to say that he would henceforth take his advice in written form, rather than listen to various hearsay evidence.[62] This coolness was doubtless brought on by a fateful step Moreton had taken in the interim. On the tenth day of November, Frewen filed an action in chancery in the High Court of Justice, naming as defendants the Powder River Cattle Company, Limited, and individually His Grace the Duke of Manchester, K.P., the Right Honorable The Earl of Wharncliffe, Lord Henry Nevill, Sir Frederick Milner, Bart., W. Tipping, and Andrew Whitton, being all of the directors of the company.[63] It was a step from which there was no backward turning.

Notes to Chapter 9

1. Earl of Wharncliffe to Frewen, January 18, 1885, Frewen Papers.
2. Earl of Wharncliffe to Frewen, August 15, 1885, Frewen Papers.
3. William Beckett Denison to Frewen, April 14, 1885, Frewen Papers.
4. Frewen to Clara Frewen, February 10, 12, 15, 1885, Frewen Papers.
5. Frewen to Clara Frewen, February 16, 1885, Frewen Papers.
6. *New York Times* (dateline Fort Keogh, Montana), March 29, 1885.
7. Plunkett diary, June 19, 1885.
8. Frewen to Clara Frewen, February 18, 1885, Frewen Papers.
9. Frewen diary, May 19, 1885, Frewen Papers.
10. Plunkett diary, March 27, 1885.
11. Charles Fitch Kemp to Frewen, November 26, 1885; and draft memorandum of agreement between the Powder River Cattle Company, Limited, and Moreton Frewen, Frewen Papers. The company's solicitors were still trying to get Moreton to put the agreement in writing in November, when he was already suing the company for other reasons. Stibbard, Gibson & Sykes to Spencer Whitehead, November 11, 1885.
12. *Democratic Leader*, April 7, 8, 9, 1885.
13. *Cheyenne Daily Sun*, April 8, 1885.
14. *Cheyenne Daily Sun*, April 9, 1885.
15. *Democratic Leader*, February 12, March 3, 26, 1885.
16. *Cheyenne Daily Sun*, August 13, 1885.

17. *Democratic Leader,* April 16, 1885.

18. *Cheyenne Daily Sun,* September 15, 1885; and *Democratic Leader,* September 12, 1885.

19. Eugene M. Jerome to Frewen, March 17, 1885, Frewen Papers.

20. Ibid.

21. Earl of Wharncliffe to Frewen, June 5, 1885, Frewen Papers.

22. Richard Frewen to Frewen, June 20, 1885, Frewen Papers.

23. Frewen to Clara Frewen, July 1, 1885, Frewen Papers.

24. *Birmingham Daily Post,* July 27, 1885; and *Times* (London), July 28, 1885.

25. Opinion of Montagu Cookson, April 15, 1885.

26. Spencer Whitehead to Frewen, August 14, 1885, Frewen Papers.

27. Earl of Rosslyn to Frewen, August 15, 1885, Frewen Papers.

28. Frewen to T. W. Peters, August 6, 1885, Frewen Papers.

29. Frewen to the Earl of Rosslyn, n.d., Frewen Papers.

30. Earl of Wharncliffe to Frewen, August 15, 1885, Frewen Papers.

31. E. W. Murphy to Frewen, October 23, 1885, Frewen Papers.

32. F. R. Lingham to Frewen, October 23, 1885, Frewen Papers.

33. Earl of Wharncliffe to Frewen, August 15, 1885, Frewen Papers.

34. Earl of Wharncliffe to Frewen, August 17, 1885, Frewen Papers.

35. Earl of Wharncliffe to Frewen, September 13, 1885, Frewen Papers.

36. Frewen to the Earl of Wharncliffe, n.d., Frewen Papers.

37. Earl of Wharncliffe to Frewen, September 19, 1885, Frewen Papers.

38. Fred G. S. Hesse to Frewen, October 26, 1885, Frewen Papers.

39. *Big Horn Sentinel,* December 12, 1885.

40. *Cheyenne Daily Sun,* November 14, 1885.

41. Richard Frewen to Frewen, October 8, 1885, Frewen Papers.

42. Frank Kemp to Frewen, October 6, 1885, Frewen Papers.

43. Horace C. Plunkett to Frewen, May 21, 1885, Frewen Papers.

44. Horace C. Plunkett to Frewen, October 11, 1885, Frewen Papers.

45. Earl of Wharncliffe to Frewen, November 10, 1885, Frewen Papers.

46. Earl of Wharncliffe to Frewen, October 2, 1885, Frewen Papers.

47. Frewen to Charles Fitch Kemp, October 6, 8, 1885, Frewen Papers.

48. Frewen to the Earl of Wharncliffe, October 11, 1885, Frewen Papers.

49. Earl of Wharncliffe to Frewen, October 25, 1885, and Frewen to the Earl of Wharncliffe, October 26, 1885, Frewen Papers.

50. T. W. Peters to E. W. Murphy, December 5, 1885.

51. Richard Frewen to Frewen, November 15, 1885, Frewen Papers.

52. Affidavit of Moreton Frewen, April 29, 1885, Frewen Papers.

53. Frewen's account with P. Lorillard & Co., October 20, 1885.

54. Morton E. Post to Frewen, December 26, 1885, Frewen Papers.

55. C. E. Lyon to Frewen, n.d., Frewen Papers.

56. W. H. Cruikshank to Richard Frewen, December 23, 1885.

57. Frewen to Charles Fitch Kemp, November 11, 1885, Frewen Papers.

58. Charles Fitch Kemp to Frewen, November 26, 1885, Frewen Papers.

59. Tally book in the possession of Fred E. Hesse.

60. "Plaintiff's Comments on the Defense for Mr. Spencer Whitehead," n.d.

61. "The Powder River Cattle Company Limited, Balance Sheet at 30th November, 1885," February 12, 1886.

62. Earl of Wharncliffe to Frewen, November 28, 1885, Frewen Papers.

63. *Praecipe* for Appearance, November 30, 1885.

· *10* ·

Of Lawsuits and Other Alarums

*T*he statement of claim filed in the High Court of Justice recited the fact that the directors had declared a dividend of 6 percent for 1884 out of the increased value of the herd; it was asserted that this action was designed to deprive Moreton of his share of the increased herd at the end of the five years. He asked the court to issue an injunction against the deferred dividend and to prevent the board from declaring any further such dividends. For their part, the directors threw down the gauntlet and advised Frewen through their solicitors that they intended to declare a further deferred dividend at the next meeting in February 1886.[1]

Although there was grousing among his friends, there was still a good bit of support. Charles E. Lyon, who had purchased Powder River shares at a premium in the expectation of 10 or 20 percent dividends, had suffered the additional indignity of having loaned Moreton cash, which had not been repaid, principal or interest. Yet he was still prepared to support Moreton's contention that the board should be essentially "swept away."

Moreton was not idle while he waited for the shareholders to convene. He and his friend Lyon both wrote to the shareholders, urging them not to give the directors their proxies, and calling for a committee of inquiry to examine the affairs of the company. Moreton put in another plug for moving the herd to better ranges in the north.[2]

There were some favorable responses. Lord Onslow said that he had already given his proxy to Wharncliffe but was now sorry for having done so, and Lord Rosslyn was still favorably disposed towards Frewen, although he asked to be relieved of the chore of attending the shareholders' meeting unless it was "needful."[3] Rosslyn had also spoken to Horace Plunkett, who was "not sanguine" about the Powder

River company's prospects; the earl was now of the opinion that the company ought to be wound up and the proceeds paid to the shareholders.[4] At Rosslyn's request, Horace agreed to give the secretary of the company the benefit of his opinion in writing, but this effort did not have the desired result.

In a thoughtful letter to Frewen, Plunkett outlined what he proposed to say to Kemp; for the most part, he endorsed Peters's management of the range. "He consulted with me, worked with me and was in my confidence." Moreover, Plunkett was not sure of the desirability of the move to Alberta, because of the great risk associated with the experiment; he said his own company could not afford the risk, even if it showed a 50 percent paper profit. Finally, he was not willing to give unqualified endorsement to the Superior feeding operations, but preferred to wait until the winter's operations were completed.

"I know my dear Moreton, you will say I have 'gone back on you,'" Plunkett continued, "but time will justify me."[5] It was a decidedly bad sign. So long as Plunkett supported Frewen, they made a formidable team; it would not be the same with Plunkett on the other side.

The board did not suffer the indignity of Frewen's lawsuit without retaliating. At the March meeting, one of Frewen's letters of the prior year was read to the board. In order to emphasize his commitment to the Superior project, he had grandly offered to buy the Superior assets back at a 10 percent premium over the company's costs, adding, "the Company are at liberty to hold me to this offer at any time they please." The board passed a resolution accepting this conditional offer for a period of two years, in case they should want to sell the Superior property.[6]

The shareholders met on February 24, 1886, and at this meeting Moreton's work bore fruit. One editor described the meeting thusly: "Mud was thrown freely by the directors at the manager, and by the manager at the directors." The Duke of Manchester had resigned from the board, and Lord Wharncliffe was in the chair; he opened with a blast at Moreton's management, stating that Frewen was largely responsible for the present condition of the company. He noted that there were shortages on the Rawhide range, which had been discovered by Peters, and that the packing house at Sherman was worthless. Lyon followed this statement by asserting that the losses were no greater than for other cattle companies and could hardly be laid at Moreton's feet.

Then Moreton gave his rebuttal. He said that Peters could not possibly know whether there was a shortage of 10 head or 10,000 on the Rawhide range, since no count had been made, and since that range was integral with the Powder River ranges. Moreover, the packing house was still intact, and therefore was not worthless, although it had never been given a fair test. After a long review of the financial results, he turned to the matter of management. "The fact is," he said, "if we shareholders are to get our dividends, we require men who will live on our ranges, not club loungers." There were supporting statements from Ted and Dick, for an unusual show of Frewen solidarity.

Peters's formal report to the meeting was in writing. He was not particularly concerned over the lack of grass on the Powder River ranges, saying, "The same thing has occurred in other years." His solution for the future was irrigation, which he thought would entail a cost of about $4.50 per acre. On the matter of Moreton's proposal to move cattle to Alberta, he said, "I can see no good in it, and certainly much risk." He thought it would cost $2.50 per head and would require the expense of separate outfits for each 2,000 head; he did not think it could be done before the end of July, which would place the last herds in Alberta as late as the first of November. He also expected that Canadian duty would have to be paid, making the cost of the move $38,500 in total. Once in Canada, the cattle could not be sold for two years.[7] At the meeting, Peters took the floor to argue against leaving the Powder River range. In addition, he threatened to leave the company if he were required to give up the Cheyenne office.

A new board was elected, and the shareholders gave Moreton the committee of inquiry he had requested, a new shareholders committee under the chairmanship of Frewen's good friend Lord Rosslyn. The meeting then adjourned for a fortnight, to await the special committee report.

The special committee consisted of Lord Rosslyn, Lord Belper, William Beckett Denison, Charles Waring, and Charles E. Lyon. It was charged with the responsibility to "look into matters to decide what was best to be done," and to cut expenses.

The committee came down on Moreton's side of the arguments and against Peters's assessment as contained in his report. Their consensus was that the range was "considerably overstocked." Peters's irrigation suggestion was dismissed out of hand, because of lack of funds. The committee's recommendation was to move a portion of the herd to Nebraska and Superior (it was expected that 3,000 to 4,000 could be accommodated there). It was noted that Frewen had secured a lease on Mosquito Creek in Alberta, which he was willing to assign to the company. The committee recommended that this be done and that 7,500 head be sent north. It was recognized that the border crossing might not be effected before winter, but it was still expected that the herd could be wintered south of the Canadian border.

On the matter of finances, the committee recommended efforts to place £15,000 of debentures, and failing that, to borrow in New York at rates not exceeding 7 percent. It was recommended that the dividend on the preferred shares be withheld, and that the company seek to redeem the preferred shares as soon as possible, and at par. The committee recommended that the expenses of the company be reduced, both in England and in America.[8]

The next meeting of the shareholders was held on March 11, and it was decided that Moreton Frewen should be sent west at once to implement the recommendations of the special committee. Lord Wharncliffe thereupon resigned. The new board, consisting of Andrew Whitton, F. A. K. Bennet, Charles Lyon, and Sir Henry Nevill, met March 13 and proposed to add Lord Rosslyn and Charles Waring to their number (both were members of the special committee). Difficulties soon developed, however, because Rosslyn was unwilling to serve on the board unless Waring also consented and that consent was not forthcoming.[9]

The representative of the preferred shareholders, William Mackenzie, whom Moreton never seems to have identified as a potential problem, then weighed in. He had been at the shareholders' meeting, and the next day he wired Lord Rossyln that there were no buyers for preferred shares, adding sourly, "Such scenes as those of yesterday would damage any company, no matter how good."[10] The following day he told the earl that the preference shareholders were in a strong position but had no wish to push things so long as they were reasonably treated. However, "if any attempt be made to scale them, as the Americans say, they will be forced to stand upon their rights."

He also pointedly noted that the preference shareholders had retained counsel to look after those rights. Although Mackenzie did not want to interfere with anything outside the province of the preference shareholders, he did offer the opinion that it was unwise to relieve Peters of the management role at this critical time, and he also thought Frewen should be kept "at arms length" until the present troubles were over.[11]

Apparently, Lord Rosslyn responded to Mackenzie that the preferred shareholders could only be paid from profits, for the latter reminded Rosslyn that the preferred shareholders had first call on the assets in the event of liquidation, remarking dryly, "If it stops paying these dividends, I think it will be in liquidation very soon." Still, he said, "I personally have no wish to go to war."[12] But war was not far away.

This all frightened Rosslyn, who told Moreton, "You must not count upon me." He had had a conversation with Andrew Whitton, who had threatened to resign if the cattle were moved to Alberta; since Rosslyn would not agree to sit if they were not moved, the two positions seemed irreconcilable. Rosslyn did agree to act as mediator with the preferred shareholders, who he thought would be willing to be paid off at par.[13]

Nevertheless, Rosslyn was willing to serve temporarily on the board to carry out the recommendations of the committee he had chaired. He wanted to get the Alberta move started, and he wanted to relieve Peters "at once."[14] The earl's correspondence with Mackenzie continued, and from that quarter there was little encouragement for reinstating Moreton as manager. Mackenzie urged that a good manager be found and that the move to Alberta not be attempted until then. On the matter of redeeming the preferred shares, Rosslyn had suggested giving these shareholders £120,000 in cattle, but Mackenzie demurred at this idea, suggesting instead £120,000 in debentures.[15] A few days later, Mackenzie wrote again, urging that the Alberta move not be made and this time making the thinly veiled threat that the preferred shareholders would prevent it if the company persisted.[16]

Rosslyn was a great ally of Moreton. Although not in the best of health, he said, "My sincerest wish is for your advantage and I think nothing at all of myself or my losses," although he admitted that he was "but a poor financier and a very bad fighter."[17] In his search for support, Rosslyn asked Waring for his comments. Waring suggested Horace Plunkett as manager in America. He agreed with the move to Alberta (now 5,000 head, not 7,500), but only under Plunkett's supervision. He also agreed that the London expenses should be reduced and that no preferred dividend be paid.[18]

Soon Dick was writing, eager to help, although he was flat broke ("I will sell for any reasonable offer.") He had met with Murphy, and he had seen Peters, but "I did not speak to him" (although he did shake hands with Mrs. Peters). He had already told Murphy to arrange for trail outfits to begin the move to Alberta; if Peters tried to interfere in any way, "there will be a good reason to oust Peters." Of course, Dick had never been one to stand on ceremony, and he seems not to have questioned how he got the authority to give these orders.[19]

Money problems continued to dog Moreton's heels, both personally and in company affairs. He was reduced to borrowing £1,000 for a month on a demand note, giving the stock of Dick's company as security.[20] The following month, two loans he had made with friends were assigned, together with collateral, to others who could not be expected to be so tolerant on deferred payment. The £5,000 note secured by 1,400 shares of the company was assigned by Lord Wharncliffe to Ralph Granville, and two notes totalling £5,000 and secured by 800 shares of the company (together with Moreton's share in the increase of the herd) was assigned by Charles Edward Lyon to his brother, A. O. Lyon.[21]

Peters wrote to Fitch Kemp in April to urge prompt action on the company's overdraft at Cheyenne, which now amounted to $19,700.[22] Dick stepped into the breach and wrote a few days later that he had arranged £12,000 for the company at 6 percent (or "really 10 percent"), on condition that he or Moreton complete the arrangements. One is inclined to be startled at the ease with which this could be done until Dick casually notes the things he has not yet done. "I have not of course got Hesse's, Carter's or Lingham's consent to use their names," said he, "and I have not yet seen Corlett. But there is no doubt you are legally manager." So it appears he had arranged the loan with the Post bank (without seeing lawyer Corlett) on the condition that he get the signatures of the three foremen, and on the assurance that Moreton was once more general manager, which was not true.[23] In the end, the board would not send money from London, nor would it authorize him to borrow in Wyoming. There soon developed the squeeze that would again force Moreton's resignation, this time for good.

Dick knew that it was far from settled that Moreton was to become manager in Wyoming, and the rumors pointed persistently to Horace Plunkett as the likeliest choice. This set Dick into a fury. "Plunkett has played Hell with my company and now will with you and yours," he told Moreton, "and I won't work with him. . . . After the gravest profession of friendship he has done more harm than either Kemp or Peters."[24]

Moreton used the "deal" Dick had arranged with Post as leverage to call a special meeting of the shareholders. Since Lord Rosslyn and Charles Waring had refused to serve on the board, he was badly in need of friendly directors. He wrote to Fitch Kemp and offered to find £12,000 ($58,000) at 6 percent on condition that he and his brother were elected to the board. In that event, he would waive the right he felt he had to resume management in Wyoming.[25] The deal Moreton was offering was, of course, not a deal at all. Even Dick had originally hedged as to whether the rate was 6 or 10 percent, but he had nevertheless sent a cable to Moreton saying, "Can get all money necessary at six if you approve home management, you or I managing here." Later, he wrote to say he had sent the cable so Moreton could "finish them," even though "it is not quite absolutely a fact that we can get all the money we want." So now we have the usually pessimistic Dick acting like the optimistic Moreton—a deadly combination indeed!

But the board had received another offer. Dick learned on April 15 that Peters had received a cable from London informing him that the money could be raised there, subject to the consent of shareholders, and that Plunkett was to be the manager in America.[26]

The formal notice of the extraordinary meeting was dated April 20, and the shareholders were informed that it had not been possible to float the debenture issue of £15,000 because of the events at the general meeting in February. As a consequence, other financing had to be arranged, consisting of £13,000 in debentures and £5,000 in a temporary loan. This financing was conditional on the election of a board consisting of F. A. K. Bennet, Edward Frewen or Sir Frederick Milner, Everett Gray, Charles E. Lyon, Lord Henry Nevill, William Tipping, and Andrew Whitton.

In preparation for the special meeting, Moreton decided to harangue the shareholders once more, in a printed pamphlet. Going over the familiar arguments, he spiced up his presentation by noting that Andrew Whitton, the largest preferred shareholder, by voting for the preferred dividend at the time when the falling price of cattle had impaired the company's capital, was taking money from the common shareholders' pockets and putting it into his own. He specifically asserted that £2,000 had been taken from him and £400 of that sum given to Whitton.[27]

Naturally, such assertions were not likely to spread oil on troubled waters. Mackenzie told Moreton that the introduction of personalities did no good for anyone. He asked why Moreton was not suggesting the movement of the *entire* herd to Alberta, if the movement of some made economic sense, so as to avoid divided supervision. "I regard with fear, I might almost say with terror, so much division," he said. "The cattle properties which do best are those that are concentrated under one management in the same locality."[28] A few days later, Mackenzie wearily asked Frewen what it was he wanted. "The board is pledged to your policy, and Plunkett is a man of whose honour there can I presume be no doubt." He had some advice for Moreton: "If I were you, I would certainly take up any mission which would pay you better, and not worry myself any more about the matter." On the matter of money "available" in the West at 6 percent, he said, "Depend upon it there is a screw loose somewhere. . . . The mere offer of money at this rate on the security of cattle should be sufficient to put you on your guard."[29]

Moreton's good friend Charles Lyon (who was rapidly sinking into bankruptcy) was not to be present at the meeting, but he gave Frewen his last measure of support. In a letter he asked to have read to the meeting, he accused Whitton, Gray, Kemp, and Stibbard of being opposed to the Alberta move, in spite of the stated intention to carry out the special committee report. He was himself on a journey to Alberta and promised to send back a report on those ranges when he got there.[30]

Joseph Richardson (who was also Moreton's creditor, but still a friend at this time) wrote to Clara, asking her to intervene to keep Moreton from expressing his opinions "quite so freely" at the meeting.[31]

The meeting was held on May 3, and it was not a congenial one. After the accounts were provisionally approved, Lord Rosslyn proposed an amendment to the slate of directors, to replace Sir Frederick Milner and Everett Gray with Edward and Moreton Frewen. The chairman ruled the amendment out of order, and the original slate passed by a show of hands (not by number of shares). It was then demanded that a poll be taken, and the slate lost. After some more parliamentary maneuvering, the two Frewens were finally elected to the board.[32]

Notes to Chapter 10

1. Stibbard, Gibson & Sykes to Spencer Whitehead, January 25, 1886, Frewen Papers.

2. Frewen to Shareholders of the Powder River Cattle Company, Ltd., February 8, 1886; and C. E. Lyon to the Shareholders of the Powder River Cattle Company, Ltd., February 5, 1886, Frewen Papers.

3. Earl of Onslow to Frewen, February 22, 1886; and Earl of Rosslyn to Frewen, February 23, 1886, Frewen Papers.

4. Earl of Rosslyn to Frewen, February 5, 1886, Frewen Papers.

5. Horace C. Plunkett to Frewen, March 3, 1886, Frewen Papers.

6. Minutes of directors' meeting, March 3, 1886, Frewen Papers.

7. T. W. Peters, "To the Directors and Shareholders of the Powder River Cattle Company, Limited," March 3, 1886, Frewen Papers.

8. "Report of Special Committee, March 1886," Frewen Papers.

9. Earl of Rosslyn to Frewen, March 13, 14, 1886, Frewen Papers.

10. William Mackenzie to the Earl of Rosslyn, March 12, 1886, Frewen Papers.

11. William Mackenzie to the Earl of Rosslyn, March 13, 1886, Frewen Papers.

12. William Mackenzie to the Earl of Rosslyn, March 20, 1886, Frewen Papers.

13. Earl of Rosslyn to Frewen, March 22, 1886, Frewen Papers.

14. Earl of Rosslyn to Frewen, March 25, 1886, Frewen Papers.

15. William Mackenzie to the Earl of Rosslyn, March 27, 1886, Frewen Papers.

16. William Mackenzie to the Earl of Rosslyn, March 31, 1886, Frewen Papers.

17. Earl of Rosslyn to Frewen, March 26, 1886, Frewen Papers.

18. "Mr. C. Waring's Suggestions, March 31, 1886," Frewen Papers.

19. Richard Frewen to Frewen, April 4, 5, 1886, Frewen Papers.

20. Spencer Whitehead to Frewen, March 29, 1886, Frewen Papers.

21. Bennett, Dawson & Bennett to Frewen, April 15, 1886; and Gedge, Kirby & Millett to Frewen, April 16, 1886, Frewen Papers.

22. T. W. Peters to C. Fitch Kemp, April 6, 1886, Frewen Papers.

23. Richard Frewen to Frewen, April 11, 1886, Frewen Papers.

24. Richard Frewen to Frewen, April 13, 1886, Frewen Papers.

25. Frewen to Charles Fitch Kemp, April 14, 1886, Frewen Papers.

26. Richard Frewen to Frewen, April 15, 1886, Frewen Papers.

27. Moreton Frewen, "The Report of the Powder River Committee, A Supplementary Statement," April 20, 1886, Frewen Papers.

28. William Mackenzie to Frewen, April 22, 1886, Frewen Papers.

29. William Mackenzie to Frewen, April 26, 1886, Frewen Papers.

30. Charles E. Lyon, April 28, 1886.

31. Joseph Richardson to Clara Frewen, April 28, 1886, Frewen Papers.

32. "Mr. Whitehead's Minute of What Took Place at the Extraordinary Meeting of the Powder River Cattle Company on the 3rd of May, 1886," Frewen Papers.

· 11 ·

Director At Last

*M*oreton wrote to Mrs. Ponsonby to explain his troubles with the Powder River company, and closed by saying, "I have made enemies by the dozen, and I shall make them yet by the score, if I am to have my face slapped and not strike back and keep striking."[1] It was all too accurate a description of his behavior in that troubled time.

Moreton was at last a director of his company, but it was at the cost of management in America; he could not disturb the Plunkett appointment. The post had been given to Plunkett at the end of March, at no salary.[2] Although Moreton was opposed to the Plunkett appointment (we don't really know why), he protested that he had always had a friendly feeling for Horace. He claimed that his opposition was solely because Plunkett was involved in at least six different outfits and would not have the time to devote to the Powder River company. If Moreton was so concerned about Plunkett's competence, one wonders why he had offered the same position to him just a year earlier. Clearly, the situation between the two men had changed. Yet, as late as March 1886, Frewen's friend Lord Rosslyn had been urging Plunkett to join the board of the company, which could not have been a sign of Moreton's disfavor. When Plunkett declined the board seat, the company continued to press him to become manager in America, but these negotiations must not have been known to Frewen. In any case, Moreton finally promised to raise no further objection to Plunkett's appointment (the life of that promise may be one of the shorter ones on record).[3]

Moreton asked Dick to see Horace. He was concerned that no explicit instructions for the northern drive had been given to Horace by the London office, and this worried him because he believed that Horace had gone on record with the shareholders as being opposed to the northern move.[4] It is not at all clear why Moreton chose this roundabout way to communicate with Plunkett, when his ready pen was sending letters to everyone else with the slightest interest in his affairs. Shortly, the two men met, and Plunkett found Moreton "perfectly furious" at his appointment.[5]

Peters gladly retired from the field of combat, leaving the uncomfortable post to Plunkett. Almost immediately there was friction. Plunkett wrote in late April to tell Moreton that he would not tolerate any interference with his instructions. He noted that Murphy, whom he had fired, seemed to have hired some men, and he asked Frewen whether these men were to be turned over to the company for use in the trail drive. Finally, he said he would be glad to receive "written" advice from Moreton.[6] Plunkett laid down the same rules for communicating with Dick, after which he enjoyed "comparative peace."[7]

Dick despaired at the Plunkett appointment, not only because Horace had once been one of his best friends, but because Plunkett and Kemp together were a formidable team — quite the opposite of Peters, whom Dick regarded as incompetent.[8] Dick, in a characteristically colorful vein, threatened Plunkett with "war to the knife."[9]

When Plunkett received the cable advising him that Moreton and Edward Frewen had been named directors of the company, he immediately assumed he would be dismissed. That such a dismissal was not issued stemmed, of course, from the promise the board had extracted from Frewen when he was elected. When Horace cabled London that the company must either appoint him for the season or dismiss him, he received a cable from Moreton (the same "perfectly furious" one) promising his support. This reversal thoroughly disgusted Dick, who had just declared "war" and was at least consistent in his actions.[10]

There was ample evidence of concern over the tumult Moreton had generated. William Beckett Denison "strongly" disapproved of what was going on: "I have wished a thousand times that I had never been fool enough to allow myself (mainly from the wish to please my son) to listen to your story in the summer of '82," he said. While the most pressing need was to secure the necessary money to keep the banks in Cheyenne from selling out the company, it seemed to him that the course that Moreton and Lyon were on was "certain to land us in disaster." He accused Frewen of pursuing purely personal motives of dislike for certain board members, to the detriment of the company. "I utterly hate the whole business, and have never before been involved in anything so distasteful as all this wrangling has been." Frewen had offered to find a buyer for Denison's shares at a 50 percent discount if Denison wished to sacrifice them at such a value. Denison responded that he would indeed like such an offer, since Moreton had "dissuaded" him from taking preference stock on the ground that the common shares would pay at least 14 percent and probably 20 percent.[11] Ernest Beckett Denison supported Moreton rather than his father, but nevertheless he could not vote against his father (he did not go to the special meeting of shareholders).[12]

Alfred Sartoris said, "No good can possibly come of all this fighting and squabbling — it only destroys what little credit we have left."[13] Lord Dunsany urged Moreton to "let bygones be bygones"; he was pleased that his son Horace and Frewen agreed on the two main points of moving north and winter feeding. He noted that Horace had had some experience in turning a "temporary failure" around and expected he might do the same with the Powder River company if Frewen would assist, rather than oppose him.[14]

Meanwhile, out on the range, the cattle were unaware of all these troubles, having often more than enough of their own. Yet, for a change, it looked as though the herds had come through the winter reasonably well. Fred Hesse reported that the Powder River ranges had had the finest weather they could wish for and the best since 1877–78; south of Buffalo, the snow never exceeded three inches in depth. He said the cattle were doing "wonderfully well," although the ranges were overstocked, and he frankly admitted, "I do not know what they live on."[15] Charles Carter, the foreman in charge of the herds on Hanging Woman Creek (in Montana), reported early in the winter that conditions there were reasonably good, although the range was overstocked as a result of putting the Rawhide herd up there. Carter reported that he had not lost a single calf from the purebred Sussex herd, although the weather in January had been very severe.[16]

Plunkett at once gave orders to get the herds moving from the Powder River to the new range in Alberta. He ordered Fred Hesse to get all arrangements made so that the border could be crossed by September 1, thus avoiding duty payment.[17] He was doing all this without Murphy's services, and Dick was mightily inflamed thereby. He cabled , complaining that Horace wouldn't employ Murphy and that the trail operation was at an "absolute standstill."[18]

Lord Dunsany was trying to find harmony as he anxiously watched the relationship between his son and Moreton. Horace was already running into trouble with the cowboys on the range, who had been talking of shooting him because of his efforts to reduce wages.[19] Dunsany was eager that management be united in a common cause to deal with these difficulties. He continued to assure Moreton that Horace wanted to move as many cattle north as Frewen did, but he urged Moreton to wire Horace before going west, to set the tone for his visit.[20]

Horace had also been able to lay bare the company's financial crisis in the West. The company had borrowed a total of $30,000 from the First National Bank of Cheyenne on two notes; both were due April 2, 1886, but had been extended. That bank also was carrying the company's overdraft, which had grown to nearly $11,000. Plunkett had had to borrow $3,000 on his own note to provide working capital. In addition, the company had borrowed $10,000 from F. A. K. Bennet on a note due June 1, 1886. The expenses for the balance of the season would amount to $25,000, making a total of over $79,000 that would have to be raised in short order. Horace thought this could almost be accomplished, counting the money Post had promised and the proceeds of sales at Superior.[21]

Disputes about Murphy continued to plague Plunkett. In early May he cabled Kemp that he would resign immediately if the home office insisted that Murphy be retained, since Murphy had pledged his services to "another" (i.e., Frewen). He also notified Kemp that the First National Bank in Cheyenne was nervous about the prospect of their notes being paid. They assumed that Post's conditions for a loan to the company at 6 percent (which he was not disclosing to the local management) would prove unacceptable to London.[22] In a long letter, Plunkett recounted his conversation with Truman Hicks, president of the First National, in which Hicks pointed out that Post could loan all the money he had at 12 percent, and was therefore likely to demand extraordinary terms to secure a loan at 6 percent.

Moreton's and Dick's dabbling was also clearly getting under Plunkett's skin. "It is hardly conceivable that any manager can succeed when his subordinates are told to disobey his orders by persons asserting that they have got control of the voting power and will soon have control of the management. Such an exhibition is an outrage on all business fairness and decency, and makes the Company ridiculous before the eyes of the whole country."[23]

Moreton was actually getting his own way in nearly everything (Whitton told Plunkett that Frewen was the dictator in company affairs), and even Ted could not see the reason for ruffling Horace further.[24] When Moreton demanded a meeting to deal with the situation, Ted responded, "Unless you have received a cable from Horace declining to carry out our instructions or refusing to accept responsibility of drive, I cannot see the necessity for a Board meeting." As to Dick's distress, he said, "Dick is mad because Murphy is thrown over . . . but there is no evidence that Horace is not carrying out our instructions."[25] Lord Dunsany guessed that the Murphy affair would cause Horace to resign, since he had only accepted the managership because he didn't want to see disorganization on the ranges near his own operation.[26]

Mackenzie, as always looking for a logical answer, was inclined to assume that Moreton would not interfere with Plunkett's management, but he wondered how that assumption squared with the statement that Post would only put up the money if Frewen was manager. "How is this?" he asked, requesting a letter pledging noninterference that he could read to his friends.[27] Moreton responded that he had promised Plunkett and the board that he would support Horace as manager. But, said he, "I am not to be understood as agreeing with his appointment. I told him very fairly before he left that I regard him as far too weak a man for a crisis." As always, Moreton was at his diplomatic best. Regarding the Post advance, he promised to say that he was satisfied with Plunkett's management, "though perhaps with a slight inward sinking."[28]

The next day Moreton again reassured Mackenzie. He cited a cable from Dick urging that Plunkett be supported to strengthen his "feebleness." Referring to Horace, he said, "He and I are such old friends that I am sure there will be no friction."[29]

Lord Dunsany continued to try to smooth things between Horace and Moreton. He pointed out that Murphy had been contacting the directors, a situation inappropriate for a subordinate. He assured Moreton that the dismissal was from no personal animosity toward him. Moreover, Plunkett had, of course, told the board why he was firing Murphy, and the latter had informed Horace that he was aware of the contents of that communication. "Of course," said Dunsany, "I don't for a moment think that you or your brother would have given Murphy that information, but you will see that the facts made it impossible for Horace to get on with Murphy."[30]

But Murphy was not quite gone after all. Late in May, Moreton told Plunkett that he was removing the Alberta drive from his responsibility ("a great relief," said Plunkett), and, of course, Murphy was to get the job.[31] However, it was not long before Murphy refused to serve, and Plunkett had to cable London to appoint another![32]

By the middle of May, Plunkett had been able to coax Post into revealing what security he would require for the $60,000 loan: a chattel mortgage on the company's properties. In addition, Post wanted Moreton to come to Wyoming to settle his personal obligations with the Post bank. Hicks of the First National promised to provide the expenses for the summer if Plunkett stayed on as manager and if $50,000 was forthcoming reasonably soon. Both Plunkett and Kemp recommended that the money be sought in London. At least Dick's meddling was apparently at an end for a (very short) time, as Plunkett reported he had withdrawn from the company's affairs.[33]

In the meantime, the London office of the company continued to work on the debentures to be sent over to Post to secure the £12,000 loan. For a time, it looked as though Plunkett had the two bankers agreeing to wait until the papers could come across the Atlantic. But there were too many people stirring in the stew. Fitch Kemp also had money needs for the London office, and when it became apparent that the loan from Post could actually be made, he cabled Plunkett that £5,000 of the Post advance should be remitted at once to London to cover obligations there.[34] This caught Horace completely by surprise, as he had been under the impression that London would leave him with the entire £12,000, as well as the proceeds of sales at Superior; he needed all of this money to keep Hicks from taking action against the company's assets.[35]

Hicks, weary of waiting, began to bounce the company's checks, which Dick considered Horace's fault: "If he had been at all decent with Post the latter would have found money for running expenses."[36]

Then Dick's ingenuity appeared from another direction, with a solution to the frantic search for funds to operate the Powder River company. His own company, the Dakota Stock & Grazing Company, Limited, had for some time been engaged in a lawsuit against

Price & Jenks. The Dakota company had bought the Price & Jenks ranch on Chadron Creek, but the deal was rescinded for nondelivery, and Dakota sued. A verdict of $54,733 was finally returned to Dakota.[37] It occurred to Dick that this windfall, which was only drawing 6 percent, could be loaned to the Powder River Company at 12 percent to alleviate its current cash distress. This he did, apparently without further consultation with anyone!

On July 17, he paid $22,000 over to the Powder River company, wrote to Fitch Kemp in London that he had done so, and tersely cabled Moreton, "Promised pay Hicks tomorrow have withdrawn money from Dakota to make part payment."[38] When Frank Kemp (who was also employed by the Dakota company) found the money missing from the Dakota accounts, he cabled the London office for instructions, and was told to hold the banks liable. The First National Bank promptly refunded the $10,000 taken from their account, and the Stock Growers National Bank followed after threat of legal action. By August 5, all of the money had again been recovered, whereupon Dick began a lawsuit against the company.[39] When Ted learned of this state of affairs, he told Moreton that Dick was completely wrong, that the action was most dishonorable, and that he would never attend another meeting of the Dakota company.[40] Things were never dull with the volatile Frewens.

Problems arose from another quarter. Because of a dispute over taxes on the cattle in Montana, Custer County threatened seizure of the herd on the Hanging Woman range. Plunkett thought that part of the trouble was that certain local cattlemen wanted to see the Powder River cattle taken off the range.[41] Dick had gone to the company lawyer in Miles City and argued that the cattle that had been moved up from Wyoming were not subject to Montana taxes since taxes had been paid in the former territory. Plunkett was able to pay the 1885 taxes under protest, but the seizure for the 1886 taxes was to prevent the company from removing the cattle from the county (there was more than $3,000 in dispute); he hoped to get the right to pay these taxes under protest as well.

While Plunkett was taking these reasonable steps, Moreton charged the western management with having needlessly paid Wyoming taxes and claimed that Horace was asserting that the cattle had merely drifted across the border.[42] While it was true that the "drift" argument had been made, it was apparently made by the company's lawyers in Cheyenne, on evidence given by Fred Hesse. In any case, this was done before Plunkett came on the scene as manager.[43]

As if the debts in Wyoming were not large enough, Moreton was now determined to redeem the preferred stock (albeit at par, not 120 percent of par), and Rosslyn cautioned him that this would require a total loan of £145,000 ($702,000)! Nevertheless, he continued to support Frewen, saying, "I hope when my account is made up at the last that I may be credited with having worked for the Powder River Co. to some purpose."[44]

Mackenzie convened the preferred shareholders and broached the possibility of a buyout in exchange for debentures. There were some who wanted their "pound of flesh," but Mackenzie thought they would be considerably influenced by what he finally decided to do. A committee was formed to look into Moreton's scheme. Moreton took the scheme to the board, who approved it, and then the lawyers were set to work to prepare the necessary legal steps.[45]

Shortly after the middle of June, Mackenzie reckoned that they had consents from over 9,500 shares of the preferred. Still, Mackenzie worried that Moreton might yet ruin the deal if he did not try harder to get along with Plunkett. "Like a good man, do leave well alone," he said. He also warned that Dick would have to be controlled, as he was "injudicious."[46] In addition to the obvious advantage of getting rid of the preferred shareholders, Mackenzie was of the opinion that Whitton, now Frewen's enemy, would also step down if Moreton played his cards right, although he warned, "If you rub his hair the wrong way, or are too anxious to get quit of him, he might resolve to 'stick by the ship.'"[47]

With so much riding on his need to exercise discretion, it is amazing that Moreton continued to act as though nothing could possibly bring him down. He became annoyed with one of Plunkett's letters and dashed off a reply that was reminiscent of the days when he had broken off his partnership with Dick. "If you will permit me to put it very strongly, it is not wise or fair to write what you would hesitate to say face to face; and you must be aware that you would not have taken the consequences involved in that letter had I been much nearer to you than five thousand miles."[48] This brought a speedy reaction. Referring to this threat, Plunkett said, "By this, I take it, you imply that fear of personal violence would have prevented my giving expression to my opinion. I don't think I am that kind of a coward." Then he added, "I am taking counsel with those who wished me to take the management and have placed my resignation in their hands so that if they think my usefulness liable to be paralysed they will relieve me of this onerous burden."[49] It was Denision who was to hold this trump card.

Lord Dunsany did not give up his peacemaking efforts, urging Moreton to try to put himself in Horace's place; he mildly chided Frewen for having a "parental affection" for the recommendations of the Rosslyn committee.[50] All these kindly soothing words did little to calm the feverish outpouring from Moreton's pen.

Dick, for his part, was not out of the fray, but instead was contributing his bit to the tension. He did a piece for the secretary of the company, which he felt would "show Plunkett up," and he was still trying to get Murphy to accept the Alberta drive job (Murphy would ultimately do so). He advised Moreton that Plunkett was "floundering . . . rather like the desperate plunges of a wounded animal," and he warned his brother not to back Horace too much, or the latter might claim he was appointed with Moreton's consent. He was himself short of money and asked Moreton to send out a "thou" (as well as some socks, handkerchiefs, and "a couple hundred cigarettes").[51] He listed debts of £19,500 ($94,000) at interest rates ranging from 6 to 12 percent.[52]

Poor Charles Lyon, who had been such a faithful follower of Moreton's, had desperately assigned his assets, including Frewen's note, to his brother, A. O. Lyon. The latter told Moreton that "nothing short of a miracle" could prevent bankruptcy, and he had been advised by counsel to repudiate the assignment from his brother and to let the creditors scramble for their share of the assets. He told Moreton to be prepared for any action they might take; "I am completely powerless."[53]

Moreton's own finances were also in a critical state. At the end of July, he sadly told Clara to put up for sale "18," the house in London. The next month, he urged her to sell the diamonds, he hoped to Jennie, who might pay "a hundred down and the rest any time later."[54] (Mama Jerome had tried to realize on her own diamonds two years earlier, but that "robber" Tiffany would only allow her 5,000 [presumably dollars] for them.)[55]

The lawsuit Moreton had filed against the company was grinding nearer to trial. It appears that he was having second thoughts about an actual trial, though, as his solicitor suggested to the company counsel that trial could be avoided if Frewen's costs were paid by the company. The company's lawyers thereupon wrote in high dudgeon to the board to say that there was little to recommend going to trial when the only reason for the trial was to see who would pay Frewen's costs.[56]

The reorganization of the company seemed at last ready to proceed. Notice was given that an extraordinary meeting of the shareholders would be held August 9 to wind up the company and to transfer the assets to a new company with £200,000 of ordinary shares at £5 each; £12 debentures paying 5 percent for one year and 6 percent thereafter were to be issued for the £10 preference shares. The debentures were to be redeemed at £3 in 1888, £4 in 1889, and £5 in 1890. The secretary noted that almost 90 percent of the preference shares had already been pledged to the exchange.[57]

At this critical juncture, Moreton decided he could no longer wait in London and set sail for America, not awaiting the outcome of the shareholders' meeting. To strengthen his hand in the West, he drafted instructions, which were finally amended and issued to him by Middleton Kemp. He was to take care of the necessary legal proof work on the Crazy Woman filing and to borrow £20,000 ($97,000) at not more than 8 percent interest. Finally, he was to look over the situation at Superior, and to do what he could to help out with the Alberta lease arrangements.[58] While these instructions were approved by a majority of the board, both Andrew Whitton and Joseph Richardson expressed concern that nothing be done to undermine Horace Plunkett's authority in managing the company's affairs in the West.[59]

Perhaps Moreton assumed that things would go easily at the shareholders' meeting, but he was wrong. Before the meeting, William Beckett Denison wrote to the shareholders, telling them that Frewen was on his way to interfere with Plunkett's management, which would certainly lead to the latter's resignation. He also reported that Dick was likewise taking an active part in company business in Cheyenne. He therefore proposed that at the shareholders' meeting resolutions be passed to cancel any authority Moreton had, to exclude Richard Frewen from company affairs, and to ask the directors for a decision on whether the company should exercise its option to sell the Superior property back to Moreton. Denison solicited proxies to accomplish this purpose.[60]

The meeting was called for the ninth, and Edward Frewen was in the chair. He disarmed Denison by reading to the meeting a cable that had been sent to Moreton and Plunkett in which Plunkett's management authority was reemphasized; Denison thereupon withdrew his first resolution. When Ted assured the shareholders that it was not the board's intention to employ Richard Frewen, Denison withdrew his second resolution. Denison did read to the meeting a letter from Plunkett, which objected to Richard Frewen's interference. Plunkett had given Denison his resignation, to be used as he saw fit. When the meeting took up the articles of the new corporation, Denison tried to replace Moreton as a director with Gray, but he eventually backed down.

The meeting could not be concluded on the ninth because of difficulty with the wording of the security to be given the preference shareholders, so it was adjourned until the sixteenth.[61] Denison, who could not attend the second meeting, proceeded to write again to the shareholders, giving his account of matters. He claimed that he had been successful in getting the board to cable Frewen substantially as he had requested in his resolution. Moreover, he also claimed that Edward Frewen had undertaken to prevent Richard from interfering further with management (this assertion was promptly denied by Ted).[62] When the adjourned meeting convened, the shareholders adopted the reorganization resolution, naming Charles Fitch Kemp liquidator of the old company. The new company was to be called, rather grandly, The International Cattle Company, Limited. (The resolutions were to be confirmed at another special meeting, on September 7, 1886).

News of the meeting and of Denison's letter to shareholders reached Moreton in Superior. Ted wrote about the proceedings and reflected that perhaps it was wise that Moreton had not been there. "I take no credit to myself," he said, "but I know if you had been present and in a rage as you naturally and predictably would have been, Beckett [Denison] and his followers would have opposed the scheme [to reorganize the company]." On the subject of Denison's letter to shareholders, he warned Moreton, "Now don't go and reply to his circular—it is not worth it."[63] This good advice fell on deaf ears.

Moreton's response was in his own letter to shareholders at the end of August. First, he noted that Beckett was the same William Beckett Denison who had been a member of the special committee and signed the unanimous report of that committee. Then he went back over the arguments he had for supporting the drive to Alberta. Finally, he defended Dick, whom Moreton claimed had done nothing to warrant the charge of interference! And his own intentions in going west, he claimed, were to appear in a Land Court (whatever he may have meant by that — apparently it had to do with proving up on the desert land entries), to secure a lease in Alberta, and to consult with Lingham. Although not included in his formal list of intentions, he did indicate that he intended to close the Cheyenne office, since Plunkett had thus far refused to do so.[64] It all sounded positively innocent.

The new company was to have seven directors, including two to represent the old preference shareholders (William Mackenzie and George D. Stibbard [the company's solicitor] were chosen). Bennet came on the board to replace Lyon, who resigned because of his personal bankruptcy. Some of these new directors held an informal meeting of the new company late in September (the articles were not then registered), and Middleton Kemp wrote Moreton a letter that reflected a feeling almost of harmony.

By August Moreton was once more in Wyoming, where he found the ranges in poor shape. In an amazingly prescient letter to Clara, Moreton said, "I am thoroughly alarmed at what I hear of the state of the ranges. I don't see how we can avoid heavy loss this winter again. It is impossible to disguise it, the business has quite broke down on these ranges. There never can be any recovery."[65] A few days later, he said, "I dread the coming winter; if it is a severe one, half the cattle in Wyoming will die for sure."[66]

Difficulties continued with the hands. In spite of the goodwill created by a lively dance held in February for the "76" hands at Crazy Woman, the continuing friction with the cowboys over wages was reported from time to time in the papers. The *Democratic Leader* reported that the cowboys had organized themselves into an informal sort of "labor league" to improve their lot.[67] In March, a cowboy wrote to say that he could not work five months for only $30 a month and then pay $30 a month for board for the rest of the year. The reduction he was protesting was $5 to $10 a month. There was some obvious satisfaction when some of the big cattlemen were quoted as saying they would keep wages at $40. When the *Cheyenne Mirror* reported that cowboys were leaving northern Wyoming for Montana because of the wage cut, the *Sentinel* denied the story, saying that wages were actually lower in Montana.[68]

The Powder River company's much-bruited northern drive finally came off, although hampered by Frewen interference. After sending a man north in May to scout the trail, Plunkett gathered over 7,000 head off the ranges and sent them north to Alberta. Starting from the Powder River country on June 25, they arrived in Alberta by the first of September, after being detained in Custer County, Montana, because of the tax dispute.[69] Ten yearlings had been drowned in crossing the swollen Yellowstone River—that was the only mishap. Plunkett expected that the cattle would have sufficient time on the new range to gain weight before winter set in.[70] It was good luck that they were gone from the range in Wyoming. Dick reported that the weather there had been "desperate": 110 degrees in the shade with hot winds, "more like the Sahara than the prairies."[71] The Wyoming and Montana ranges were to suffer more before the year was out. Moreton gloated that Peters had been wrong in arguing that it would take two years to get the cattle admitted to Canada; nor did he give Plunkett any credit for the move, calling the Irishman a "cur."[72]

The company had a lease on seventeen townships on Mosquito Creek and Little Bow River, about fifty miles north of Fort McLeod and fifty miles south of Calgary. The lease was for twenty-one years, at one cent per acre. For the benefit of his friends back in Wyoming, W. E. Holleman (who had been on the drive) observed that wages in Canada were no better than those in Wyoming—$40 for regular hands and $45 for "old hands." The Canadian cattle outfits followed the practice of letting the hands go after the spring roundup, then hiring again in the fall for two or three weeks.[73]

Murphy, now in Alberta, sent back glowing reports about the condition of the cattle on the Mosquito Creek range. He told Moreton that there was ten times as much grass per acre as on the Powder River range (Frewen thought the multiple was six, but still excellent).[74] It was some of the last good news that would come from the company's operations.

Although the exodus of many herds left the Powder River ranges less crowded, Plunkett advised the London office that there were a lot of grasshoppers on the range; he expected to have to scatter the cattle far more than usual, with consequent difficulties in gathering them the following year.[75]

Moreton found Cheyenne "deserted." A number of the companies had moved their offices out, or were contemplating doing so, although the Swan company was bucking the trend by announcing its intention to build a "commodious" new office in the spring of 1887. When A. H. Swan returned to Cheyenne after three months in England, he confidently proclaimed his affairs "entirely satisfactory." The calf crop was thought to be larger than in the two prior years, although not "extraordinarily large" because of the poor character of the grass, bleached by the rains of the previous fall. Prices for cattle were very low.[76]

There were still signs of growth in the territory. While activity at the land office was less hectic than it had been (there were now only three employees in the surveyor general's office, compared with thirty-six to thirty-eight in 1883), much of the desirable land in the territory had already been surveyed and platted. The continued construction of the Northwestern railroad raised the question whether the hopes of Douglas to become the great central metropolis could be realized. This new town, located across the Platte River from Fort Fetterman, had been named after the famous senator, in the hope that it would do for Wyoming what Lincoln had done for Nebraska (or at least that was the understanding of the *Democratic Leader*).[77] The town was being promoted by C. H. King & Co. and Richards Brothers, who had the contract for 500,000 brick to erect storehouses and a bank. King had a store at Fetterman, and Richards had a bank there.[78] Yet, there was already disturbing talk that a location eighty miles beyond, on the Searight ranch, would claim the honors for central Wyoming.[79] The new town was to be named for a young lieutenant who lost his life at the battle of Platte Bridge: Caspar Collins.

In spite of these lingering signs of continued growth, the main economic force in the territory, the cattle industry, was headed towards the most disastrous winter of its history. By mid-December light snow borne by fifty-mile winds was sweeping through the capital. As if to give some sort of omen, perhaps the most distinguished member of the cattle industry, Governor George W. Baxter, was abruptly removed from office in December by the president for illegal fencing of public lands. He was replaced by Colonal Thomas Moonlight, who had once been in command of Fort Laramie.[80]

As usual, when faced with adversity, Moreton took comfort from the fact that the other companies were in worse shape than the Powder

River; they were "all broke, the whole gang of them," he said. "No one in Cheyenne has got a bob left; I never saw such a depressed place."[81] The Powder River company was leaving Cheyenne for its new headquarters in Superior, and Moreton did not look back. "I am glad to believe that I shall never or hardly be in that beastly place again."[82] By the middle of September the company's headquarters were established at Superior, apparently to the surprise of Plunkett, who had not expected the move to occur so soon.[83]

If Moreton was glad to leave Cheyenne, feelings there were decidedly reciprocal in some quarters. The company had alienated the First National Bank, and, for a time, even Moreton's old friend Morton Post seems to have soured on his unorthodox financing schemes. Post's cashier, A. J. Parshall, wrote to Frewen at Superior to give him notice that the two notes Dick had arranged were soon due, and that payment was expected. Parshall noted pointedly that there were other customers who were in need of the money, and the bank did not want to deny them in favor of the Powder River, "who . . . have never in any instance done as they agreed with us."[84]

There was also criticism of Frewen and his countrymen from another quarter. The *Boston Daily Advertiser* had carried an article claiming that the cattle business was ruined, quoting "Englishmen" as the source for this opinion. Thomas Sturgis and a number of other prominent bankers in Cheyenne signed an open letter rebutting the statement. They took particular umbrage to the notion that anyone would rely on the opinion of Englishmen to learn about the western cattle business. It was noted that of the 450 members of the Wyoming Stock Growers Association, only 14 had direct or indirect use of foreign capital.

Then came the unkind part. The foreign-financed enterprises were conducted by young men from the "aristocratic" classes, "unaccustomed" either to economy or work, their business in many instances only a "grand picnic." The average foreign investor only spent a few months of each year on the range. As to true conditions in the West, the letter concluded with the sanguine prediction that no great liquidation was coming, and as bankers they could say that not 1 percent of the cattle raisers were insolvent, "or anything near it."

As to the trek by some to Montana and the British possessions, this was put aside as the search for paradise in the next country; the writers were nonetheless grateful for the relief this had provided to their own range, which was now "well grassed" and as capable of supporting cattle as it was five years before.[85] It was a spirited response, and it was a great pity that it contained so little truth, as the next few months would amply prove.

As usual when he was on the range, Moreton's enthusiasm returned, and soon he told Clara to advise Ted that they would soon have "lots of cash to make things smooth."[86] He was even predicting dividends again, although only "moderate," and he cautioned Clara not to mention his prediction to a soul.[87] In soberer moments, he still realized that all depended on the winter. If it was mild and the balance of the herd could be moved to Alberta, the company would survive, but "if it is a hard one and our losses heavy, then the company is ruined."[88]

On this, his last trip to the western range, Moreton took time out for a meeting with a historic figure. Old Sitting Bull had come back with eighteen lodges of Sioux to the Custer battleground, and Frewen saw him there. "Wasn't it interesting," mused Moreton, "only ten years ago."[89] It is tempting to imagine that the two talked of battles lost, but no one has recorded what passed between them.

Dick's affairs were rapidly coming unglued. The Dakota Stock and Grazing Company went into liquidation in 1886 and was winding up the business when Dick made his abortive attempt to help the Powder River company with Dakota funds. Although the funds were speedily recovered from the banks, litigation immediately commenced. At about this time, some Dakota cattle were delivered under circumstances that Dick thought were fraudulent, and he made the charge of fraud against Frank Kemp, who was manager of the Dakota company. While it was soon apparent that the transaction was innocent of any fraud, there were enough allegations to cause Horace Plunkett to write to Middleton Kemp, defending Frank (he had originally recommended Frank Kemp as manager), and Ted Frewen was greatly distressed at Dick's intemperate charges.[90]

In early October, Moreton made a trip of inspection to the Alberta range, on Mosquito Creek. He and Murphy had ridden twelve miles into the mountains when they were caught in a heavy snow storm. Eight inches of fresh snow were dumped on the ground and more was coming down. On the way home, they lost their way in the storm and camped in a clump of timber, where they watched the snow fall for twenty hours, until there were two and a half feet on the ground. As they were striking camp, a rifle cartridge was accidentally dropped into the fire. It exploded, and the shrapnel was driven into Moreton's leg. Nevertheless, he rode out, and they were six hours making nine miles. At the next camp they were still fifty miles from the nearest doctor, at Calgary. Not relishing such a journey, Frewen determined to try his own surgical techniques. "I thought I would feel for the bullet myself and see how deep it was in," he told Clara. "To my great delight I found the substance within half an inch of the surface and with a good deal of 'labor and sorrow' I got it out. I will keep the trophy for you. I have kept the wound well washed and open and bread-poulticed and today it looks quite healthy. . . . I have no doubt I shall be well in a few days."[91] And he was!

By the first week of October, Moreton had completed his whirlwind trip to the West, leaving a good deal of unfinished business. Morton E. Post wrote from Cheyenne, noting that Moreton had promised to leave debentures as security for the company's past due loans but had not done so. Moreover, Post thought the money market in New York, Chicago, and the West generally made it impossible to sell the company's debentures in the fall of 1886. He was still expressing "fullest confidence" in Moreton's ultimate success. Yet, he wanted the money due him.[92]

Plunkett gave Moreton a brief report in late October. It was not favorable. The winter prospects were, in a word, gloomy. The Wyoming ranges were not in good shape, but he had lacked the men and money to move any more of the cattle to Alberta; in any case, he was concerned at the risk of moving them so late.

As to finances, Horace reminded Moreton that the company still owed Post $30,000, Bennet about $11,000, and Fred Hesse had run up debts of $14,000.

In Chicago, on the way home, Moreton met William Mackenzie, who had come over to get a first-hand view of the western operations of the company for which he was now a director. Apparently the two got along well. Moreton told Clara, "Mackenzie is here; he is an excellent fellow, very keen about Lingham and sizes Plunkett up about as I do, a thorough old woman and deceitful at that! But keep this all to your little self."[93] As usual, Moreton's assessment of the situation was slanted in his favor. Of the same meeting, Plunkett noted that Mackenzie "supported me fully."[94] Frewen's friendship with Mackenzie was a somewhat rocky one, in which the canny Scottish stockbroker would try to offer good conservative advice to Moreton, almost always without success.

As if fate were sending him a message that things would not go well, when Moreton stopped at the Chicago Club that fall, he was asked to pay for the stationery he was using (undoubtedly in some quantity)![95]

Notes to Chapter II

1. Frewen to Mrs. Ponsonby, October 26, 1886, Frewen Papers.
2. Horace Plunkett to Charles Fitch Kemp, May 10, 1886, Frewen Papers.
3. Frewen to Joseph Richardson, April 1, 1886; and Frewen to Charles Waring, April 1, 1886, Frewen Papers.
4. Frewen to Richard Frewen, April 16, 1886, Frewen Papers.
5. Plunkett diary, April 21, 1886.
6. Horace C. Plunkett to Frewen, April 24, 1886, Frewen Papers.
7. Plunkett diary, April 26, 1886.
8. Richard Frewen to Frewen, April 24, 1886, Frewen Papers.
9. Plunkett diary, April 29, 1886.
10. Plunkett diary, May 3, 9, 12, 1886.
11. William Beckett Denison to Frewen, April 25, 1886, Frewen Papers.
12. Ernest Beckett Denison to Frewen, April 29, 1886, Frewen Papers.
13. Alfred Sartoris to Frewen, April 26, 1886, Frewen Papers.
14. Baron Dunsany to Frewen, April 27, 1886, Frewen Papers.
15. Fred G. S. Hesse to Frewen, March 1, 1886, Frewen Papers.
16. Charles Carter to Frewen, December 9, 1885, and January 27, 1886, Frewen Papers.
17. Horace C. Plunkett to Fred Hesse, April 24, 1886, Frewen Papers.
18. Richard Frewen to Frewen, May 4, 1886, Frewen Papers.
19. Plunkett diary, June 18, 1886, Frewen Papers.
20. Baron Dunsany to Frewen, May 5, 1886, Frewen Papers.
21. Horace C. Plunkett to Charles Fitch Kemp, May 7, 1886, Frewen Papers.
22. Charles Fitch Kemp to Frewen, May 10, 1886, Frewen Papers.
23. Horace C. Plunkett to Charles Fitch Kemp, May 10, 1886, Frewen Papers.
24. Plunkett diary, June 29, 1886, Frewen Papers.
25. Edward Frewen to Frewen, May 11, 1886, Frewen Papers.
26. Baron Dunsany to Frewen, May 11, 1886, Frewen Papers.
27. William Mackenzie to Frewen, May 12, 1886, Frewen Papers.
28. Frewen to William Mackenzie, May 13, 1886, Frewen Papers.
29. Frewen to William Mackenzie, May 14, 1886, Frewen Papers.
30. Baron Dunsany to Frewen, May 20, 1886, Frewen Papers.
31. Horace C. Plunkett to Charles Fitch Kemp, June 16, 1886.
32. Horace C. Plunkett to Charles Fitch Kemp, June 25, 1886.
33. Horace C. Plunkett to Charles Fitch Kemp, May 13, 14, 1886.
34. Charles Fitch Kemp to Frewen, May 19, 1886, Frewen Papers.
35. Horace C. Plunkett to Charles Fitch Kemp, June 16, 1886.
36. Richard Frewen to Frewen, June 17, 1886, Frewen Papers.

37. *Democratic Leader,* April 21, 1885.

38. Richard Frewen to Charles W. Middleton Kemp, July 17, 1886; and Richard Frewen to Frewen, July 17, 1886, Frewen Papers.

39. Charles W. Middleton Kemp to Dakota Shareholders, August 6, 1886.

40. Edward Frewen to Frewen, August 18, 1886, Frewen Papers.

41. Horace C. Plunkett to Charles Fitch Kemp, June 25, 1886.

42. Frewen to Charles Fitch Kemp, July 26, 1886, Frewen Papers.

43. Horace C. Plunkett to Charles Fitch Kemp, July 15, 1886.

44. Earl of Rosslyn to Frewen, May 8, 1886, Frewen Papers.

45. William Mackenzie to Frewen, May 18, 25, 1886, Frewen Papers.

46. William Mackenzie to Frewen, June 18, 1886, Frewen Papers.

47. William Mackenzie to Frewen, May 26, 1886, Frewen Papers.

48. Frewen to Horace C. Plunkett, June 12, 1886, Frewen Papers.

49. Horace C. Plunkett to Frewen, June 29, 1886, Frewen Papers.

50. Baron Dunsany to Frewen, June 8, 1886, Frewen Papers.

51. Richard Frewen to Frewen, July 17, 1886, Frewen Papers.

52. Richard Frewen to Frewen, July 11, 1886, Frewen Papers.

53. A. O. Lyon to Moreton Frewen, May 19, 1886, Frewen Papers.

54. Frewen to Clara Frewen, July 30, August 29, 1886, Frewen Papers.

55. Frewen to Clara Frewen, May 1, 1886, Frewen Papers.

56. Stibbard, Gibson & Co. to Charles Fitch Kemp, May 26, 1886.

57. Charles W. Middleton Kemp to the Shareholders, July 30, 1886.

58. Charles W. Middleton Kemp to Frewen, July 30, 1886, Frewen Papers.

59. Andrew Whitton to Charles W. Middleton Kemp, July 29, 1886; and Joseph M. Richardson to Charles W. Middleton Kemp, July 29, 1886.

60. William Beckett Denison to the Shareholders, August 5, 1886.

61. Spencer Whitehead to Frewen, August 10, 1886, Frewen Papers.

62. William Beckett Denison to the Shareholders, August 12, 1886; and Edward Frewen to William Beckett, August 15, 1886.

63. Edward Frewen to Frewen, August 18, 1886, Frewen Papers.

64. Frewen to the Shareholders, August 30, 1886, Frewen Papers.

65. Frewen to Clara Frewen, August 29, 1886, Frewen Papers.

66. Frewen to Clara Frewen, September 9, 1886, Frewen Papers.

67. *Democratic Leader,* April 11, 1886.

68. *Big Horn Sentinel,* February 13, March 20, 27, and April 24, 1886.

69. *Big Horn Sentinel,* July 24, 1886.

70. Horace C. Plunkett to Charles Fitch Kemp, July 7, 1886.

71. Richard Frewen to Frewen, July 11, 1886, Frewen Papers.

72. Frewen to Clara Frewen, August 31, 1886, Frewen Papers.

73. *Big Horn Sentinel,* October 16, 1886.

74. Frewen to Clara Frewen, October 11, 1886, Frewen Papers.

75. Horace C. Plunkett to Charles Fitch Kemp, August 12, 1886.

76. *Cheyenne Daily Sun,* July 13, 1886.

77. *Democratic Leader,* June 16, 1886.

78. *Democratic Leader,* May 11, 1886.

79. *Cheyenne Daily Sun,* July 1, 1886.

80. A sometime Republican, Moonlight had been a Democrat since running unsuccessfully for governor of Kansas. *Cheyenne Daily Sun,* December 9, 1886.

81. Frewen to Clara Frewen, September 5, 1886, Frewen Papers.

82. Frewen to Clara Frewen, September 1, 1886, Frewen Papers.

83. W. S. Oliver to Frewen, September 13, 1886, Frewen Papers.
84. A. J. Parshall to Frewen, September 6, 1886, Frewen Papers.
85. *Cheyenne Daily Sun,* December 31, 1886.
86. Frewen to Clara Frewen, September 1886, Frewen Papers.
87. Frewen to Clara Frewen, September 26, 1886, Frewen Papers.
88. Frewen to Clara Frewen, October 11, 1886, Frewen Papers.
89. Frewen to Clara Frewen, September 1886, Frewen Papers.
90. Horace C. Plunkett to Charles W. Middleton Kemp, September 2, 1886.
91. Frewen to Clara Frewen, October 11, 1886, Frewen Papers.
92. Morton E. Post to Frewen, October 7, 1886, Frewen Papers.
93. Frewen to Clara Frewen, November 19, 1886, Frewen Papers.
94. Plunkett diary, November 13, 1886.
95. Frewen to Clara Frewen, November 10, 1886, Frewen Papers.

·12·

The Liquidator Liquidates

$\mathcal{H}$orace Plunkett wrote his report to the shareholders of the company while en route back to Europe in December 1886. "I am shortly about to resign the management of the Powder River Cattle Company," he said, "because I find it a position compared with which the throne of Bulgaria is a bed of roses."[1] While we do not know what caused him thus to malign the Bulgarian throne, it is true that he had had difficulties.

Even before this report reached the shareholders, there was more difficulty with the reorganization of the Powder River company into the International company. Plunkett received a cable from London saying that he was getting a power of attorney to borrow money in the name of the company. The cable closed with the cryptic statement, "All property of company is vested in me," but the cable was unsigned! Nevertheless, it was clear that Charles Fitch Kemp was the liquidator, and that he was now vested with complete power to manage the company's assets. Telling Moreton of this news, Plunkett recalled the company's debts: in total, the company owed $90,000 and had only $25,000 in sight. Horace said, "Raise all you can. We are in a mess."[2]

Cables and pleas back and forth across the ocean were unavailing in providing cash, and on November 22 the board met to consider the situation. Ted was there, and he reported to Moreton, "I pray I may never have to go through such a day of humiliation." Andrew Whitton read Everett Gray's proposal to raise the necessary cash for the continued operation of the company. He was offering £18,000 ($87,000) at 10 percent, on condition that Moreton Frewen and his friends (i.e., E. F. Gardner and F. A. K. Bennet) retire from the board and that Moreton give up voting power on his stock. The board was informed that Mackenzie had secured Moreton's consent to these conditions (although not in writing), but Ted was totally uninformed; he and Stibbard nearly came to blows.[3]

Moreton's consent had, in fact, not been secured. He was in New York, and Plunkett cabled him there to urge his acceptance of the terms being offered, placing his interests into Mackenzie's hands.[4] The board then met again on December 3, and a further letter from Everett Gray was read to the assembly. He recited the history of Moreton's unfilled promises to raise the necessary money at favorable interest rates. He then repeated the offer to lend £18,000 at 10 percent (possibly with some at 8 percent), on condition that Frewen, Gardner, and Bennet retire, that Moreton give his resignation "absolutely in writing," and that he give up the voting power of his shares for eighteen months. Gray also insisted that Moreton agree not to interfere with the affairs of the company.[5]

Morton Post, who was in New York, sent a letter over to Moreton as he was preparing to sail for England, again demanding payment of the loan from the Post bank (it was now over $100,000). "Under the present management, I can see nothing but disaster and failure in the near future for the company," he said. As with much of the Post correspondence of this period, we must assume Moreton may have instigated the letter.

The response to Gray's offer was nearly three weeks in coming. Finally, on December 21, Ted, Mackenzie, Stibbard, and Fitch Kemp signed a letter to Moreton (who was back in London), warning him that unless he accepted the terms, the property of the company would be attached and sold.[6] The same day Moreton replied, agreeing to the terms. "I do this," he said, "because I gather from your letter the assets of the Company are otherwise likely to be realized during this winter and therefore at as you express it, 'a ruinous sacrifice.'"[7] It was done.

Or was it? In spite of the straightforward words Moreton used on the twenty-first, he was still quibbling the next day about giving up his voting rights, which he called "quite unnatural" (he tried to limit the waiver to the period that the loan was outstanding, assuming optimistically—as always—that this might be less than eighteen months). Mackenzie, who agreed with Moreton's assessment of the clause, warned him that he must accept it anyway, since some of the money had been raised on these precise conditions, which could not be deviated from. "Another thing," Mackenzie added, "there must be no circulars or appeals of any kind to shareholders. It would spoil all my chances." He was getting to know Moreton quite well.[8]

When it seemed that nothing more could go wrong, Moreton, like a balky mule, decided to resist. Mackenzie asked Ted to use his influence, and instead he got a wire back supporting Moreton (although Ted continued privately to urge Moreton to accept). On December 24, Mackenzie again urged Frewen to accept the voting rights clause, noting that Andrew Whitton had put up £2,000 ($10,000) of his own money, which was more than any of Moreton's friends had put up![9]

Moreton had not been idle while Mackenzie was anxiously awaiting his response to Gray's offer. Finally, he wrote to Mackenzie, noting that he had talked with shareholders, and they were of the opinion that he should take over management in the West; it would therefore not do for him to promise Gray to give it up. He even imagined that he could be held liable for damages for doing so![10] He was encouraged on this course by Lord Rosslyn, who told him he might well decide to give up interference but should never give up the voting rights. At the same time, his lordship politely declined to put up any further funds for the company's use ("Mackenzie writes for £10,000 as if I were Rothschild," he said).[11]

Finally, all the pleading bore some fruit, and Moreton wrote to say that he would accept the conditions, provided that the liquidator and the board were parties to the agreement, and not Gray personally.[12] Before the month was out, however, there were changes in his outlook, and Mackenzie was again pleading for firm, unequivocal acceptance of the terms. He noted that Moreton was wrong in attributing to Gray and Whitton bad faith in the matter. "There is somebody behind both him and Whitton who keeps us all up to his requirements," Mackenzie said. Moreton showed this letter to Rosslyn, who suggested that the fly in the ointment was Wharncliffe. He added his own support for the intransigence Moreton was again showing.[13]

Mackenzie suggested a solution that should have solved the problem: he would be named as proxy to vote Moreton's shares. Unfortunately, this was objected to by the lending group, leading Mackenzie to remind Moreton that there was "somebody else" behind this problem. Then Moreton's old friend, Lord St. Oswald was substituted as proxy, which Mackenzie hoped would satisfy everyone. This brought forth an amazing wire from Moreton: "Will assign to Beckett

[Denison], Wharncliffe or any Scot, not Lord St. Oswald."[14] In light of Rosslyn's speculation about Wharncliffe, this is a very difficult communication to explain. The objection to St. Oswald can be explained, if not comprehended, because we have Moreton's own reasoning for it. He told Mackenzie that he would not involve Lord St. Oswald in "this damned cesspool" because of his fondness and respect for the man, and because of the trouble he expected in the near future. "I would as soon quarrel with my father and use his name in circulars."[15]

Nevertheless, Mackenzie (who was also surprised at the wire) told Moreton to go down to Stibbard's office, write Denison's name in place of St. Oswald, and sign the papers. Stibbard made the same offer to Frewen.[16] And finally he did sign.

Moreton gave Clara his own version of this fall from power. He blamed it on the fact that when he went west, he had had no authority to borrow. This was true, although there was never any indication that he had secured terms that were acceptable in London. "I am quite decided not to come back on the board as things are," he wrote from Montreal. "I am not going to be treated after this fashion."[17] One wonders if Clara really believed he could get back on the board if he wanted to!

At Superior the situation was critical, although Plunkett did not hold Lingham personally responsible. Lingham had unexpectedly received 1,500 head of cattle in poor condition to be fed, for which no preparations had been made. "They are now in the open yard with snow up to their bellies," Lingham said, "with the account at the bank overdrawn, and no money to either buy feed or pay the freight on them."[18] Plunkett estimated that the company would as a result realize from 6,000 head only what it should have got from 5,000 head. This problem was created by the divided lines of communication and authority, which had been permitted, and indeed, fostered, by the board and by Moreton.

Plunkett was relatively pleased about the Alberta range. The grass was very good, although the country was too open for a good winter range.

Plunkett's report irritated Moreton exceedingly, but a less partial reader must be impressed with the temperate tone and the number of references laudatory to Moreton's judgment. To be sure, Plunkett sketched the comic-opera efforts of Richard Frewen to take over operations, acting, as Dick supposed, on behalf of Moreton. But then

Horace said, "He acted with characteristic openness, and the most that can be said against him is, that his zeal somewhat outstripped his discretion." He even thought Murphy had done a good job (none the worse for having been fired so many times!), and he complimented Lingham at Superior, remarking of all these men, "It is only fair to point out that they are all of Mr. M. Frewen's appointment."

On the future prospects for the company, Plunkett did not expect that it would be able to pay dividends for the next five years, but he did think that the debenture holders would be well advised to let the management continue to try to realize maximum value from the remaining assets, rather than demand immediate liquidation (the interest had not been paid). As we shall see, he shortly changed his mind about this recommendation.

Moreton called the report "discreditable, dishonorable, a breach of trust." He was highly critical of Plunkett for having divulged the finances of the company to the shareholders, not seeing the irony of such a complaint by one who had placed a letter with the newspapers urging that all cattle be sold! Ted Frewen told Mackenzie that Plunkett's kind words for Moreton and Dick were nothing more than evidence that Horace was a "regular shuffler & thoroughly inconsistent. He abuses my brothers (for which I don't blame him) & then proceeds to pat them on the back, as if he was afraid he'd said too much."[19] There may be something to Ted's analysis; there is an unreal sense about the way Plunkett responded with gentleness to the sharpest barbs thrown at him by Dick and Moreton.

In February, Plunkett met with the board, who were still trying to get him to reconsider his resignation. He told them that his terms would include payment of £600 for 1886 (his original appointment was without pay) and similar payment for 1887. He wanted absolute control, and he now insisted that he would only take the job to liquidate the operation, not to continue it.[20]

Naturally, the accounts prepared in the spring of 1887 did not include the effects of the winter just ending. The accounts were sent out by Fitch Kemp on March 22, 1887. He informed the shareholders that he had not been able to transfer the assets to the new company because the liabilities of the old company could not be paid off; he had therefore secured permission of the court to borrow a total of £30,000 ($145,000) on the security of the old company's assets to continue operations.

He did note that reports from the range were ominous, and that serious losses might require the cattle account to be written down further. As it was, the calf brand in 1886 had only been 6,485, more than 1,300 fewer than the previous year (which also represented a decline from 1884). Still the books showed a total of nearly 43,000 head, including the 6,800 on the Alberta range. Sales from all locations only totalled 3,472, about 1,000 fewer than the previous year, and only £17,700 ($86,000) were realized from these sales. Cash expenses amounted to nearly £20,000 before interest on the new debentures, so that there was a substantial loss to be carried to the balance sheet. The total deficit to be applied against the £200,000 of ordinary shares was nearly £96,000 ($465,000). The ordinary shareholder was disappearing rapidly as a financial element in the company. Instead, the old preference shareholders, who had a £100,000 position before the exchange of their shares for debentures, would have a £120,000 position after the organization of the new company was completed, and this position would be secured by second mortgage debentures. The direction of the company had passed from the hands of a board on which Moreton had a few friends, to a liquidator he now despised. Frewen's efforts had actually worsened the situation.

Kemp's report did pay tribute to the wisdom of some of Moreton's suggestions, such as the drive to Alberta, but it pointedly noted that the Superior operation had proved unprofitable (Plunkett expected that it would lose £7,000 [$34,000]).[21] He also noted that Frewen had agreed not to interfere with the management of the company until after July 1, 1888 (the period covered by assignment of his proxy to William Beckett Denison). Kemp urged the shareholders to give Plunkett such assurances of confidence and support as would cause him to withdraw his resignation.

But Moreton had other hopes. He had made an arrangement to secure marketing rights for a lubricator that could be attached to railway cars and maintain lubrication, preventing "hot boxes." His trip to the West in 1886 was in part to further this project. He was in Montreal in August, and there he got encouragement from the Canadian Pacific: they would install one of these devices on a transcontinental passenger train and run it to the Pacific and back without a break in service. In Omaha, he talked with the Union Pacific, and he saw the Northern Pacific at St. Paul. By October, the results of the Canadian Pacific test were in, and favorable; Moreton was sure they would now use it.[22]

Notes to Chapter 12

1. Horace C. Plunkett, "Report to the Shareholders of the Powder River Cattle Company, Limited, by the Manager," December 18, 1886, Frewen Papers.

2. Horace C. Plunkett to Frewen, November 15, 1886, Frewen Papers.

3. Edward Frewen to Frewen, November 24, 1886, Frewen Papers.

4. Horace C. Plunkett to Frewen, December 3, 1886, Frewen Papers.

5. Everett Gray to Charles Fitch Kemp, December 3, 1886, Frewen Papers.

6. Edward Frewen, William Mackenzie, George D. Stibbard, and Charles Fitch Kemp to Frewen, December 21, 1886, Frewen Papers.

7. Frewen to Charles Fitch Kemp, December 21, 1886, Frewen Papers.

8. William Mackenzie to Frewen, December 22, 1886, Frewen Papers.

9. William Mackenzie to Frewen, December 24, 1886, Frewen Papers.

10. Frewen to William Mackenzie, December 24, 1886, Frewen Papers.

11. Earl of Rosslyn to Frewen, December 25, 1886, Frewen Papers.

12. Charles Fitch Kemp to Frewen, December 28, 1886, Frewen Papers.

13. William Mackenzie to Frewen, January 4, 1887; and Earl of Rosslyn to Frewen, January 5, 1887, Frewen Papers.

14. Frewen to William Mackenzie, January 6, 1887, Frewen Papers.

15. Frewen to William Mackenzie, January 6, 1887, Frewen Papers.

16. Stibbard, Gibson & Sykes to Frewen, January 7, 1887, Frewen Papers.

17. Frewen to Clara Frewen, November 25, 1886, Frewen Papers.

18. F. R. Lingham to Charles W. Middleton Kemp, November 24, 1886, Frewen Papers.

19. Edward Frewen to William Mackenzie, January 17, 1887, Frewen Papers.

20. Plunkett diary, February 15, March 1, 1887.

21. Plunkett diary, April 27, 1887.

22. Frewen to Clara Frewen, August 9, 19, 31, September 26, and October 16, 1886, Frewen Papers.

·13·

War and Winter

*M*oreton certainly had a fine sense for timing his disasters. Just when it seemed that enough money could be raised to pay off the debts of the old company, he devised a new plan to thwart the reorganization of the company. He told Mackenzie that he wanted to prevent the assets of the old company from being handed over to the new company because he did not trust the new board.[1]

Although he could not have known it at the time, this additional burden on the poor struggling Powder River company was coming on top of the worst winter the Wyoming range cattle industry had ever experienced. The weather was by no means the only problem of that terrible winter, as overcrowding on the range and lax business practices of some of the operators also took their toll, but the cumulative effect when spring came was a loss from which many never recovered.

Although nearly everyone who deals with the winter of 1886–87 knows that it was bad, there is limited contemporary information that is reliable. The newspapers of the day were wary of offending the cattle interests by speculating on the rigors of the weather, and only very general reports in the eastern press told a partial story. All seem agreed that there was a lot of wind, which the *Boomerang* called "ceaseless," and it was impossible to ignore the deaths of ranch hands at Sundance, Evanston, and Stinking Water. Yet, when Dr. Larson studied the contemporary reports, he found that there were massive gaps in the available information.[2]

The bartender at the Cheyenne Club is supposed to have soothed the grieving cattlemen there by reminding them that their herd tallies bore no direct relationship to the number of animals on the range, anyway: "Don't worry boys; after all the books won't freeze."[3] (He may, indeed, have said that, but the idea was not original with him;

two years earlier, I. S. Bartlett quoted Colonel Luke Murrin's camp-
fire conversation about cattle losses: "Never mind, boys, keep the books
warm. Keep the books warm.")[4]

Nevertheless, the newspapers still wanted to avoid most news
that would damage the already sick industry; the *Democratic Leader* was
indignant at a Chicago *Tribune* story estimating losses in Montana
at 40 to 65 percent.[5] The *Northwestern Live Stock Journal* contented itself
with weather reports for Montana and other distant places, saying
the Wyoming cattle were in fine condition, until finally the *Big Horn
Sentinel* growled that readers might occasionally prefer a few truthful
remarks.[6]

Range cattle, some looking "as if they had all seen their last day,"
had been roaming the outskirts of Cheyenne since the first week of
January, and by March the police gave up trying to keep them under
control in the city itself.[7] The usual warming chinook winds were blow-
ing by January 22, but they didn't last long enough to be a real benefit,
and soon the melted snow was ice again. In early February a storm
blockaded the Wyoming Central railroad near Lusk, and high winds
prevented clearing the tracks, so that provisions had to be packed in
to the trapped passengers.[8]

For a time, the word from Calgary (via Murphy in North Platte)
was that the cattle there were "all fat," and that there had been no
snow, although it was very cold. Considering the losses that were
beginning to be known on the Wyoming range, Murphy wondered
if Moreton couldn't concoct some scheme to get his hands on the
Alberta herd and leave the others to the company. "Can't you report
them all dying up there, or some such scheme, and get them to let
you have that outfit?" he asked. As to the Wyoming ranges, he said,
"The prospects are now that we will lose 60 per cent of all cattle in
Wyoming, and sure 50." In his bitterness, he took considerable satisfaction from this retribution, which had been none of his doing.[9]

By February, the severity of losses on the ranges was beginning
to be reported in the eastern press, although the postmaster at Albright,
Montana, said that the foremen of the big outfits were only stirring
from their chairs in front of the stove to tell the editors that "all is
well." A report from Ft. Keogh, Montana, reported "enormous" losses,
while another from Assinaboina noted reports of losses of 25 percent,
but said that most were "thankful if they have enough left to start
anew in spring." Hay was scarce at $50 a ton.[10] Although there were

various reports of losses on the western ranges, the facts were late coming in, and even experienced cattlemen such as Morton Post were still saying that the situation was being exaggerated.

The new year opened with the northern ranges covered with six inches to two feet of snow (in Cheyenne there was not yet enough snow for sleighing; that situation would shortly change). On the Powder River ranges, the cowhands were riding a line to keep the stock out of the river bottoms, where feed was very scarce. There were two weeks of "ceaseless" storms in the north, and the *Sentinel* now estimated that losses there would be at least 20 percent, even if the weather now turned warm; otherwise, 50 percent was more likely.[11] A Sundance rancher found a calf six months old completely hemmed in by the snow around a single tree. Before it was rescued, the poor starving animal had stripped the bark from the tree as far up as it could reach. It was a fortunate survivor.[12]

The Powder River herds were trying none too successfully to cope with one of the severest winters in history. Although Plunkett had agreed with Moreton's 1882 assessment that the Powder River range was one of the finest in the northwest, in his report at the end of 1886, he termed it a "wilderness." As a consequence, most of the other cattle outfits had moved out, so that the Powder River cattle had plenty of room, although little grass.

Snow was one to three feet deep, and the temperatures were ten to twenty degrees below zero; the cattle were dying. Men at the Powder River company were quoted as saying that they would drive more cattle north into Alberta, where the herds were faring well, but this forelorn hope required that the poor animals should survive their present troubles. In any case, despite Murphy's euphoric reports from afar, conditions in Alberta were really not as favorable as the sufferers in Wyoming thought. A letter from Calgary at the end of February reported that the winter there had been the worst in twenty-five years; the Powder River cattle up there had drifted badly, and many had died.[13]

By the middle of February, the weather again turned milder for a time, and the snow began to disappear on the northern ranges. The beleaguered cattlemen could at least take comfort in the thought that the heavy snowfall would mean good grazing in the summer. But there was more. In a storm that was one of the worst of that awful winter, the northern ranges were swept with a heavy snowfall in the third week of April, with devastating effect on the calf crop.[14] With that, the winter was finally over.

The tragedy on the range was being played out far away from the warfare between Moreton Frewen and the Powder River Cattle Company. The main actors in that other play were certainly unaware of the gravity of conditions in Wyoming, although, as we know, Moreton was concerned about the general situation. Yet, there had been bad winters before, and the Powder River ranges had demonstrated their great resilience in the face of adversity. Consequently, Frewen's exertions were directed toward his battle with the company, and specifically toward keeping the reorganization from taking place.

Mackenzie, who was still working to get the money to keep the company alive (at least for a couple of years), tried to head off this new threat to stability. After a good deal of pleading and cajoling, Moreton retreated a trifle to suggest that his grievances could be handled by arbitration. Mackenzie seized on this with relief, offering to review his arbitration proposal.[15]

Moreton now charged off in this direction. The liquidator, Fitch Kemp, had been regularly needling him about taking up his obligation to purchase the Superior property, and Moreton in early April suggested the arbitration route for his general claim on his contract.[16] Kemp promptly appointed his arbitrator, listing the company's claim against Moreton for £1,254 ($6,000) (including the old claim for the unpaid portion of Peters's salary). At this point, Moreton declined to appoint his arbitrator; he delayed because he was already contemplating another action.

"One thing is certain, the property must be got out of the hands of that salvage corps in Walbrook," he said to Mackenzie, referring to the address of the company headquarters in London.[17] He told Mackenzie that he intended to sue, and the Scotsman wrote back to tell him that he could not collect damages on his contract. Asked for advice on the same subject, Morton Post urged Moreton to wait until he knew more about losses on the range; he did say that he thought Frewen had good grounds for a suit.[18]

The general meeting of the shareholders of the old company was held March 29, 1887, with Lord St. Oswald in the chair; he emphasized that he had not been involved in past controversy, and he hoped to keep "within due limits" the opinions to be expressed—this proved a vain hope. After hearing Kemp's report, Moreton rose to tell the shareholders of a conspiracy to victimize him. He blamed his failure to borrow the necessary money on the fact that no power of attorney was ever issued by the liquidator; yet when he returned, having thus failed to secure the funds, he found the Gray offer, conditioned on his resignation. In this way, "a pistol was held to my head, and my votes snatched from me."

In his inimitable way, he gave the shareholders his opinion of Plunkett. "I know Mr. Plunkett well; he has been my neighbour on Powder for many years. A more unfortunate choice, as I wrote at the time, could not have been made. He is altogether too weak a man, in my judgment, for the critical times on which we had fallen in this business. The result, anyhow, is that, left to shift for themselves on an absolutely exhausted range, our property is at this moment squandered, dead or dying along the hill sides or streams of the Big Horn Mountains." He was now of the opinion that losses on the Wyoming and Montana ranges would run to one-third.

He also complained about the company accounts. There were £120,000 of debentures on the balance sheet, and he argued that these debentures had no existence until the transfer to the International company was complete.[19] In this matter, he was certainly technically correct.

Plunkett was at the meeting and noted that there were only thirty shareholders present. He called Moreton's attack on him "savage," but thought few cared about the speech. Many of them pressed Horace to continue in management in America.[20]

Moreton also told the assembly that he was intending to appeal his rights under his agreement with the company (the 1882 agreement) to "a western jury." This prompted the company to go to the British courts immediately to seek an injunction against him, since disputes under his contract were to be settled by arbitration. Mr. Justice Kay handed down his judgment a month later, in which he restrained Frewen from any proceedings in America against the company.

Moreton immediately cabled Post to inform him of the British court's restraining order on him, so it is obvious that Post was more of a co-conspirator with Moreton, rather than merely a creditor of the company. He responded that he would "be careful."[21] Indeed, Moreton referred to Post as his partner on more than one occasion, and he warned Ted that he intended to go to America to give evidence in whatever action Post might decide to take.[22]

The liquidator was continuing to negotiate with Plunkett, and it was now being proposed that Plunkett receive a salary of £1,000, on the condition that he remit half of that sum to Frank Kemp. Moreton complained that Horace was not being required to commit full time to the position.[23]

Moreton then tried to get Plunkett to renounce the manager's position by appealing to Horace's father, Lord Dunsany. Incredibly, he tried to carry off this difficult bit of persuasion by seeking to demonstrate Horace's incompetence to the baron, noting that the Powder River company had paid dividends while Moreton was managing it, while under Horace's management it had not. Also, he claimed that he always had good men working for him, while Horace's ranch was always in the hands of "thieves and drunks."[24] Not surprisingly, these pleadings failed to impress Dunsany, so Frewen tried again. Claiming that Plunkett had cost the Frewen brothers fully £50,000 in the Dakota and Powder River companies, he urged his lordship to prevail on Horace to withdraw, presumably on grounds of equity.[25]

The baron replied that Horace did not agree that he caused the Frewens a loss; indeed, he thought his management was a benefit to the company, and Dunsany noted that this opinion was shared by others who had much money staked on it. As to Moreton's oft-expressed claim that Horace had injected himself wrongly into the company's affairs, Dunsany noted that Plunkett's own operations would have been much affected by any bankruptcy of the Powder River company on its range. Nevertheless, Dunsany did wish Horace would give up the manager's position, but he said that Horace was determined to improve the company's situation. In the interest of full communication, Dunsany sent Moreton's letter on to Horace![26]

It is obvious that the reason Moreton decided to throw everything behind some kind of lawsuit was the realization that the deal he had made to restructure the company had backfired: the preferred shareholders now could get debentures and could take all of the remaining assets. "If we are forced to repay the £120,000 in lump sums between now and 1889–1890, infallibly we common shareholders will get nothing whatsoever. Our capital is wholly gone," he told Mackenzie. "Your preference people having milked the cow dry, are now anxious to kill her for beef!"[27] At least he had not lost his sense of humor. He now had a new reorganization to propose. The debentures should be paid off in series before 1894 (he later told Ted 1896), with interest at 6 percent until redeemed, the office expenses in England should be further reduced, and George D. Stibbard should sever his connection with the company ("Mr. Stibbard I won't see except in a law court, that is flat," Moreton told Ted).[28]

Mackenzie was also getting reports from the West, which indicated to him that there had been very heavy losses in Montana and Wyoming. By early June, Maurice J. Lothian had heard that native stock suffered 7 percent losses, trail stock and eastern cattle 10 to 25 percent; in northern Montana losses were 25 to 40 percent.[29] Mackenzie also had learned of heavy losses in Alberta (Murphy continued to estimate that they would not run over 5 percent, but he was having trouble with the Indians).[30] Plunkett got to the Powder River range in May, and there Fred Hesse told him that the company's herds there were literally melting away. Two months later, Horace had concluded that the losses would run 75 percent on stock cattle and a minimum of 10 percent on steers — "A calamity, indeed."[31]

Mackenzie learned that the Canadians were not inclined to let more cattle in without payment of duty, and he bitterly remarked, "I never knew of such an unfortunate company."[32] The matter of the duty remained vague. Moreton told Ted that he had "little doubt" that the remaining cattle on the Wyoming and Montana ranges (the "survivors") could be got into Canada duty free.[33] He even briefly contemplated going to Ottawa to assist in this matter, but when Mackenzie reminded him that he had no authority to act on behalf of the company, he quite uncharacteristically cancelled the trip.[34]

Moreton did not cancel his Ottawa journey entirely out of deference to Mackenzie's remonstrance about lack of authority; he had another trip in prospect that was more interesting to him.

Notes to Chapter 13

1. Frewen to William Mackenzie, January 20, 1887, Frewen Papers.

2. Taft Alfred Larson, "The Winter of 1886–87 in Wyoming," *Annals of Wyoming* 14(1) (January 1942), passim.

3. Edward Everett Dale, in John Clay, *My Life on the Range* (New York, 1961), xiv.

4. *Cheyenne Daily Sun*, February 15, 1885.

5. *Democratic Leader*, March 27, 1887.

6. *Big Horn Sentinel*, January 29, 1887.

7. *Democratic Leader*, January 8, March 3, 1887.

8. *Cheyenne Daily Sun*, February 12, 1887.

9. E. W. Murphy to Frewen, January 12, 1887, Frewen Papers.
10. *New York Times,* February 14, 17, 19, 1887.
11. *Big Horn Sentinel,* January 15, 1887.
12. *Cheyenne Daily Sun,* February 4, 1887.
13. *Big Horn Sentinel,* February 6, March 5, 1887.
14. *Big Horn Sentinel,* April 23, 1887.
15. Frewen to William Mackenzie, April 2, 1887, Frewen Papers.
16. Frewen to Charles Fitch Kemp, April 2, 1887, Frewen Papers.
17. Frewen to William Mackenzie, April 12, 1887, Frewen Papers.
18. Morton E. Post to Frewen, March 31, 1887; and William Mackenzie to Frewen, March 21, 1887, Frewen Papers.
19. *The Financial News,* April 1, 1887.
20. Plunkett diary, March 29, 1887.
21. Morton E. Post to Frewen, April 29, 1887, Frewen Papers.
22. Frewen to Edward Frewen, April 22, 1887, Frewen Papers.
23. Frewen to William Mackenzie, April 19, 1887, Frewen Papers.
24. Frewen to Baron Dunsany, April 4, 1887, Frewen Papers.
25. Frewen to Baron Dunsany, April 22, 1887, Frewen Papers.
26. Baron Dunsany to Frewen, April 29, 1887, Frewen Papers.
27. Frewen to William Mackenzie, April 15, 1887, Frewen Papers.
28. Frewen to Edward Frewen, April 22, 1887, Frewen Papers.
29. Maurice J. Lothian to Frewen, June 8, 1887, Frewen Papers.
30. E. W. Murphy to Frewen, April 13, 1887, Frewen Papers.
31. Plunkett diary, May 25, July 2, 1887.
32. William Mackenzie to Frewen, March 21, 1887, Frewen Papers.
33. Frewen to Edward Frewen, April 22, 1887, Frewen Papers.
34. Frewen to William Mackenzie, April 29, 1887; William Mackenzie to Frewen, May 3, 1887; and Frewen to William Mackenzie, May 4, 1887, Frewen Papers.

· 14 ·

Eastern Interlude

*T*he prospect that so easily diverted Moreton from his trip to Ottawa was arranged by the good offices of Lord Randolph Churchill. In a sense, it was only fair that Lord Randolph should do a favor for Moreton, since the political downfall of Churchill had ruined yet another of Frewen's chances, if Anita Leslie has the story right.

Churchill had been at the very pinnacle of his public life in the fall of 1886; he was Chancellor of the Exchequer in Lord Salisbury's cabinet, after having dictated his own terms for taking the post. One day, Queen Victoria invited him to spend the night at Windsor Castle. While there, in a move worthy of Moreton Frewen, he sat down at a desk and, using the queen's own stationery, wrote Salisbury his letter of resignation. After sending off the letter and a copy to the *Times,* he then went to bed, not bothering even to tell Jennie (nor did he tell his hostess, who was not amused, to say the least). Although Lord Randolph had apparently not expected that Salisbury would accept the resignation, the prime minister did just that. It was the end of Churchill's political career. The man selected to replace him at the exchequer was George Joachim Viscount Goschen, and when Lord Randolph was told of the appointment, he said, "I forgot Goschen," causing the viscount to go through life as the man whom Lord Randolph forgot.[1] Anita Leslie says that Moreton had secured the position as secretary to Goschen and could have expected a high post, had it not been necessary for him to withdraw because of the circumstances of Goschen's elevation.[2]

Nevertheless, Lord Randolph still had some friends, and when Moreton needed help, Randolph sent him to Joseph Rock, the agent for the Nizam of Hyderabad, to undertake an assignment with Sir Salar Jung, recently dismissed prime minister for the Nizam. Best of all, the job would really pay a salary! He was to get £500 ($2,400) for about six months of his time, plus his expenses.[3]

After dashing off a new circular to the Powder River shareholders, Moreton left for the East. By late May he was in Cairo, wondering what effect his new circular was having, and giving Clara orders for the party he was planning for Sir Salar Jung in July. It had been a part of Moreton's assignment to keep Jung out of England during the queen's jubilee celebration. Now that the celebration was past, a visit might safely be contemplated. The nabob had his heart set on attending the Goodwood Races, and this would require renting a suitable house in the area and plans for entertainment. Moreton was obsessed by the need to devise a suitable guest list (in one letter he wrote, "Where can I find Kinsky?" referring to Count Kinsky, Jennie's perennial admirer).[4] Instructions flew: avoid the "masher" gang, "we ain't that kind of party, get some one clever."[5] He suggested inviting Louisa, Duchess of Manchester, although she and the other old Duchess M (presumably Marlborough) may not get on. After suggesting to Clara all sorts of important people, he ended unconvincingly, "but ask who you like, don't be too particular about their being swells."[6] As to Clara herself, she must have a nice gown or two, in spite of the need to economize; she must look well for this occasion. Who knows, it might lead to a permanent job in India![7]

Presently he received another serious assignment from Sir Salar. That gentleman had grown attached to the sister of Princess Nazli of Egypt, niece of the Khedive Ismail, and he wanted Moreton to so arrange for the marriage that he could pick the lady up on his way home the following winter (rather as one might arrange to buy a handsome sofa!). Frewen at once embarked on the duty, and the communications were launched. For this service Sir Salar offered Moreton a pair of studs, which he refused, not to appear as a "boodler."[8] Then a snag appeared — the parents of the intended bride were "vile." "As are all the Turks, they would sell her like a bale of cloth." But suddenly, it was all agreed: the marriage was arranged, although not until November.[9]

Despite Moreton's salaried position, he continued to have money problems. He was looking for the £70 he needed to pay the costs assessed against him when Justice Kay ruled against him. Although Sir Salar owed him £300, he did not want to ask for any more from him (having already received an advance of £200). He dispatched Clara to negotiate a £200 loan from another friend.[10] Soon, he was writing to Stuart Wortley (Lord Wharncliffe's nephew) that he could not pay the loan he had got from that source, which he claimed was at an effective interest rate of over 16 percent.[11] Then the Powder River company served him with a petition in bankruptcy for old bills owing there, causing him to threaten dire consequences in the West (of which more later).[12] Yet, his optimism had not deserted him; he still thought the Superior land development would make him rich (£50,000 or so).[13]

While he was occupied in the East, word reached Moreton that Alec Swan's operation had gone down. Frewen remarked, "If such as he are busting, there is little hope for us smaller fry of amateurs." Swan had been surety on a $25,000 note to the German Savings Bank of Davenport, Iowa, and when the note was unpaid, the bank attached the Swan assets while Swan was in Europe. Swan bravely declared that the attachment had nothing to do with the current conditions in the cattle industry, and a few days later the *Sun* confidently opined that Swan would soon resume his business.[14] But it was not to be.

The *New York Times* noted that just four years earlier Swan had been known as the cattle king of Wyoming. The First National Bank of Cheyenne was a principal creditor of Swan's, who sat on its board. Even the president of the bank was surprised — he thought the Swan firm "very wealthy."[15] In financial extremity, Swan did not behave as his friends would have hoped: he made a midnight assignment of his assets to a receiver, so as to avoid the levy of the bank. Although the bank sold his stock, it was badly injured by the losses. Calling Swan the best cattle man in all the northwest, Moreton briefly turned over in his mind the thought of bankruptcy for the Powder River company.[16] The following year, Frewen heard of the failure of the Sturgis outfit, with losses of a million and a half mentioned; here was another "good businessman" who had gone broke in the cattle business. Peters's operation in Wyoming had also fallen on bad times. Peters, it seems, had turned to drink (according to Lingham). Lord Wharncliffe was a loser there, too, which gave Moreton a certain spiteful sense of pleasure.[17]

Then, in October, the Cheyenne business community was shocked to learn that Morton E. Post & Co. had suspended operations. To inspire confidence in the shaken city, Francis E. Warren, former territorial treasurer and governor, and A. J. Parshall, the cashier of the bank, were appointed trustees to oversee the liquidation; the bonds of the trustees were signed by the major bankers in Cheyenne. The severity of the cattle disaster was told by the numbers: once holding deposits of a million dollars, the bank was down to a quarter of that size by the time it suspended. Prominent among the assets were the notes of Moreton Frewen ($100,000) and his brother Richard ($20,000). The *Cheyenne Daily Leader* reported hopes that Moreton's notes could be realized at 50 percent.[18]

As if to add a final insult to the misfortunes of the industry, the government in May designated cavalry troops from Fort McKinney to assist in the removal of illegal fences on the public domain.[19]

But Moreton had other schemes in progress. He dashed off a letter about a scheme to build a Hudson's Bay railroad in Canada. And, of course, there was also his ice maker and the lubricator for the railroads.[20] Neither was he neglecting his warfare with the Powder River company. The circular he had written before departing for the East started off by recounting his experiences in the western cattle business. He did not stint on a few choice remarks about the lack of experience of others, charging that many who were offering opinions came home every winter to England, and thus did not know anything about that season in Wyoming. In this group he placed Horace Plunkett, saying Plunkett had never seen a winter storm on the prairies and had as little conception as the Grand Lama as to what happened in the winter.

As to the financial troubles, Moreton rehashed the old story. He claimed that two banks in the West had been prepared to finance the company, but that this was prevented by the connivance of Kemp, Gray, Stibbard, and Whitton, who exacted his resignation and transfer of his proxy as conditions for the loan.

In an extensive attack on Plunkett's management, Frewen noted that Plunkett's own Frontier Cattle company had gone into liquidation the previous summer, and that it had paid only one dividend, of 1½ percent.[21] Actually, Plunkett's company had been the victim of multiple difficulties. His foreman had been arrested for horse stealing, which left the EK without a foreman at roundup time. Later, the cowboys saw Horace as a leader in the effort to reduce their wages, and some were talking of shooting him. While the owners were attempting to divide the property among themselves, a prairie fire hit the range, causing damage to fences and forage; only two weeks later the terrible winter of 1886–87 struck, with snow over the tops of the fences. The ungathered cattle were sold in the spring of 1888 for $15,000.[22]

Moreton's circular was soon followed by one signed by Maurice John Lothian, who said he was the owner of 500 shares. This paper was in fact drafted by Moreton, and he was intensely worried that by mistake it might be issued before his own circular was out — a potentially awkward situation, since it referred to his circular. In an effort to make it look independent, Lothian's circular said, "Personally, I ought to say that I know very little of Mr. Frewen. . . ." The Lothian paper supported the need to move as many cattle as possible to Alberta and to continue feeding at Superior. It questioned the hiring of Plunkett (because of cost). Finally, the paper listed sixteen western cattle, land, and timber companies, showing the dividends paid the previous year (mostly nil; the 10 percent dividend to the preferred shareholders for the Powder River company was the highest on the list); this information was designed to show the effect of overstocking on the industry in general.

The Lothian circular closed with four recommendations: that Frewen give up his legal proceedings; that the debenture holders be deferred until 1894 at 6 percent; that expenses be cut; and that Frewen be asked to sever all connection with the company, either as director or manager. The shareholders were warned that unless some settlement could be made, the company's assets would likely be attached by the debenture holders.[23]

The day before the circular was issued, Lothian wrote to Moreton, telling him that his circular was made to look a bit like an attack on Frewen. He urged Moreton to strike while this information was fresh in people's minds, and before they scattered for summer holidays.[24]

Some friends were not happy with the latest barrages. Alan Gardner, who had lost his board seat when Moreton was forced out, told Ted that he wished Moreton would let the whole thing drop, although he hoped Ted would stay on the board to keep the "vultures from gorging themselves."[25] Ted did not comment to Moreton on the pamphlets, except to say they were out. He noted that the financial condition of the company was worsening; Superior feeding was becoming a perfect "sink" for cash.[26]

The response from other shareholders was not encouraging. Lothian was disappointed that only seventeen shareholders, representing 4,275 shares, had written in support of his suggestions (including Clara Jerome, with 1,600 shares).[27] Perhaps there was a weariness with warfare.

In August, Moreton wrote to Denison about the reports that had finally been assembled about the condition of the western herds. He had heard that on both sides of the Big Horn Mountains herds were "nearly blotted out." Herds that once numbered 5,000 were down to 50 or so. The trail herds were particularly hard hit. As to the Powder River company, Plunkett now estimated that there were only 12,000 head on the Wyoming and Montana ranges, as compared with a book count of 33,000; the loss had been about 75 percent. The calf brand was only 1,200.

Moreton's previous hints about legal trouble with the company became clearer; he said that he had recently dissolved a "partnership," with the result that his late partner would now contest company titles in the West. The partner in question was obviously Post, who was conniving with Moreton to get around the prohibition of the British courts against any action by Frewen against the company.[28] Since Frewen was enjoined from acting against the company in the American courts, his solution was to have Post cause an action there. Moreton would then agree to come to America to give evidence and thereby get the legal hearing he had been wanting. "Unless I cable you on Wednesday the 5th October, make me bankrupt."[29] Obediently, Post cabled on September 30, "Have instructed attorney Cheyenne attach desert claim. Will reach Chicago Friday, Superior Saturday. Post." In October, word reached the company's Cheyenne lawyers that the Post bank had attached Moreton's desert land entry in Johnson County to recover on a $20,000 promissory note.[30]

Moreton also threatened to interfere with the sale of the Superior property. Plunkett had sold the property for $50,000, but the land was partly in Frewen's name (as was the ranch headquarters on Crazy Woman). Moreton warned that he intended to notify the purchasers that the company did not have good title to the Superior property, and to seek an injunction to halt the sale.[31]

These bold threats did bear fruit, but not of the sort he had anticipated. To secure his cooperation, the company prepared to force him into bankruptcy over the debts he owed it. Ready to pay the few hundred pounds he thought he owed to forestall the bankruptcy action, Moreton was surprised to learn that the company claimed a much larger sum was owed. A writ was issued to restrain him from leaving the country. Although he was able to get a deferral, he was effectively checkmated. In a letter to Clara, he wrote, "I believe it is all up." It seemed that Wharncliffe was again his nemesis. A provision of the agreement with the earl in which he had borrowed £5,000 ($24,000) made the principal due if the interest was not paid. The interest was in arrears. Therefore, the entire £5,000 could be claimed, and Wharncliffe was claiming it!

Mackenzie made another stab at getting the situation calmed. He warned Moreton that chances of success in the American courts were slight, and even if he did win, the action to upset the Superior transaction was merely wasting the few assets the company had with which to pay him.[32] While this advice was on its face given in good faith, Frewen had by this time come to believe that Mackenzie was chiefly motivated as the representative of the old preferred shareholders, and not solely as a friend to him.

While the lawyers continued to write to each other, sending copies off to their respective clients, Moreton bestirred himself to go off with Sir Salar Jung again, this time having persuaded the poor man to return to Hyderabad, despite the dangers he might incur there. To help with the duties of the journey, the faithful Lingham had once again signed on with Moreton. Soon, Frewen was writing Clara from exotic India, and his hopes were rising again: "I am feeling filled with confidence now."[33]

The Powder River company accounts for the year 1887 were dated March 29, 1888. Sales of cattle amounted to 4,399 head, on which only £9,200 ($44,500) were realized. The remaining herds were estimated to total 17,805, including a calf brand of 3,305 (1,586 in Alberta). While Fitch Kemp conceded that the Alberta herd was doing well, the need to pay duty on any further transfers from the southern ranges made it uneconomic to contemplate more movement from the south. Since the Superior feeding operation had realized only a little over £1 per head, the company was determined to sell that facility for $50,000, half in cash. Because of continuing inability to settle with the creditors of the old company, the new company had still not been organized.

Early in 1888, Bennet wrote to Moreton in India, bringing him up to date on company affairs. It now looked as though the range cattle industry had suffered losses of 50 to 99 percent. Bennet cited the example of one man who was able to gather only 79 head from a herd of 5,300 turned loose the previous fall. Beef prices were low, only two and a half to three cents per pound. Even without considering that the common shares of the Powder River company were worthless because of the reorganization of that company, Bennet felt that these events left him with ten years of his life "wasted." He reckoned that half the population north of the Platte had left the country, but that those remaining were ample for the limited work remaining. In spite of the economic troubles, only one bank had failed, the Post institution in Cheyenne. Closing this litany, Bennet said, "Hoping the East will treat you better than the West has done."[34]

At the end of 1887, Plunkett, too, gave up the western adventure and went home for the last time. A farewell dinner was held for him at the Cheyenne Club. He would serve in Parliament, and in 1903 Queen Victoria knighted him. His western experiences left a mark on him: he said they had been an education, although he thought he had learned more about men than about cattle. The country never held the fascination for him that it had for Moreton — Plunkett called it strange and unfriendly. The saddest comment was that he had no real friends there. Earlier, he had stated his assessment of the Wyoming people thusly: "They don't like us naturally, and on the whole I don't like them."[35]

Notes to Chapter 14

1. Elizabeth Longford, *Queen Victoria* (New York, 1964), 493.
2. Leslie, *Lady Randolph Churchill,* 140.
3. Frewen to Joseph Rock, May 6, 1887, Frewen Papers.
4. Frewen to Clara Frewen, May 25, 1887, Frewen Papers.
5. Frewen to Clara Frewen, May 25, 1887, Frewen Papers.
6. Frewen to Clara Frewen, July 1, 1887, Frewen Papers.
7. Frewen to Clara Frewen, May 25, 1887, Frewen Papers.
8. Frewen to Clara Frewen, May 26, 1887, Frewen Papers.
9. Frewen to Clara Frewen, July 1, 1887, Frewen Papers.
10. Frewen to Clara Frewen, June 4, 1887, Frewen Papers.
11. Frewen to Stuart Wortley, August 22, 1887, Frewen Papers.
12. Frewen to William Mackenzie, August 31, 1887, Frewen Papers.
13. Frewen to Clara Frewen, June 7, 1887, Frewen Papers.
14. *Cheyenne Daily Sun,* May 17, 21, 1887.
15. *New York Times,* May 17, 18, 1887.
16. Frewen to Clara Frewen, May 28, 1887, Frewen Papers.

17. Frewen to Clara Frewen, from Bombay, undated but probably 1888, Frewen Papers.

18. *Cheyenne Daily Leader,* October 11, 1887.

19. *Cheyenne Daily Sun,* May 20, 1887.

20. Frewen to C. A. Drummond, May 7, 1887, Frewen Papers.

21. Moreton Frewen, "Statement to the Shareholders of the Powder River Cattle Company," May 12, 1887.

22. Savage, "Plunkett of the EK," 212–13.

23. Maurice J. Lothian, "To the Shareholders of the Powder River Cattle Company," May 24, 1887, Frewen Papers.

24. Maurice J. Lothian to Frewen, May 23, 1887, Frewen Papers.

25. Alan Gardner to Edward Frewen, May 23, 1887, Frewen Papers.

26. Edward Frewen to Frewen, June 8, 1887, Frewen Papers.

27. Maurice J. Lothian to Frewen, June 8, 1887, Frewen Papers.

28. Frewen to William Beckett Denison, August 17, 1887, Frewen Papers.

29. Frewen to Morton E. Post, September 24, 1887, Frewen Papers.

30. Corlett, Lacey & Riner to Stibbard, Gibson & Sykes, October 27, 1887.

31. Frewen to Charles Fitch Kemp, September 9, 1887, Frewen Papers.

32. William Mackenzie to Frewen, October 1, 1887, Frewen Papers.

33. Frewen to Clara Frewen, December 5, 1887, Frewen Papers.

34. F. A. K. Bennet to Frewen, January 11, 1888, Frewen Papers.

35. Plunkett diary, July 21, 1881, November 2, 1887; and Trevor West, "Biography of Horace C. Plunkett," manuscript.

·15·

Eheu Fugaces

*M*oreton was fond of the quotation *Eheu fugaces,* which comes from the Horace lines, *"Eheu fugaces, Postume, Postume, labuntur anni."*[1] Ever impatient with his slow progress, he never had enough time to achieve what he had hoped; each year closed before the bonanza was realized.

The 1888 New Years greeting to Clara and the "chickens" (as he called the children) came from Aurangabad, where Moreton was contemplating new sallies at the Powder River company. He wanted her to dig out his letters from 1881 and find the "strongest" quotes about how well the cattle were doing on the range after the hard winter.

Moreton was in great good humor, even getting "fat." While stirring up political affairs in Hyderabad he still had time to go sightseeing, which excited him a good bit more than it did Lingham.[2] Another ranchman from America, the Marquis de Mores, had come to the East for shooting.[3] He travelled in great style, going off to Nepal with eighty elephants, if we can believe Moreton's report.[4]

Back in London, his solicitors were juggling the claims of creditors to keep disaster at bay. Indeed, it must be assumed that one of the incentives for his travel abroad during these months was to keep out of the reach of creditors; a frequent excuse given by his solicitor was that Mr. Frewen was out of the country. In the year ended in March 1888, the solicitors handled payments of £3,000 ($15,000) for him, including £800 ($3,900) apparently borrowed on short term from Count Kinsky so that the more pressing claims of the Powder River company could be met.[5]

Moreton continued to threaten the company with actions, and Post did attach the Crazy Woman property and had it put up for sale, while the company continued to press for an assignment of that property so that it could obtain its return. The British court did order such an assignment, but Frewen's solicitor happily recounted that the judge was not sure this would be legal in the United States and had therefore merely ordered such assignment as would be legal. Moreover, Moreton's solicitor convinced the judge that if Frewen were merely acting as a trustee for the company, his costs in the matter should be paid by the company, and the judge agreed![6] All of this only gave Moreton another excuse for delay, while he tried to get what he wanted from the company.

It was not entirely clear what he wanted, because the target kept changing. Even his own explanation is maddeningly confusing. He said of the Crazy Woman filing, "I regarded the property as mine and as entered for my benefit; at the same time I am quite prepared to admit that I had at the time the wish and the intention to convey the land to the company after title became vested in me." Of course, he had instigated the Post attachment of the property and now said, "I am quite prepared to convey the title to the company if the land is mine; but if it is now the property of the M. E. Post Co., then I am no longer to do so."[7] There was apparently never any dispute that the company's money was used to pay the filing fees and to make the necessary improvements to perfect claim to the property; moreover, it was indistinguishable from the other claims filed for the company by its employees, and Moreton never raised any question about the company's right to claim those properties. This was one of the least attractive reflections of his character.

At one point, his solicitor negotiated with all of his larger creditors, including the Powder River company, to give them between 20 and 30 percent in prompt payment and the promise of deferred payments for the balance. For a time, it looked as though the company would accept it, but finally "someone" among the creditors of that company insisted that no such settlement be made with Frewen unless he absolutely agreed to give up all his claims against the company, and this he would not do.

He was threatened with bankruptcy time after time, and although Lord Rosslyn tried to intervene on his behalf to prevent company action against Moreton, the Powder River company finally lost patience and tried to serve him with a bankruptcy motion covering the £933 ($4,600) judgment the company had secured against him; his solicitor paid the judgment to avoid the action.[8] Now that the money claim of the company was paid, Moreton refused to complete the property conveyance for the Crazy Woman acreage and associated ditches (the Moreton and Dick ditches). There were these occasional respites in the money struggle, but the problems never wholly went away. The house in London had to be sold, and at the end of July, bankruptcy proceedings were threatened by former friend Richardson, who was pursuing a claim of £6,000 ($29,000) against Moreton.[9]

Morton Post, who had played such a large part in the American side of Moreton's war with the company, had now fallen upon bad times himself. With an optimism almost Frewen-like, he moved to Ogden, Utah (which he thought would soon outstrip Salt Lake City and become a second Denver), where he was associated with the Inter-State Land and Town Company. The treasurer of that company was none other than Alexander H. Swan (who was also down on his luck).[10] From Ogden, Post sent hopeful letters to Moreton about coal speculations, and Frewen stirred himself to see if the funds could be raised to invest in them.[11] Somehow, Moreton found $6,400 to forward for this purpose.[12] Post also had hopes of recovering some of the money owed him by the Frewens, although the tone of his letters was always friendly.

Dick, who owed Post money, negotiated to transfer 1,000 of his shares in the Dakota company to Post in discharge of the notes he had signed. The Dakota company was now in liquidation, and it was expected that about £1 per share would be realized (there were no preferred shareholders to gobble up everything). Dick had altogether 3,000 shares, which he had loaned to Moreton, who had pledged them to secure some of his own debts; to release them would require money Moreton did not have. All of this was true, but it was also true that Moreton had apparently promised to release them to Dick and now would not do so. As always when Dick felt aggrieved, he took up his pen and wrote to his brother. "I can't quite understand," he said, "if you can't pay any portion of your debts, how you can afford to keep up a house in Park Lane." This letter struck fire, and another tumultuous Frewen family row erupted. Moreton wrote to Dick, Dick wrote to Moreton, Moreton wrote to Ted to get his opinion, Ted gave his opinion, Moreton was outraged, and so on. The record is fuzzy, but apparently Post was all but forgotten in the meantime; he would look elsewhere for money to get back on his feet.

Despite the forced conveyance of the Crazy Woman property to the Powder River company, Post still felt that his claim on it would prevail when he wrote to Moreton in February 1889.[13] The following year, the lawyer handling the bankrupt estate of the Post bank in Cheyenne wrote to Moreton's solicitors in London to inquire about the Crazy Woman property. The foreclosure that Post had arranged was still one of the assets of the defunct bank, but the Wyoming lawyer was uncertain whether Frewen had ever been entitled to it, or whether he had made the filing only as a trustee for the company.[14] So it was that the last ranch headquarters of the proud old Powder River Cattle Company was little more than a bone to be picked over by bankruptcy attorneys.

In 1888, it became apparent that Fitch Kemp, named as the liquidator of the Powder River company in order to transfer its assets to the International company, was in fact only to be the final liquidator of the old company. When he sent his report to the shareholders in the middle of the year, he summarized the situation. The preference shareholders now were entitled to a total of £125,000 ($611,000) (£100,000 face, plus dividends in arrears), and the assets did not exceed £90,000 ($440,000). Moreover, there were other debts of £23,000 ($112,000), making it absolutely certain that the ordinary shareholders had lost their entire investment.

The Alberta herd, that great hope in Moreton's mind, was being sold to satisfy the creditors, and about £48,000 ($235,000) would be realized, of which £10,000 would be in cash. Kemp was getting the permission of the court to conclude that sale.[15] The creditors had called a meeting of the preference shareholders in March 1888, to ask them to advance enough money to pay off the debts of the old company; this the preference shareholders declined to do. As a consequence, the creditors delayed throwing the company into bankruptcy only on Kemp's assurance that the Alberta herd would be sold promptly, and that they would be paid from the proceeds.[16]

Kemp's report to the shareholders stimulated another hot Frewen response. We need not spend much time recounting its substance, because so much of it had already been said before. Moreton still thought that the pressing debts could be paid entirely out of beef sales, the remaining Wyoming and Montana herds could be moved to Alberta, and in five years all would be well. Frewen and his friends solicited proxies of protest against sale of the herd, but when the matter came before the court for approval, Frewen's solicitor sadly reported that the efforts of Lord Rosslyn and others to have it set aside had

fallen on deaf ears. The judge was impressed that the proposed sale
had been approved by preference shareholders holding 64 percent of
that issue.[17] It was going to be a liquidation after all.

Moreton had one last plan to shake those rascals in London who
were oppressing him. In late August he went to the United States,
against the advice of Mackenzie, who was still pleading for a realistic
attitude in a matter where the conclusion was evident. Moreton was
defiantly planning some sort of legal action in Denver, and for this
purpose he had cabled ahead to Post to meet him. Then, suddenly,
he threw the whole thing up. To Clara he explained why: "It would
have involved getting into the witness box twice a year for probably
three years to come . . . and if after enormous legal expenses, I had
got only a few thousand dollars, it would have been a blow." But he
was not depressed. "Although I have had my journey for nothing,
yet I am glad I came: it settles that matter once for all."[18]

The following year, Kemp reported again on the liquidation, this
time only to the preference shareholders. He noted that he had asked
the ordinary shareholders if they wanted a meeting and had received
no answer. Only 1,499 head had been sold during the year; the calf
brand was 3,040. It was estimated that there were still 13,040 head
in the remaining herds. The total assets available to pay off the preference shareholders were estimated at almost £88,000 ($430,000) (of
which £40,000 was attributed to the cattle and horses), and there was
£4,000 ($20,000) owing to creditors. The directors were continuing
to draw their £1,000 in fees. It was a sad ending.

Still, the company was not totally worthless. In February 1889,
Lothian reported to Moreton that a few ordinary shares had traded
at five shillings ($1.22), and some of the preference shares had sold
for more than £2 ($9.78) in the Dundee market.[19]

In the middle of 1889, Fred Hesse negotiated the sale of the Wyoming herds. The deal called for the transfer of all the cattle owned
by the company that could be delivered in the years 1889 and 1890,
up to a total of 15,000 head. We do not know what the terms of the
sale were, but there were apparently unusual penalty clauses, and
Hesse was obviously nervous about it. He wrote to Plunkett, who
was still manager of the company in the West, "I am very pleased
that you have confidence in me in the face of what I suppose to the
shareholders looks like a most reckless piece of business."[20]

Unfortunately, Plunkett was not pleased with the deal, and Hesse had to remind him that the purchaser (Wibaux) was "the only man, I suppose in America, who could or would have bought as large a herd of she stock as ours." Hesse admitted that Wibaux had demanded more than any other purchaser.[21] The company eventually realized $139,000 on the Wibaux sale, for a total of 7,419 cattle and 100 horses.[22]

At the end of 1889, Hesse summarized the assets that were left. There were still about 3,500 head of cattle, and 200 horses (the latter had been sold but not delivered). The breeding stock were still there, 70 Sussex cattle and 61 Shorthorns, and there was some land. The 160 acres filed on by Tom Morgan on the Powder River was in the company name, as were 800 acres filed on by Warren and Carter on the Tongue River. Hesse also listed the 480 acres in the Frewen filing. Excluding the value of land and buildings (which Hesse found hard to assess in the depressed market), the company had $7,255.98 in assets, from which liabilities and expenses of $3,830.44 had to be paid.[23]

But the old company and its ranges still refused to die. Before the end of the year, Hesse had found another 500 head of cattle, and a year and a half later they were still turning up! In the middle of 1891, Hesse wrote, "76 cattle are turning up very well, and I believe we should get enough out of them to pay the whole thing."[24] By this time, Hesse himself was apparently the major creditor of the old company, having covered obligations from his own funds.[25]

A poignant footnote to Moreton's relationship with the grand old ranch on the Powder River was written in a letter from one of Frewen's old employees there in the fall of 1888. The cattle, the few that remained, were big and fat, he said, although no one now had the money to prosper from a benevolent nature that provided an abundance of rain and grass. The old man hoped that Moreton could get the board of directors in far-off London to give him Old Jim, his horse of ten years' association. But Moreton was without the power even to arrange a soft berth for a worn-out cow pony.[26]

This was not the end of Moreton's adventures; there was more, much more. By the end of October, he was on the water again, headed for India, and by Christmas his spirits had revived sufficiently to contemplate going on with the Hudson's Bay railroad business and hunting coal beds in Wyoming in partnership with Post.[27] Although he never returned to the Wyoming range, he found excitement and hope in South Africa, Australia, and elsewhere, and eventually he came back to England to live out his last years. Anita Leslie remembered him as a gray-haired old man surrounded by his marvelous memories. What a storyteller he must have been to the little ones!

No one came into contact with Moreton Frewen without forming a strong opinion of him. If he had been only an empty vessel, a shameless con man, how can we explain the people who passionately devoted their lives to him? Old Mack, the faithful valet who was often unpaid (if we are to believe Anita Leslie), or Murphy, or Lingham — who certainly could have found a boss who would more consistently advance his career — these, and more clung to him and wrote him letters asking why he did not answer, knowing full well that the burdens on him had for a few days quenched even his nearly boundless enthusiasm. For all of the carping about the strange British aristocrats on the range, there is at least some evidence that Frewen's relationships with the Wyoming cowboys were good. Plunkett did seem to have much more difficulty choosing good foremen than Frewen did. And it was Plunkett the boys wanted to shoot, not Moreton!

On the negative side, Moreton made equally strong enemies. One lady wrote him after he had made conciliatory overtures to her, "You make a great mistake if you think that the change which there certainly is in my feelings about you is in any way due to the misfortunes you may have had in the cattle line." She was, instead, offended by "reports" he had been spreading, and that he had "behaved very badly" toward Horace Plunkett (a friend and cousin of her husband).[28]

He was apparently not particularly close to his children, although that circumstance was not at all rare in the Victorian era (Moreton's nephew, Seymour Leslie, was so unaccustomed to seeing his father about the house that, on seeing him in bed with Leonie, the boy said, "*Qui est ce monsieur, maman?*").[29] Moreton's daughter Clare, who became an accomplished sculptor, had a particularly stormy life with her father. She infuriated him, as well as cousin Winston and the establishment of Britain, by dashing off to communist Moscow in 1920 to sculpt Lenin and Trotsky. As she had hoped, this earned her a place in the public eye.[30]

Of course, there was more to Moreton than boundless optimism; otherwise, we would have to count him an empty-headed fool. His schemes were often odd, even bizarre, but he had carefully considered each of them. Moreover, he killed them when he saw they had no further promise. And they did not all fail. Later in life, the vile-tasting antiseptic he promoted went on to become a commercial success (under the brand name "Milton")—although not for him—and the mining properties in Australia also returned handsomely (to others) the investments made in them. That he did not die rich, after all, was not the fault of his ideas, but the fact that he came upon them when other events had too completely overwhelmed any chance for a great success; selling out too quickly, he was forced to devote the meager returns to reducing some of the more pressing claims upon him. In later life, he finally had a brief opportunity to try his hand at politics: he was the member from N. E. Cork in 1910-11.[31]

While undoubtedly there were those who did not like the British gentleman who seemed to be playing at the business of ranching, it is instructive to remember another incident. At the time of the Johnson County invasion, when the cattlemen were pinned down at the TA Ranch by the Johnson County defenders and in some fear for their personal safety, one of them (Herbert E. Teschemacher) took the trouble to get a message out to Moreton to ask him to plead with the president for help.[32] While such a request may have stemmed only from a sense of desperation, in which any straw might be grasped, there must also have been some feeling that the man to whom the request was sent would be capable of producing positive results.

The Powder River company is a special case. It is hard to find much fault with a good deal of what Moreton said about this property. He always knew that the open ranges were not something one could count on forever; if money was to be made by grazing them, it must be made opportunistically. When the settlers took over the more attractive regions, those ranges would have to be vacated. He thought that the more arid portions of the range would never be amenable to irrigation, and in that judgment he was certainly correct. What he did not correctly forecast at the beginning was the extent to which other cattlemen would crowd in upon "his" range. He blamed President Cleveland for the beginnings of that disaster, since the presidential order forced cattle from the Indian Territory range onto other ranges farther north. But even without this event, overstocking would have occurred anyway.

When overstocking became apparent to him, Moreton saw the need to move, and his moves, first to Montana and later to Alberta, were, again, soundly based. He was probably correct in the later assertion that more cattle could have been pushed into Alberta in the early stages, before the Canadian government insisted on duty payments.

Of course, these ranges would also have become overstocked, but he had not promised that there was any way to prevent that. A few more years of profits could have been gleaned.

It is a bit more difficult to do a post mortem on the conflicting advice given to the directors in London. Peters was clearly wrong on two counts: he thought the ranges were no worse than they had often been and would recover; and he thought that irrigation was the salvation of the range cattle industry. Subsequent events proved that the ranges were dangerously depleted; the winter of 1886–87 wrote the final chapter on that argument. And irrigation was too expensive for an industry with such thin margins.

One can certainly sympathize with the board in London, who got much conflicting advice about the strange business they owned in America. Yet, once the decision was made to liquidate, it was inevitable that the common shareholders would lose their entire investment. Moreton raged that the board and the London office continued to live off the carcass of the old company, and he may have been irrational in that feeling, but he was not entirely wrong. And it was Horace Plunkett who made it necessary to liquidate, by insisting that he would manage only to that end. We cannot know what might have been absent that factor, but some of the big outfits, such as the Swan company, struggled on after reorganizing and securing the land to continue on the range. Could the old Powder River company have done so, too?

Plunkett's position changed over time. He had been cautious about the Alberta drive at the beginning, and his voice was undoubtedly a strong factor in causing the board to pause at the critical point when more animals might possibly have walked to safety in the British dominions. But as soon as he saw the Alberta ranges, he knew they were better than those in Wyoming and Montana, and he fully supported efforts to use them, to the extent that was still possible. His efforts to move 7,000 cattle were competent and did not deserve Moreton's criticism. Plunkett, who had once marvelled at how much good there was in Moreton, came to regard the man as an unscrupulous liar; they had once been friends, but for years afterwards they were enemies.[33] Long after the Wyoming episode, the two met by accident in Ireland at the home of Frewen's nephew, Shane Leslie. Leslie says they kept "utter silence."[34]

One footnote to Moreton's relationship with Plunkett should not go unnoticed. Early in 1908, Plunkett returned from a trip to the United States to learn that Moreton's creditors were getting ready for one final assault on the bones of his financial carcass. He told Frewen that he had ordered his solicitor to withdraw. "While my claim against you is one the justice of which I personally believe in," Horace said, "it is not one which I desire to press in circumstances so different to those out of which it arose, now nearly a quarter of a century ago. . . . Should you ever as I hope you may, be in a position of affluence you will then be free to consider whether it should be revived at your instance."[35]

Gradually, the gulf between the two men closed, and correspondence again started up (not about cattle, to be sure, but about Ireland and politics).[36]

Finally, the end came, on September 2, 1924. Moreton was 71, and he was still working on the book that would be published as his autobiography after his death, oddly titled *Melton Mowbray & Other Memories*. While Clara mourned the loss of this man so filled with enjoyment of life, a letter arrived out of the past he had loved in far-off Wyoming. It was from Charley Oelrichs. He said, "I have always held him in great affection, and his death has brought to my mind, very vividly, memories of the long past, and in which he was most prominent, the many experiences which we shared in the far west, in the early days of the ranches, and later, his delightful companionship, during the frequent trips to my country. Were I known to the journalists of this country, and had the gift of expression that he himself had so abundantly, I could supply for publication later on, many interesting incidents of Moreton's first years in America."[37]

He did not enrich himself financially, but he did enrich the memories of those who knew him. His had been a tumultuous life, filled with excitement, joy, and a good bit of trouble. Jennie once summed up her feelings about her own marriage to Randolph (which also had its share of troubles) in a way that undoubtedly mirrored her sister's feelings about Moreton. She said, "If I had to lead my own life over again with dear R. just as it was, I would—in preference to anyone else—& so would you with Moreton."[38] And so she would have.

Notes to Chapter 15

1. "Ah me, Postumus, Postumus, the fleeting years are slipping by." Horace, *Odes* 14, 1.

2. Frewen to Clara Frewen, February 19, 1888, Frewen Papers.

3. Frewen to Clara Frewen, January 1, 1888, Frewen Papers.

4. Frewen fragment (letter to Clara), undated but probably 1888, Frewen Papers.

5. Account with Spencer Whitehead, June 26, 1888.

6. Spencer Whitehead to Frewen, October 31, 1888, Frewen Papers.

7. Moreton Frewen, undated memorandum attached to affidavit of John A. Riner, March 28, 1889, Frewen Papers.

8. Affidavit of George Davey Stibbard, July 24, 1888; and Earl of Rosslyn to Clara Frewen, May 28, 1888 (Charles Fitch Kemp blandly responded to the earl that he was "far from being actuated by any hostility toward Mr. Frewen."). Frewen Papers.

9. Joseph Richardson to Frewen, July 28, 1888, Frewen Papers.

10. Morton E. Post to Frewen, May 25, 1889, Frewen Papers.

11. Morton E. Post to Frewen, May 13, 1889, Frewen Papers.

12. Morton E. Post to Frewen, May 25, 1889, Frewen Papers.

13. Morton E. Post to Frewen, February 16, 1889, Frewen Papers.

14. John C. Baird to Frewen, August 27, 1890, Frewen Papers.

15. "To the holders of Ordinary Shares in the Powder River Cattle Company, Limited," July 25, 1888, Frewen Papers.

16. Charles Fitch Kemp to Spencer Whitehead, July 17, 1888.

17. Affidavit of Charles Fitch Kemp, August 4, 1888.

18. Frewen to Clara Frewen, August 26, 1888, Frewen Papers.

19. Maurice J. Lothian to Frewen, February 2, 1889, Frewen Papers.

20. Fred G. S. Hesse to Horace C. Plunkett, June 6, 1889, Hesse letterpress.

21. Fred G. S. Hesse to Horace C. Plunkett, June 6, 1889, Hesse letterpress.

22. Fred G. S. Hesse to Horace C. Plunkett, September 9, 1889, Hesse letterpress.

23. Fred G. S. Hesse to Charles Fitch Kemp, December 11, 1889, Hesse letterpress.

24. Fred G. S. Hesse to Horace C. Plunkett, December 21, 1889, and July 22, 1891, Hesse letterpress.

25. Savage, "Plunkett of the EK," 214.

26. Tom Morgan to Frewen, September 10, 1888, Frewen Papers.

27. Frewen to Clara Frewen, December 25, 1888, Frewen Papers.

28. S. Cloncurry to Frewen, April 28, 1889, Frewen Papers.

29. Leslie, *Lady Randolph Churchill,* 208.

30. Leslie, *Clare Sheridan,* 121.

31. Burke, *Burke's Landed Gentry.*

32. David M. Emmons, "Moreton Frewen and the Populist Revolt," *Annals of Wyoming* 35(2) (October 1963): 165.

33. Plunkett diary, November 24, 1884, and July 13, 1887.

34. Shane Leslie to Margaret Digby, February 17, 1950.

35. Horace C. Plunkett to Frewen, January 15, 1908, Frewen Papers.

36. There are a number of letters from Frewen to Plunkett dated 1917 in the Plunkett Papers.

37. Charles M. Oelrichs to Clara Frewen, September 28, 1924, Frewen Papers.

38. Leslie, *Lady Randolph Churchill,* 216–17.

Bibliography

The chief source for this book consists of letters and papers accumulated by Moreton Frewen in connection with his ranching operation in the Powder River country, now at the American Heritage Center at the University of Wyoming, Laramie, Wyoming. These papers are very extensive for the period when he was in active management of these operations, and become more sparse thereafter. Quotations from the Frewen letters and diary are cited as "Frewen Papers." One liberty has been taken with the originals: Moreton Frewen was strangely indifferent to punctuation, and the usual marks have been inserted to make his writing easier to read.

Other manuscript collections consulted include the papers of the Wyoming Stock Growers Association and the minutes of the Cheyenne Club, both also at the American Heritage Center in Laramie. Mr. Fred E. Hesse of Buffalo, Wyoming, permitted me to quote from the letterpress of his grandfather, Fred G. S. Hesse, and from the tally book in his possession, and I am grateful for that courtesy.

Dr. Trevor West is preparing a definitive biography of Horace C. Plunkett, and he has kindly assisted with references to the Frewens from the Plunkett papers.

Newspapers

Big Horn Sentinel
Birmingham Daily Post
Cheyenne Daily Leader
Cheyenne Daily Sun
Democratic Leader (Cheyenne)
Financial News

Laramie Daily Sentinel
Manchester Guardian
New York Times
Times (London)

Secondary Sources

Anderson, R. A. *With Horace Plunkett in Ireland.* London, 1935.

Andrews, Allen. *The Splendid Pauper.* New York, 1968.

Barton, William H. "David D. Dare and the American Dream." *Annals of Wyoming* 41(2) (Fall 1979).

Blake, Robert. *Disraeli.* New York, 1967.

Brough, James. *The Prince & the Lily.* New York, 1975.

Burke, Sir Bernard. *Burke's Landed Gentry.* London, 1930.

Canton, Frank M. *Frontier Trails.* New York, 1930.

Chaffin, Lorah B. *Sons of the West.* Caldwell, Idaho, 1941.

Churchill, Randolph S. *Winston S. Churchill.* 2 vols. Boston, 1966.

Condit, Thelma Gatchell. "The Hole in the Wall." *Annals of Wyoming* 29(1) (April 1957).

Cooksey, C. R. (Mose). "Robbers' Roost Station." *Annals of Wyoming* 38(1) (April 1966).

Dary, David. *Cowboy Culture.* New York, 1981.

Digby, Margaret. *Horace Plunkett, An Anglo-American Irishman.* Oxford, 1949.

Emmons, David M. "Moreton Frewen and the Populist Revolt." *Annals of Wyoming* 35(2) (October 1963).

Engebretson, Doug. *Empty Saddles, Forgotten Names.* Aberdeen, South Dakota, 1982.

Flannery, L. G. "Pat," ed. *John Hunton's Diary.* 6 vols. Glendale, California, 1970.

Frewen, Moreton. *Melton Mowbray.* London, 1924.

Frink, Maurice. *Cow Country Cavalcade.* Denver, 1954.

Guice, John D. W. *The Rocky Mountain Bench.* New Haven, 1972.

Historical Sheridan and Sheridan County. Sheridan, Wyoming, 1959.

Jackson, W. Turrentine. *The Enterprising Scot.* Edinburgh, 1968.

Kelly, Charles. *The Outlaw Trail.* New York, 1959.

Kerr, W. G. *Scottish Capital on the American Credit Frontier.* Austin, Texas, 1976.

Langtry, Lillie. *The Days I Knew*. New York, 1925.

Larson, Taft Alfred. *History of Wyoming*. Lincoln, 1965.

————. "The Winter of 1886–87 in Wyoming." *Annals of Wyoming* 14(1) (January 1942).

Latham, Dr. H. *The Pasture Lands of North America: Winter Grazing*. Omaha, Nebraska, 1871.

Leslie, Anita. *Clare Sheridan*. New York, 1977.

————. *Lady Randolph Churchill*. New York, 1969.

————. *The Remarkable Mr. Jerome*. New York, 1954.

Longford, Elizabeth. *Queen Victoria*. New York, 1964.

Lorillard and Tobacco. New York, 1977.

Lott, Howard B., ed. "Diary of Major Wise, an Englishman, Recites Details of Hunting Trip in Powder River Country in 1880." *Annals of Wyoming* 12(2) (April 1940).

————. "The Old Occidental." *Annals of Wyoming* 27(1) (April 1955).

Magnus, Philip. *King Edward the Seventh*. New York, 1964.

Malone, Dumas, ed. *Dictionary of American Biography*. New York, 1933.

Martin, Ralph G. *Jennie*. 2 vols. New York, 1971.

Masters, Brian. *The Dukes*. London, 1975.

Mercer, Asa S. *The Banditti of the Plains*. Norman, Oklahoma, 1954.

Meschter, Daniel Y. *Wyoming Territorial and Pre-Territorial Post Offices*. Cheyenne, 1971.

Murray, Robert A. *Military Posts in the Powder River Country of Wyoming, 1865–1894*. Lincoln, Nebraska, 1968.

————. *Military Posts of Wyoming*. Fort Collins, Colorado, 1974.

Pine, L. G. *Burke's Peerage*. London, 1953.

Savage, William W., Jr. "Plunkett of the EK." *Annals of Wyoming* 43(2) (Fall 1971).

Seymour, Flora Warren. *Indian Agents of the Old Frontier*. New York, 1941.

A Survey of Wyoming County Courthouses. 1972.

Trevelyan, George M. *British History in the Nineteenth Century and After (1782–1919)*. London, 1937.

Woods, L. Milton. *Sometimes the Books Froze: Wyoming's Economy and Its Banks*. Boulder, Colorado, 1985.

————. *The Wyoming Country Before Statehood: Four Hundred Years Under Six Flags*. Worland, Wyoming, 1971.

Urbanek, Mae. *Wyoming Place Names*. Boulder, Colorado, 1967.

Index

Adair, John, 24
Albany County, Wyoming, 4
Alberta range. *See* Canadian range
Alston, W. C., 39, 53, 54, 89
Anson, Lord, 66
Ashton, Sam, 39, 114
Assinaboina, Montana, 175
Auger, General Christopher C., 2
Aurangabad, India, 191

Babbitt, Colonel, 124, 125
Baillie-Grohman, William A., 37-38
Barton & Dillon (cattle company on the Powder River), 51
Bat caves (MF's guano mining scheme), 46-47, 49-50, 60, 77, 112
Baxter, George W. (governor of Wyoming), 160
Beard, George L., 49
Belper, Lord, 66, 140
Bennet, F. A. K., 124, 188-89; International Cattle Company, Ltd. board of directors, member of, 158; PRCC board of directors, member of, 141, 144, 167, 168; PRCC debt to, 150, 163
Big Horn, Wyoming, 8, 9
Big Horn Basin (Wyoming), 4, 6-7, 51
Big Horn Mountains, 4, 6, 37, 101, 114, 178, 187
Big Horn Ranche (Frewen Brothers cattle ranching operation), 31
"Book Count," 14, 118, 174-75; of the PRCC herds, 91, 117, 133, 135, 172, 187
Boughton, Edward Shuckburgh Rouse, 41

Bozeman Trail, 5
Brickwall (MF's birthplace), 20
Buffalo, Wyoming, 8-9, 53, 54, 80, 101, 149

Cactus Club, 14. *See also* Cheyenne Club
Camp Connor (Wyoming), 5
Canadian Pacific Railroad, 172-73
Canadian range, 127, 131, 138, 140, 141, 145, 186, 194, 198-99; cattle drive to, 142, 147, 149, 155, 158, 159; Charles Fitch Kemp on, 172; Horace Plunkett on, 139, 170, 199; lease for, 141, 156, 158, 159; Moreton Frewen on, 158, 163, 198-99; PRCC herd on, 172, 188, 194; sale of herd on, 194-95; and winter of 1886-87, 175-76, 180
Canadians (and MF's cattle export scheme), 106-109. *See also* Frewen, Morton, and cattle export scheme; Pope, John Henry; Lansdowne, Lord; MacDonald, Sir John
Canyon ranch, 81-82, 85, 102, 111
Carbon County, Wyoming, 4
Carey, Joseph M., 12, 15, 124; as president of the Wyoming Stock Growers Association, 79, 106
Carlingford, Lord, 96, 97, 107
Carter, Charles (foreman for PRCC in Montana), 143, 149
Carter County, Wyoming, 4. *See also* Sweetwater County
"Castle Frewen," 55. *See also* Powder River ranch house
Cheyenne Club, 14-15, 54, 100, 174, 189

Cheyenne National Bank, 49

Cheyenne, Wyoming, 1–2, 3, 54, 100, 123, 160

Chicago, St. Paul, Minneapolis, & Omaha Railway, 135

Churchill, Lady Randolph (Jennie Jerome), 26, 27–28, 69, 92, 155, 200

Churchill, Lord Randolph, 22, 27–28, 66, 69, 182, 200

Churchill, Winston S., 19–20

Clay, John, 75, 79, 109

Collins, John W., 48–49

Conrad, John H., 80

Cookson, Montagu, Q. C., 128

Corlett (lawyer for PRCC in Wyoming), 143

Crazy Woman crossing (of the Bozeman Trail), 8

Crazy Woman range, controversy over ownership, 191–92, 193; MF's land filing on, 67, 73, 81, 102, 156, 187; MF's ranch house on, 31, 112; for PRCC herd, 77, 81, 131, 191–92, 193–94

Crazy Woman's Fork, 37

Crook, General George, 6

Crook County, Wyoming, 6, 7, 8, 101

Cruikshank, W. H., 135

Custer, Colonel George A., 6

Custer County, Montana, 159

Dakota Stock & Grazing Company, Limited, 90, 152–53, 162, 193

Dare, David, 49, 81

Denison, Ernest Beckett, 66, 68, 149

Denison, William Beckett, 65–66, 67, 169–70, 172, 187; conflict with MF, 121–22, 148–49, 156–57; and Horace Plunkett's resignation as manager of PRCC, 155; PRCC special committee of inquiry, member of, 140, 157–58

Denver, Colorado, 36, 60, 73, 81, 195

Devoe, Henry N. (Johnson County commissioner), 53, 54

"Dick" irrigation ditch, The, 102, 193

Dodge, General Grenville M., 2

Douglas, Wyoming, 160

Draper (cattle owner on the Powder River), 71

Dry Fork (MF's ranch house on), 31

Dunraven, Earl of, 90

Dunsany, Lord (Horace Plunkett's father), 41, 46, 67, 116; as mediator between MF and Horace Plunkett, 149, 150, 151, 155, 179

East, James, 46

Edward, Prince of Wales, 22–23, 92

EK Ranch (Horace Plunkett's ranch), 70, 89, 185–86

English Derby, 55

Fencing (of public lands), 10, 81, 86–87, 184; federal government on, 87, 126, 130; and range cattle industry, 185

First National Bank of Cheyenne, 159, 161, 184

Fitzwilliam, Charles, 40

Foley, Tim, 32

Foley herd, 32

Fort C. F. Smith, Wyoming, 5

Fort Casper, Wyoming, 51

Fort Fetterman, Wyoming, 6

Fort Keogh, Montana, 175

Fort Laramie Treaty of 1868, 5

Fort McKinney, Wyoming, 8, 37

Fort Philip Kearny, Wyoming, 5, 8

Fort Reno, Wyoming, 5, 8

Fremont County, Wyoming, 101

Frewen, Anna Louisa (Louise) (MF's sister), 55

Frewen, Charles Hay (MF's uncle), 20–21

Frewen, Clara (Clara Jerome) (MF's wife), 22, 25, 26, 92, 122, 183; in childbirth, 85, 129; courtship with MF, 27–29; and death of MF, 200; engagement and marriage to MF, 29; and MF's debts, 92, 155; and Pierre Lorillard, 56, 75; as shareholder in PRCC, 67, 187; visit to the Powder River ranch house, 55, 60

Frewen, Clare (MF's daughter), 129, 197

Frewen, Edward, and cattle ranching in Wyoming, 33, 34, 63–64; and debt to Stebbins & Post bank, 52;

and disapproval of Richard Frewen, 153, 162; and Gilbert Leigh's funeral, 115; inheritance, 20; and MF, 25, 34, 39, 140, 151, 167, 168, 171, 178, 179, 180, 186, 193; on PRCC affairs, 167, 186; PRCC board of directors, member of, 144, 145–46, 148, 157, 168, 186; PRCC, shareholder of, 67, 72, 84

Frewen, Hugh Moreton (MF's son), 85

Frewen, John (MF's half brother), 20

Frewen, Moreton, autobiography (*Melton Mowbray & Other Memories*), 19, 200; and bat caves (guano mining scheme), 46–47, 49–50, 60, 77, 112; birth of, 20; and the board of directors of the PRCC, 79, 83–84, 90, 163–64, 172; and the board of directors of the PRCC, conflict with, 71–72, 75, 115–16, 117, 121, 128, 133, 135, 138, 139–40, 177, 187, 188; board of directors of the PRCC, member of, 145–46, 147, 148, 151, 157, 167–70, 185, 186; and Canadian range, 127, 135, 138, 145, 147, 149, 152, 156, 158, 159, 162–63, 180, 194, 198–99; and canyon ranch, 81–82, 102, 111; cattle export scheme of, 95–97, 103, 106–109, 111, 116, 125, 130; and cattle ranching in Wyoming, 23, 24, 31–34, 36, 50–51, 52, 56, 63–64, 70–71, 80–81, 97–98, 123, 130, 132, 158, 162–63, 198; character of, 19, 23, 93, 95, 196–97; on Cheyenne, 160–61; Cheyenne Club, member of, 14–15; Clara (wife), relationship with, 28, 55, 60, 92–93; courtship, engagement, and marriage of, 27–29, 53, 55, 60; and Crazy Woman range, 73, 81, 102, 112, 156, 187, 192–93; death of, 200; debts of, 52–53, 89, 103, 134, 143, 152, 183–84, 185, 187–88, 191, 192, 193; exploits of, 24, 59–60, 83, 162–63; family of, 20, 25–26, 34, 85, 197; on Gilbert Leigh's death, 114–15; and Goschen, 182; Horace Plunkett, relationship with, 41, 70, 89, 116, 123, 132, 139, 147, 148, 150, 151, 154–55, 156, 159,

167, 171, 178, 179, 185, 199–200; horse racing, enjoyment of, 21–22, 29, 55; hunting, 24, 37–40; and Indians, 24–25, 32, 36, 38, 82–83; inheritance, 20–21; and the Johnson County invasion, 198; and land filings for PRCC, 101–103, 158; lawsuits against PRCC, 136, 138, 155–56, 178, 187, 188, 191–92, 195; and Lillie Langtry, 22, 23, 26, 32, 101; and McCulloch evaluation of PRCC property, 72–75; on the Maverick Law, 99; as manager of the PRCC, 67–68, 90–91, 111, 115, 117–18, 123–24, 128, 144, 186; mining schemes of, 44–45, 134–35, 193, 196, 198; and Montana range, 133–34, 153–54; Morton Post, partnership with, 187; nicknames, 19; old age, 196–97; optimism of, 25, 36–37, 42, 95, 162, 197; organizing the PRCC, 63–70; others' opinions of, 197; on overstocking of ranges, 98, 198; on outlaws, 17, 33, 87–88; and Pierre Lorillard, 56–58, 60, 75–76; political life of, 116, 134, 198; as post master at Powder River, 37; and the PRCC, 198–99; and PRCC special committee of inquiry, 138, 140–41, 155, 157–58; and PRCC, financial troubles of, 121, 143–44, 153, 163, 167–70, 185, 194–95; and the Powder River country, 24, 31, 33, 40; and the Powder River ranch house, 28, 31, 34–35, 37, 57, 59–60, 73, 104, 111–12, 114, 196; and Powder River range, 13, 73, 84, 196; railroad schemes of, 172–73, 185, 196; relationship with Americans (in Wyoming), 34, 37, 39–40, 197; Richard Frewen, partnership with, 31–33, 52, 57–59, 63–64; Richard Frewen, relationship with, 25, 33, 52, 57–59, 109–110, 133, 140, 153, 155, 158, 193; reorganization scheme for PRCC, 154, 157, 158, 174, 177, 178, 179–80; and roundups, 83, 84, 88; on settlers in Wyoming, 85; and shareholders of the PRCC, 77, 90–91, 96, 138–39, 144–45, 157–58, 177–78, 183,

185–86, 194; as a shareholder of the PRCC, 72, 75, 167–70, 185; and Shearburn affair, 47–48; and Sherman Hill refrigeration plant, 45–46, 60, 64, 70, 85, 97, 140; shipping cattle to London, 127–28; with Sir Salar Jung (in India), 49, 182–83, 188, 191, 196; Sitting Bull, meeting with, 6, 162; in South Africa, 196; and store on the Powder River, 8, 111; storm at sea, 122; Superior cattle feeding operation, 111, 117–18, 120, 122–23, 135, 136, 139, 149, 156, 177, 187–88; Superior land development project, 109–111, 126, 184; Thomas W. Peters, relationship with, 53, 89, 128–29, 135; and the telephone, 35–36, 111; and Uncle Charles Hay Frewen, 20–21; to the United States, first visit of, 24; Winston Churchill on, 19–20; on winter of 1886–87 in Wyoming, 178, 187; on woman suffrage, 3; writings about, 19; in Wyoming, 1, 8; Wyoming Stock Growers Association, member of, 13–14

Frewen, Richard, and bat caves (guano mining scheme), 47, 50, 112; and Canadian range, 131, 143, 155; and cattle disease, 96; and cattle ranching in Wyoming, 32, 131, 159; Cheyenne Club, original member of, 14; and concessions in Yellowstone National Park, 46; and Dakota Stock & Grazing Company, 90, 152–53, 162, 193; death of, 25; debts of, 112–13, 185, 193; and Duluth iron ore project, 135; and Edward Shearburn, 47–48; in Egypt, 48; health of, 57; Horace Plunkett, relationship with, 46, 132, 144, 147, 148, 149, 151, 152, 155, 170–71; inheritance, 20; as letter-writer, 25, 26; MF, partnership with, 31–33, 52, 57–59, 63–64; MF, relationship with, 25, 33, 52, 57–59, 109–110, 133, 140, 153, 155, 158, 193; and Murphy, 134, 155; and PRCC affairs, 143–44, 152–53, 155, 156, 158, 161, 170–71; relationship with Americans (in Wyoming), 40; and Superior land development

project, 110–11, 126; travels to Wyoming, 24, 25; William Mackenzie on, 154; at Wyoming Stock Growers Association meeting, 124

Frewen, Stephen (MF's brother), 20, 23, 25, 26, 52, 116

Frewen Brothers (partnership between MF and Richard Frewen), 76. *See also* Frewen, Moreton; and Frewen, Richard

"Frewen Castle," 14. *See also* Powder River ranch house

Frontier Land & Cattle Company (Horace Plunkett's cattle company), 41, 185

Gardner, E. F. (Alan), 86, 167, 168, 186

Gilchrist, Andrew, 41

Goschen, George Joachim Viscount, 182

Gray, Everett, 64, 145, 157; board of directors of PRCC, member of, 65, 144; MF, conflict with, 75, 121, 167–68, 169, 178, 185

Grey, Albert, 95

Hanging Woman Creek range, Montana, 80, 149. *See also* Montana range

Hanna, Oliver Perry, 8, 39

Hart, Mrs. Verling B., 101

Hathaway, William E., 36, 53

Hesse, Fred, 106, 123, 134, 154; Canadian range, cattle drive to, 149; Edward Frewen's cattle operation, foreman for, 33; and land filings, 102–103; and PRCC accounts, 196; and PRCC debts, 163, 196; PRCC's Wyoming ranges, foreman for, 99, 124, 143; PRCC's Wyoming herds, sale of, 195; Powder River roundup, foreman for, 79; on range conditions, 131, 149; on winter of 1886–87, 180

Hicks, Truman, 150, 152

"Hole in the Wall," 17

Hoyt, John W. (governor of Wyoming), 46, 53

Hyderabad, India, 188

Hyderabad, Nizam of, 49, 182

Iliff, John Wesley, 2
Indians, 5, 54; Battle of the Little Big Horn, 5–6; and MF, 24–25, 32, 36, 38, 82–83; United States government treaties with, 4, 5
International Cattle Company, Ltd., 157, 158, 171, 188, 194. See also Powder River Cattle Company, reorganization
Inter-State Land and Town Company, 193
Irrigation, 85, 102, 140, 199

Jackson, W. E., 53
Jay Em, Wyoming, 80
Jerome, Clara. See Frewen, Clara
Jerome, Eugene, 110, 126
Jerome, Jennie. See Churchill, Lady Randolph
Jerome, Lawrence, 113–14
Jerome, Leonard Walter, 25, 27, 28, 29, 58, 90, 92, 96, 100
Jerome, Leonie. See Leslie, Leonie
Johnson, Edward Payson, 7
Johnson County, Wyoming, 7, 8, 53, 70, 101, 131
Johnson County invasion, 198
Jung, Sir Salar, 182, 188

Kay, Justice, 178, 183
Kemp, Charles Fitch, on Canadian range, 188; PRCC, liquidator of, 157, 167, 177, 179, 194, 195; PRCC, manager of, in London, 113, 133, 135, 143, 144, 145, 150, 152; report to shareholders of the PRCC, 171–72, 194, 195
Kemp, Charles W. Middleton, and the Dakota Stock & Grazing Company, 90, 162; and MF, 156, 158; and the PRCC, 65, 67, 72, 84–85, 90, 156, 158
Kemp, Frank, and Cheyenne Club, 15; Dakota Stock & Grazing Company, manager of, 153, 162; and MF, 15, 58, 79, 97, 113, 133; PRCC, assistant manager of, in Wyoming, 15, 73, 97, 132, 133–34; and PRCC "book counts," 77 n.1; Richard Frewen on, 113, 144
Kinsky, Count, 191

Langtry, Lillie, 22–23, 26, 32, 100–101
Lansdowne, Lord (Canadian Governor General), 96–97, 107–108
Laramie County, Wyoming, 4
Larson, Taft Alfred, 174
Leadville, Colorado, 36, 60
"League, The," 98
Leigh, Gilbert, 24, 55, 109, 114–15
Leng, John, 76
Leslie, Anita, 92, 182, 196–97
Leslie, John, 22
Leslie, Leonie (Leonie Jerome), 19, 22, 26, 197
Leslie, Shane, 199
Lingham, F. R., Horace Plunkett on, 171; and MF, 120, 122, 158, 197; and MF's cattle export scheme, 95, 107; with MF in India, 188, 191; MF on, 163; PRCC, foreman for, 143; and Superior, 110, 131, 170; on T. W. Peters, 129, 184
Little Bow River, Alberta, Canada, 159. See also Canadian range
Livestock feeding, 100, 131–31. See also Superior, and cattle feeding operation
Lone Star Dance Hall, 54
Lorne, Lord, 107
Lorillard, Pierre, and MF, 29, 60, 79; MF's calf sale to, 56–58, 71, 75–76; MF's debt to, 86, 89, 134; on the PRCC, 86
Lothian, Maurice John, 180, 186–87, 195
Lowther, Hugh (later Lord Lonsdale), 21, 23, 32, 40
Lyon, A. O., 143, 155
Lyon, Charles E., 148; MF's debt to, 134, 143, 155; personal bankruptcy of, 143, 145, 155, 158; PRCC, member of the board of directors of, 141, 144; PRCC, special committee of inquiry, member of, 140; PRCC, shareholder of, 86, 138, 139–40; supports MF, 138, 139–40, 145, 155

McCulloch, John, 72–75
MacDonald, Sir John (Canadian Prime Minister), 109, 116, 123
Mackenzie, William, 68, 171; International Cattle Company, member of

board of directors of, 158; on MF's
resignation from board of directors
of PRCC, 167–70; PRCC board of
directors, member of, 163–64;
PRCC, preferred shareholders, rep-
resentative of, 66–67, 141–42, 154,
179; to MF, 86, 145, 151, 177, 188,
195; on the winter of 1886–87 in
Wyoming, 180
Manchester, Duke of (William Drogo
Montagu), 79, 90; MF's lawsuit
against, 136; PRCC board of direc-
tors, chairman of, 63, 65, 68, 139
Mandeville, Lady, 65
Marney, S. A., 99
Maverick Bill, 11
"Maverick" brands, 88
Maverick Law, 98, 125
Mavericks, 10, 125
Melton Mowbray & Other Memories
(MF's autobiography), 19, 200
Mercer, Asa S., 99
Milner, Sir Frederick, 133, 136, 144,
145
Montana range, 80, 133, 149, 153, 159,
178
Moonlight, Colonel Thomas (gover-
nor of Wyoming), 81, 160
"Moreton" irrigation ditch, The, 102,
193
Morgan, Elliott S. N., 53
Morris, Esther, 1
"Mortal Ruin" (MF's nickname), 19
Morton E. Post & Company, 80;
bankruptcy, 184–85, 194; and Crazy
Woman range, 191–92, 194; MF's
debt to, 89, 134; PRCC, loans to,
43–44, 152, 161, 163. *See also*
Stebbins, Post & Co.
Mosquito Creek, Alberta, Canada,
141, 159. *See also* Canadian range
Murphy, E. W., attachment to MF,
197; and Canadian range, 143, 152,
155, 159, 175, 176, 180; Horace
Plunkett on, 132, 148, 149, 150, 171;
and Montana range, 133–34;
PRCC, foreman for, in Wyoming,
80, 124; on T. W. Peters, 129
Murrin, Colonel Luke, 175

Nevill, Lord Henry, PRCC board of
directors, member of, 65, 68, 69,
129, 136, 141, 144; MF's lawsuit
against, 136
Nichols, Beach & Co. (cattle company
on the Powder River), 51
"97" brand (Edward Frewen's brand),
64
Northern Pacific Railroad, 109, 111, 172
North Platte River, 4
Northwestern Live Stock Journal, 99
Northwestern Railroad, 160
Nye, Edgar Wilson (Bill), 88

Obrenovich, Milan, King of Serbia,
92
Odder, Michael, 86–87
Oelrichs, Charles M., 15, 71, 200
Oelrichs, Harry, 15, 71, 84, 100
Onslow, Lord, 138
Outlaws, 15–17, 33. *See also* Range
Cattle Industry, and cattle rustling

Parshall, A. J., 161, 184–85
Partridge, Si, 125
Peck, Judge William Ware, 7–8
Pease, Dr. Eugene L., 7
Pease County, Wyoming, 7. *See also*
Johnson County
Peters, Thomas W., 39, 184; on Cana-
dian range, 128–29, 140, 159; and
desert land entries, 133; Johnson
County, organization of, 53, 54;
and MF, 53, 89, 128–29, 135;
PRCC, manager of, in Wyoming,
123–24, 135, 139, 140, 143, 144, 148,
177, 199; and Superior cattle feeding
operation, 128–29
Piney River, 5, 51
Plunkett, Horace, 41, 42, 189; and
Canadian range, 139, 147, 149, 152,
159, 163, 170, 199; and cattle ranch-
ing in Wyoming, 41–42, 82, 112, 131,
132; cattle feeding operation of, in
Nebraska, 131–32; Cheyenne Club,
member of, 14–15; and Dakota Stock
& Grazing Co., 162; and EK ranch,
70, 89, 185–86; and Frontier Land
& Cattle Co., 41–42, 185; and

Gilbert Leigh's death, 115; on McCulloch's evaluation of the PRCC, 75; MF, relationship with, 41, 70, 89, 116, 123, 132, 139, 147, 148, 150, 151, 154-55, 156, 159, 163, 167, 168, 171, 178, 179, 185, 199-200; and Murphy, 148, 149, 150, 151, 171; on PRCC, financial condition of, 138-39, 150, 152, 163, 167; PRCC, joint management with, 132; PRCC, manager of, in Wyoming, 97, 144, 145, 147, 148, 151, 152, 156, 159, 163, 170, 171, 178, 179, 186, 195-96, 199; and PRCC herd, Montana taxes on, 153; relationship with Americans (in Wyoming), 40, 150, 189, 197; resignation as manager of the PRCC, 154-55, 157, 167, 171, 172; and Richard Frewen, 46, 132, 144, 147, 148, 149, 151, 152, 155, 157, 170-71; and Sherman Hill refrigeration plant, 97; and Superior cattle feeding operation, 126, 139, 149, 170, 187; on T. W. Peters, 129, 139; on western management, 116; and William Mackenzie, in Wyoming, 163; on winter of 1886-87 in Wyoming, 176, 180

Plunkett & Roche, 89

Pole, Chandos, 88

Pope, John Henry, 97, 107, 109

Post, Morton E., 48, 71; and Crazy Woman range, 191-92, 193-94; and coal mining speculation, 193, 196; and the Interstate Land and Town Co., 193; and lawsuit against PRCC, 187, 191-92, 195; and loan proposal to PRCC, 144, 150, 151, 152; and MF, 81, 161, 177, 178, 187; MF's debt to, 134, 152, 193; PRCC debt to, 72, 163, 168; Richard Frewen's debt to, 193; on winter of 1886-87 in Wyoming, 176. *See also* Morton E. Post & Co.; Stebbins, Post & Co.

Powder River Cattle Company, Ltd., accounts, 84, 90, 117, 118, 135-36, 150, 171, 172, 185, 188, 194, 195, 196; acquisition of "J-rolling-M" brand, 80; board of directors of, and MF, 135, 139, 185 (*See also* Frewen, Moreton, and board of directors of PRCC); Canadian range, 141, 142, 159, 194-95 (*See also* Canadian range); cattle shipment to London, 127-28; and Crazy Woman range, 191-94 (*See also* Crazy Woman range); and cooperative management with Horace Plunkett, 132; debts of, 154, 163, 168, 172, 178, 194; dividends of, 84, 91-92, 111, 117, 171; extraordinary meeting of, 144; and First National Bank of Cheyenne, 161; and Hanging Woman range (Montana), 80 (*See also* Montana range); herds of, 74; land filings in Wyoming of, 101-102, 126 (*See also* individual ranges); in liquidation, 194; and (proposed) loan from Morton E. Post & Co., 152; and McCulloch's evaluation, 73-74; MF and, 198-99; MF's debt to, 184, 187-88, 191; MF's lawsuits against, 155-56, 187, 188, 191; origin of, 63, 64, 67-68, 69-70; preferred shareholders, 130 (*See also* Mackenzie, William); and Rawhide range, 80; reorganization of, 154, 156-57, 158, 167, 171, 172, 174, 177, 178, 179-80, 188-89; special committee of inquiry of, 138, 140-41, 142, 155, 157-58; and Superior cattle feeding operation, 188 (*See also* Superior, cattle feeding operation); Superior headquarters, 161; shareholders meetings, 120, 130, 141, 177; and weather, herd losses due to, 83; and winter of 1886-87 in Wyoming, 175-76, 180, 187

Powder River Crossing (MF's store at), 36

Powder River Live Stock Company, 70

Powder River ranch house, 14, 31, 55, 67, 73, 74, 77, 81, 111-12, 125, 196

Powder River range, conditions, 131, 149, 158, 163; and land filing, 196; for PRCC herd, 74, 77, 117, 125; roundup, 79; and winter of 1886-87, 176, 180

Powder River region, and Indians, 54; Johnson County, 6; and MF, 8, 77, 125; military posts in, 5; outlaws in, 33, 79–80; and post office, 36, 37; and the range cattle industry, 51, 63; roundup, 11–12, 55; settlement of, 80; as Sioux hunting ground, 4–5

Prairie Cattle Company, 66

Preferred shareholders (of PRCC). *See* Mackenzie, William

Range cattle industry, and branding, 10; and cattle rustling, 16, 87, 131; and disease, 10, 96, 107; and fencing of public lands, 10, 81, 86–87, 126, 184; and foreign investment, 79, 161; growth of, 42; and Indians, 82–83; and land filing practices, 102; and MF's cattle export scheme, 107; and the open range, 2, 9, 73, 198; origins of, in Wyoming, 2, 9; and overstocking, 10, 97–98, 112, 141, 149, 158, 161–62, 163, 174, 186, 198; owner/cowboy relations, 99, 158–59; and the press, 125–26; and pressure from settlers, 50; and roundups, 10, 12, 55; and weather, 10, 41, 51–52, 56, 83, 123, 131, 149, 160, 163, 172, 174, 187; and winter of 1886–87 in Wyoming, 160, 174, 187, 188–89

Rawhide herd, 71, 74, 117, 135, 149

Rawhide range, 71, 74, 76–77, 80, 81, 84, 139–40

Rawlins, General John A., 2

Red Cloud, 5

Refrigeration plant. *See* Sherman Hill refrigeration plant

Richardson, Joseph, 145, 156, 193

Richmond, Duke of, 96

Roche, Alexis Charles Burke, 41, 42, 70

Roche, James Boothby Burke, 24, 41, 55

Rock, Joseph, 182

Rosslyn, Lord, 134, 144, 154; against sale of Alberta herd, 194; on Horace Plunkett, 147; as MF's ally, 142–43, 145, 169, 192; PRCC board of directors, member of, 141, 144; PRCC

special committee of inquiry, chairman of, 140, 142; PRCC, shareholder of, 67, 128, 138–39

Roundups, 10, 12, 55; institutionalized, 98; MF and, 83, 84, 88; and PRCC ranges, 79, 84

St. Oswald, Lord, 169–70, 177

Sartoris, Alfred, 64–65, 79, 149

Servia, H.M.S., 64, 70, 96, 122

"76" brand (MF's brand), 32, 88

Shearburn, Captain Edward E., 47–48, 52, 59

Sheep ranching (in Wyoming), 85

Sheridan, General Phil, 6, 24

Sherman Hill refrigeration plant, 45–46, 60, 64, 70; failure of, 85, 97, 139, 140

"Silver Tongue" (MF's nickname), 19

Sitting Bull, 6, 162

Stearns & Patterson (cattle operation on the Powder River), 51

Stebbins, William R., 48, 80

Stebbins, Conrad & Co., 80

Stebbins, Post & Co., 54; bankers for Frewen Brothers, 33; and Edward E. Shearburn fraud, 47–49; and Frewen debts, 52, 57, 58; and PRCC accounts, 70, 77. *See also* Morton E. Post & Co.

Stewart, Bob, 82, 102

Stibbard, George D., 170; conflict with MF, 145, 168, 180, 185; International Cattle Company board of directors, member of, 158; PRCC, solicitor for, 158

Sturgis, Frank, 71

Sturgis, Thomas, 112, 131–32, 161; conflict with MF, 57–58, 71, 75; Wyoming Stock Growers Association, secretary of, 12, 13, 82, 97, 99, 106

Sturgis Brothers (cattle operation), 184

Superior, 115; as headquarters for PRCC, 161; land development scheme, and MF, 110–11, 126, 184; PRCC property, and cattle feeding operation, 111, 117–18, 120, 121–23, 126–27, 131, 135, 136, 149, 156, 170, 172, 186; PRCC property, MF's obligation to buy, 139, 156, 177; PRCC

property, sale of, 187, 188; PRCC
property, as transfer stockyards,
109-111
Swan, Alexander H. (Alec), 51, 72, 81,
160; bankruptcy, 184; cattle holdings
of, in Wyoming, 86; and fencing
controversy, 86-87; and Interstate
Land and Town Co., 193; and
Maverick Law, 99
Swan, Louise, 81
Swan Brothers (cattle operation), 42
Swan Land & Cattle Company, Ltd.,
72, 160; bankruptcy, 184; dividends
of, 92, 118; and fencing controversy,
86-87; and land title, 126; and
Maverick Law, 125; reorganization
of, 199
Sweetwater County, Wyoming, 4

Tate (MF's foreman), 24, 32
Taylor, Colonel Stuart, 57, 58-59, 76
Terry, General Alfred, 6
Teschemacher, Herbert E., 125, 198
Texas bat caves. See Bat caves
Thayer, John M. (governor of Wyo-
ming), 7
Thornhill, Jack, 24
Tipping, William, 65, 68, 136, 144
Tongue River range, 51; land filing
on, 102, 196; MF's ranch on, 32;
PRCC ranch on, 74, 77, 85, 112;
roundup, 84
Trabing, Augustus, 8, 15-16
Tupper, Sir Charles (Canadian High
Commissioner), 107

Union Pacific Railroad, 1, 2, 46, 172
Uinta County, Wyoming, 4

Van Tassell, Rensselaer Schuyler, 71,
80, 81, 100
Victoria, Queen of England, 92
Vivian, Gray & Co., 63, 103

Waring, Charles, 65, 140, 141, 143, 144

Warren, Frances E. (governor of
Wyoming), 2, 126, 184-85
Wharncliffe, Lord, 64, 84, 184; conflict with MF, 141, 169-70; and MF,
120-22, 123, 129-30, 132-33; and MF's
debts, 143, 188; MF's lawsuit
against, 136; PRCC board of directors, member of, 76, 136, 139, 141;
and Superior cattle feeding operation, 126-27, 129-30
Whitehead, Spencer, 115-16, 128
Whitton, Andrew, 76; conflict with
MF, 115, 128, 129, 142, 145, 154, 167,
169, 185; on Horace Plunkett, 156;
MF's lawsuit against, 136; PRCC
board of directors, member of,
68-69, 129, 136, 141, 144; PRCC
herds, inspection of, in Wyoming,
83-85, 115; on PRCC herds, moving
to Canadian range, 142
Wibaux (purchaser of PRCC's Wyoming herds), 196
Winn, Algernon James, 61, 81, 131
Wise, Major Lewis Lovatt Ashford,
39
Winter of 1886-87, 160, 174-77, 178,
180, 187, 188-89, 199
Wolseley, Sir Charles, 24
Woman suffrage, 3-4
Wortley, Stuart, 184
Wyoming ranges, 175, 178, 195-96. See
also Crazy Woman range; Powder
River range; Rawhide range;
Tongue River range
Wyoming Stock Growers Association,
74; annual meetings of, 54-55, 79,
99, 124-25; on cattle diseases, 96,
108; on cattle rustlers, 79-80, 87,
131; and foreign capital, 161; on free
range, 9-10; and Maverick Law,
98; and MF's cattle export scheme,
106; origin of, 11; political power of,
12-14; and roundups, 11-12, 79
Wyoming Territory, 1, 2-3, 4, 160

Yellowstone National Park, 5, 63

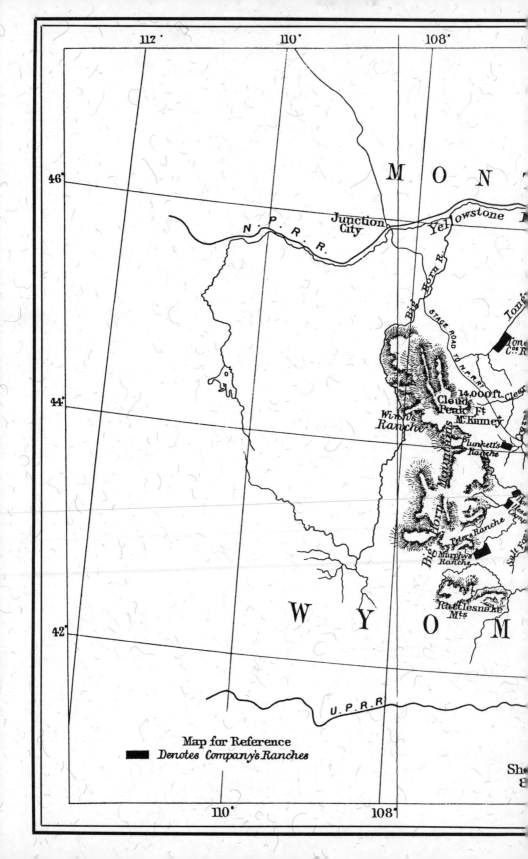

Map for Reference
Denotes Company's Ranches